DI

MANUSCRIPT

We are seeking comments by interested readers to be included in the book once it is published. When you send in your comments please give your name (first and last) and the city and state where you live to the following:

Snail mail: 703 Hamilton Court
Altamonte Springs, FL 32701

E-mail: JimHarmanCPA@aol.com

Thank you for taking the time to read this important book. We believe the message in this book should be read by everyone in the body of Christ. Please see the next page for more information on how you can order multiple copies of the finished book to give to your congregations or to your friends and loved ones. This valuable book would be a great teaching tool in the churches throughout the land.

Dear Brothers and Sisters in Christ:

Most of our followers are aware of the importance of distributing what our Lord described as *"meat in due season."*

> *Who then is a faithful and wise servant, whom his lord hath made ruler over his household, to give them meat in due season? Blessed is that servant, whom his lord when he cometh shall find so doing. Verily I say unto you, That he shall make him ruler over all of his goods"* (Matthew 24:45-47).

Those who take our Lord's word to heart will be found distributing vital meat to their friends and family members who are in a desperate need to be fed such essential nourishment.

After reading this draft manuscript of Lyn Mize's book **The Open Door**, we encourage you to consider ordering multiple copies to give away to friends and loved ones who need to hear the message in this timely book. If you would like to do so, we would be happy to have them sent directly from the printer to you for the <u>cost of printing and shipping</u> as follows:

# Copies***	Cost
5	$ 40
10	$ 75
20	$115
30 or more	$ 5 per copy

We strongly believe that the Lord is returning very soon and we may not have very much time left to be found distributing vital "meat in due season." Please send your order to the addresses below.

God bless you as you continue looking for that Blessed Hope!

Jim Harman

Snail mail:	703 Hamilton Court
	Altamonte Springs, FL 32701
E-mail:	JimHarmanCPA@aol.com

*** Due to staffing challenges at our printers the minimum order at the current time is 20 books. Smaller orders will take a little longer.

THE
OPEN DOOR

Lyn Mize

Prophecy
Countdown
Publications

The Open Door

Prophecy Countdown Publications, LLC
P.O. Box 941612
Maitland, FL 32794

www.ProphecyCountdown.com
www.ffwfthb.org

ISBN: 978-1-7332995-2-7

All references from Scripture are from the King James Version unless noted otherwise.

Scripture quotations from the Thomson Chain Reference Bible, New International Version (NIV), Copyright 1973, 1978 and 1984 by International Bible Society.

Numerical references to selected words in the text of Scripture are from James H. Strong Dictionaries of the Hebrew and Greek words.

Certain words such as Kingdom and Judgement Seat are capitalized to emphasize their importance, but not in accordance with Traditional fashion.

Credit and Copyright for pictures inside this book:
    Page 116 – Bride with veil (#504) courtesy of: www.EricaKoesler.com
    Page 167 – *The Bride* by Dorothy Luscombe
    Page 176 – Pictures of the Beast, the False Prophet and the Antichrist courtesy of Pastor Randy Shupe: www.PastorRancyShupe.com

Back Cover image of the New Jerusalem by Steve Creitz, www.ProphecyArt.com

Publisher's Preface

Meat In Due Seasons Ministries originally published *The Open Door* in April 1994. Lyn Mize was a gifted disciple of Christ who was able to bring out the deeper truths often missed by other authors. I met Lyn at Ray Brubaker's International Prophecy Conference back in 1992 and we became good friends and fellow students of the Bible until he went to be with the Lord in December 2011. When we first met, we exchanged manuscripts of the books the Lord had given to each of us to write. His was called: *The Open Door* and mine was called: *The Coming Spiritual Earthquake*. We both were amazed how each of our books had the same message that the Lord was coming for His church in two phases: First Fruits (at the beginning of the Tribulation) followed by the Main Harvest (three and one-half years later). Lyn's studies and writings have far surpassed my own, and much of his work can be found on his First Fruits Ministry website that can be found at: www.ffwthb.org

Since his book *The Open Door* is no longer in print we felt it should be made available to the body of Christ as the Lord's return quickly approaches. Lyn Mize's exceptional book is being reproduced with only minor edits to the original.

What sets Lyn Mize's teachings apart from most other ministries is his belief that not all believers will be taken in the rapture at the start of the tribulation period. When we first met we were both so excited that the Lord had revealed this vital teaching to both of us!

This view of phased raptures was also held by such noted and well respected Bible teachers as: Ray Brubaker, Mikkel Dahl, Robert Govett, G.H. Lang, Hudson Taylor, Witness Lee, D.M. Panton, G.H. Pember, George N.H. Peters, Joseph A. Seiss, A.B Simpson and John Wilkinson who are all now deceased.

This position is not held by most of today's church and the purpose of both of our ministries has always been to help believers to prepare to be part of those First Fruit believers who will be taken before the start of the tribulation period.

Along these same lines,   Lyn also taught that much of the church is in danger of being excluded from reigning and ruling with Christ in the coming millennium. He also correctly points out that not all Christians will be part of the bride of Christ.

Proverbs 27:17 says: *"As iron sharpeneth iron, So a man sharpeneth the countenance of his friend."* I was blessed to have Lyn Mize as a close friend. I always considered him to be one of my best friends and an important personal mentor.

Even though we were like minded regarding most biblical doctrine, we did not agree on everything. Lyn held to the traditional seven year tribulation period that is taught by most bible teachers of today. This differs from our view, which shows that Daniel 9:27 is a prophecy about Christ and not about the Antichrist. Despite our differences, we always respected each other and we did not let these non-essential teachings to interfere with our close personal friendship.

Readers should be forewarned that Lyn had a rather startling interpretation of who the coming Antichrist is. While I agree with his analysis (chapter 10) and believe that he is correct, I would only differ from his belief that the Antichrist is still alive at the present time. However, I believe that God will bring him back to life at just the right moment, immediately after the removal of the First Fruit believers. We are including Lyn's astonishing analysis regarding the Antichrist for those who fail to participate in the soon to occur rapture.

Don't allow your skepticism over some of Lyn's beliefs detract you from the essential material that is included in this valuable book. His main purpose, as well as ours, is to encourage the reader to become the overcomer Jesus will be looking for when He returns. A careful and diligent reading and studying of the material in this book will help insure that Jesus tells you: "Well Done" when you stand before Him at the Judgment Seat.

James Harman
Publisher
Prophecy Countdown Publications, LLC

Dedication

   This book is dedicated to all those Christians who aspire to be part of the Bride of Christ. This includes all those Christians who are watching and listening for their Beloved as they hear His voice as He comes leaping upon the mountains and skipping upon the hills.

   They can see Him through the lattice and eagerly wait for Him to say, "Rise up, my love, my fair one, and come away. For, lo, the winter is past, the rain is over and gone; The flowers appear on the earth; the time of singing of birds is come, and the voice of the turtledove is heard in our land; The fig tree putteth forth her green figs, and the vines with the tender grape give a good smell. Arise, my love, my fair one, and come away."

Song of Solomon

In Memoriam

Dorothy Caines
Kenneth Caines
M. Dooley Lowe
William E. Mize

Table of Contents

Foreword

Who then is a faithful and wise servant, whom his lord hath made ruler over his household, to give them meat in due season? Blessed is that servant, whom his lord when he cometh shall find so doing. Verily I say unto you, That he shall make him ruler over all of his goods (Matthew 24:45-47).

In 2009 Lyn Mize wrote the foreword to my book *The Kingdom* and he graciously stated, "…it is my firm conviction that Jim Harman will be one of those faithful and wise servants that provides "meat in due season." With Lyn's sudden passing away to be with the Lord in 2011, little did we know that I would be distributing this magnificent book as a partial fulfillment of his prediction.

I'm convinced that the book you are holding in your hands or reading on your devise holds a vital message that the entire body of Christ needs to digest. While most pastors and teachers are capable of instructing their flock in the "milk" doctrines of the faith, very few are providing their congregations with a healthy diet of "meat" (Hebrews 5:13-14) that is so vital to their spiritual well being.

Lyn Mize was a gifted student of God's Word who had a special ability of being able to discern the deeper truths hidden beneath the surface. Lyn was able to mine the special nuggets and gems, giving us a rich and delicious meal to nourish our soul.

If you are like me you may be tempted to turn to the last chapter of this book first. While his analysis of the Antichrist is intriguing, please don't neglect a careful and diligent study of the truths Lyn has provided for you in the first nine chapters. They can help you become the mature disciple Jesus will be looking for when He returns.

Some of Lyn's teachings may be difficult to swallow for many, but I encourage you to please take the time to pray and meditate on those sections that may upset you. Allow the Holy Spirit to help you as He did for the Berean believers:

Now the Berean Jews were of more noble character than those in Thessalonica, for they received the message with great eagerness and examined the Scriptures every day to see if what Paul said was true (Acts 17:11 – NIV).

Admittedly, when first reading some of Lyn's beliefs we may initially be offended (John 6:60-61) and quickly object. But those who have teachable hearts and open minds will be able to allow the Holy Spirit to reveal that a great deal of what Lyn Mize has to offer should be seriously considered by all believers in Christ.

The rapture of the faithful Christians is rapidly approaching, but a great multitude of believers (Revelation 7:9, 14) will be taken by surprise. A careful reading of this book by Lyn Mize can help insure this does not happen to you.

Jesus went away almost 2,000 years ago and He is in the process of preparing a Holy City for those overcoming believers who are diligently making themselves ready for that glorious day when we stand before Him at the Judgment Seat. Lyn Mize has given us an excellent resource that can be instrumental in helping us qualify to become part of those who will reign and rule with the King of the Universe in this magnificent Holy City.

Wherefore the rather, brethren, give diligence
To make your calling and election sure:
For if ye do these things, ye shall never fall:
(2 Peter1:10 – KJV)

James T. Harman
Prophecy Countdown Publications, LLC
www.ProphecyCountdown.com

Introduction

There is one place in the Bible that states what a person must do in order to be saved. That verse states very simply the one and only step for a person to be saved. The verse is as follows:

> Acts 16:31 (KJV) *And they said,* **Believe on the Lord Jesus Christ, and thou shalt be saved,** *and thy house.*

This requirement for salvation could not be any simpler. There is not a step two to God's plan of salvation. There is only one step, and those well-meaning preachers, teachers and authors who add additional steps to God's plan are adding to the Bible. Some tracts give as many as twelve steps for salvation.

If there was ever an *easy believism* to salvation, the Bible emphatically states it. Salvation does not require repentance, baptism, submission to the control of the Holy Spirit, fellowship with other Christians, fellowship with God, or faithfulness to God. These six things *should* accompany salvation, and they are essential for receiving the inheritance that is reserved in heaven for the faithful Christian, but they are not requirements for salvation, either before or after the new birth experience.

The thief on the cross next to Jesus did not perform any of the above acts, yet Jesus assured him that he would be in paradise with Jesus that very day. The thief was not promised a position in the kingdom as he requested. The Gospel of John was written (John 20:31) so that man would believe and be saved, and the word repent is not found in this book of the Bible.

The Old Testament picture of salvation is the story of the brazen serpent (Num. 21:8-9), and the requirement for salvation was simply to look and live. A simple glance at the brazen serpent was all that was necessary to demonstrate belief in its power to save. The brazen serpent on the pole was a picture of Jesus on the cross so a simple glance at the cross in belief is all that is necessary for salvation. The individual does not have to repent, pray, acknowledge, walk, obey, do, work, read, learn, study, abstain, fast, love, hate, or perform any of the other Biblical action words that describe the works that a Christian *should* do after he is saved in order to *earn rewards* for his efforts.

It is true that salvation is by grace, and works of any kind do not play a part in this salvation that depends solely on the mercy of God. Then why are there so many Scriptures that talk about repentance, obedience, faithfulness, abiding, studying, praying, walking, working, loving, doing, and abstaining? The answer to that question is what this book is all about. In one sentence, the answer is as follows: **Salvation is by grace, but rewards are according to works!**

And, behold, I come quickly;
and my reward is with me,
to give every man
according as his work shall be.
Revelation 22:12

Chapter 1

THE COMING RAPTURE

The Open Door

I have said that this open door in heaven, and this calling up of the Apocalyptic seer through that door into heaven, indicate to us the manner in which Christ intends to fulfill His promise to keep certain of His saints "out of the hour of temptation;" and by what means it is that those who "watch and pray always" shall "escape" the dreadful sorrows with which the present world, in its last years, will be visited.
Joseph A. Seiss – *The Apocalypse: Lectures on Revelation*

> Rev 3:8 (KJV) I know thy works: behold, I have set before thee an ***open door***, and no man can shut it: for thou hast a little strength, and hast kept my word, and hast not denied my name.

God has promised a special "open door" to the faithful Christians of the Philadelphia church in Revelation. This open door is the promised Pretribulation Rapture that will keep these faithful Christians from the "hour of temptation."

> Rev 3:10 (KJV) Because thou hast kept the word of my patience, I also will keep thee from the ***hour of temptation***, which shall come upon all the world, to try them that dwell upon the earth.

A few verses later in Revelation 4:1 the Apostle John looks up and sees this open door into heaven.

> Rev 4:1 (KJV) After this I looked, and, behold, a door was opened in heaven: and the first voice which I heard was as it were of a trumpet talking with me; which said, Come up hither, and I will show thee things which must be hereafter.

This is the Pretribulation Rapture of the church as seen by the great majority of Christians today, but most overlook that this open door was promised only to the faithful Philadelphia Christians. Other Christians such as those in the church of Thyatira are told that they will be cast "into great tribulation" if they do not repent. They do not receive the open door.

> Rev 2:22 (KJV) Behold, I will cast her into a bed, and them that commit adultery with her into great tribulation, except they repent of their deeds.

The timing of the Rapture is one of the most controversial issues in the Church today. The student of Bible prophecy should ask himself why so many faithful Christians believe in a Midtribulation Rapture if the Pretribulation Rapture of the entire Church is the correct view. The answer is simply that there are Scriptures that confirm a Midtribulation Rapture. Christians on both sides of the issue fail to consider the idea that perhaps the Bible teaches both a Pretribulation Rapture and a Midtribulation Rapture.

It is interesting that the pretribulation rapturists expend great efforts in trying to rebut the Scriptures that confirm a Midtribulation Rapture, and the midtribulation rapturists do the same thing with the Scriptures that confirm a Pretribulation Rapture. An honest and forthright exposition of Scripture reveals teachings for both. The Firstfruits Rapture (i.e., the taking out of faithful, mature, Philadelphia Christians) is pretribulational, and the Main Harvest Rapture (i.e., the final taking out of the remaining Christians who have been refined and purified by the tribulation) is midtribulational. This is confirmed both doctrinally and typologically throughout the Scriptures as will be seen.

The Pretribulation Rapture is the most popular view held in the Church today, but popularity is not an accurate measure of Scriptural truth. If popularity determines truth, then we should all convert to Islam since that is the fastest growing religion in the world today.

Perhaps one of the reasons the Pretribulation Rapture is the most popular view is that it requires the least accountability in living the Christian life. It is very comforting for the average Christian to believe that he can sit back and enjoy the pleasures of life and dabble in the things of the world, while all the time believing that he will be miraculously removed before any hard times or persecution sets in during the tribulation. Any teaching that Christians might experience hardship, persecution or maybe even martyrdom is resisted by the majority of Christians today. It is difficult for Christians to understand that our present comfort is not the primary goal of our heavenly Father in accordance with the following Scripture:

> 1 Pet 1:7 (KJV) That the trial of your faith, being much more precious than of gold that perisheth, though it be tried with fire, might be found unto praise and honour and glory at the appearing of Jesus Christ:

God the Father promised to meet all of our physical needs if we seek the Kingdom of God (i.e., the millennial kingdom) (Matt. 6:33), but the Scriptures are replete with examples of faithful followers of Christ suffering the most horrible circumstances imaginable. The first news that Paul received after his conversion was that he was going to have to suffer a great deal for the sake of Jesus Christ. The Church in America today does not really grasp what suffering is all about, and many consider it suffering to drive a used car and live in a modest house.

Prosperity is a difficult test that God has provided for the Church in America, and the great majority of Christians are failing miserably. Pastors are among the casualties. Some are even preaching a gospel of prosperity, which states that financial success is a sign of being a faithful Christian. This false doctrine is so far removed from what the Scriptures teach that no rebuttal is necessary. The primary point to be made is that the Church is not exempt from persecution and hardship. In fact, the Lord even allows the ones He loves the most to go through fiery trials in order to purify them and increase their heavenly rewards.

In the final analysis, Christians will be ever so thankful to the Lord Jesus Christ for the three and one-half years of suffering during the tribulation after they see the rewards for faithfulness that will be received at the Judgment Seat of Christ. The tribulation will be a final period of refining and purifying for those Christians who have not allowed themselves to be cleansed and purified during the present time.

The truth is that only a small segment of Christians are preparing themselves for the coming of the Lord Jesus Christ. The majority of the Church is concerned with building large churches with gymnasiums, plush seats, carpets, stained glass windows and numerous other superficial accoutrements designed to impress our fellow Christians and other local churches. This describes the church age called Laodicea in Revelation 3:14-19. In verse 20 Jesus says He stands and knocks at their door, but most Christians do not open their door to Him. Jesus Christ rejects this church at the Firstfruits Rapture. The Philadelphia church, however, is given an "open door" in verse 8, and this is the Firstfruits Rapture. The Sardis church and the church of Thyatira will also be rejected by Jesus Christ at the Firstfruits Rapture. Chapter 8 will discuss the seven churches including their identity and the types of Christians they represent.

Faithful Christians can see why the Pretribulation Rapture is so popular since the largest segment of Christianity today is made up of Christians in churches typified by Sardis, Thyatira, and Laodicea. These are the backslidden and lukewarm Christians who are opposed to any suggestion that faithfulness will be the criterion for rewards, let alone a special rapture prior to the tribulation. Pointing out the numerous Scriptures that clearly depict a Firstfruits Rapture is not convincing to many lukewarm Christians since searching the Scriptures to see if these things are true is not a part of their lifestyle. They simply quote the Scriptures that point to a Pretribulation Rapture and glibly say that salvation is by grace and not works. For them, everything good in the Bible is for the saved, and everything bad is for the lost. They even use Revelation 3:10 as a proof text for the Pretribulation Rapture, but they overlook that the promise of being *"kept from the hour of trial"* is only directed to the faithful Philadelphia Christians (Rev 3:7). The churches of Laodicea, Sardis and Thyatira are often labeled as mere professing Christians, tares, the false church or some other tag that relegates them to the ranks of the lost. The fact that Jesus himself clearly identifies these groups of believers as part of his Church apparently makes little difference.

In consideration of the above, this is not written to the great majority of Christians who have their minds made up and are not really interested in searching the Scriptures for the meat of the Word. This is written to Christians who are open to the Word and who are hungry to learn. The reader should study and pray for understanding about what the Scriptures have to say about the rapture of the Church.

Not a New Idea

Many of the great men of God in the Philadelphia church age of the 18th and 19th centuries understood and taught the doctrine of the Firstfruits Rapture. They were men like J. Hudson Taylor, founder of the China Inland Mission, Dr. A. B. Simpson, founder of the Christian and Missionary Alliance, John Wilkinson, founder of the Mildmay Mission to the Jews, and Joseph A. Seiss, one of the greatest prophecy scholars who ever lived. Once the doctrine of Firstfruits Rapture has been explained in detail to a person who is truly desirous of knowing what the Scriptures teach, that person is typically converted to a belief in the phased rapture of the Church. The teaching is clear.

The remainder of this chapter will be presented in three sections with the first section providing an exegesis (i.e., interpretation) of the Scriptures addressing the rapture. The second section will present the argument from a typological standpoint of the Old Testament. The third section will address the criticisms from some of the more famous prophetic scholars of what they call the "partial rapture theory." The term partial rapture is not appropriate for describing the Firstfruits Rapture since it implies that only a portion of the Church will be raptured. The term phased rapture is more descriptive since the entire Church will be raptured in two phases. This section will point out how the opponents of the Firstfruits Rapture use the straw man as a technique in their attempts to refute the phased rapture position.

Section I—Why a Special Rapture?

An excellent starting place for pretribulation rapturists to understand the concept of the Firstfruits Rapture is the variety of resurrections and raptures in the Bible. Enoch and Elijah were both translated into heaven without seeing death. The Head of the Church, Jesus Christ, has already been resurrected and is currently in heaven performing his function as our High Priest (Heb. 3:1-2). These easily understood truths pave the way for a more detailed understanding of the two phases in the rapture of the Church.

The doctrine of the Firstfruits Rapture is closely related to the doctrines of Grace and Works. The doctrine of Grace pertains to the salvation of the spirit, and the legal term *justification* is the most descriptive term of what took place at the moment of salvation. *Positional sanctification* has also been used to describe the believer's position in Christ as a saved individual. By contrast, the doctrine of Works is related to the believer's spiritual growth and maturity, and the most frequently used term for this process is *sanctification* or *progressive sanctification*. 1 Peter 1:9, describes this progressive sanctification the "**salvation of the soul**."

2 Timothy 2:15 tells us to "rightly divide" the Word. The difference between Grace and Works is one of the most fundamental divisions in Scripture. By grace our spirits are saved by faith in Christ. We then have *positional sanctification*. Our souls are being saved by obedience to Christ. We are being *progressively sanctified*. This *progressive sanctification* will determine our rewards and final standing in the Kingdom of God. The following Scriptures refer to this process of progressive sanctification:

> Phil 1:6 (KJV) Being confident of this very thing, that he which hath begun a good work in you will perform it until the day of Jesus Christ:
> 1 Peter 4:19 (KJV) Wherefore let them that suffer according to the will of God commit the keeping of their souls to Him in well doing as unto a Faithful Creator.
> James 1:21 (KJV) Wherefore lay apart all filthiness and superfluity of naughtiness, and receive with meekness the engrafted word, which is able to save your souls.

The biggest question in this process of sanctification is the cooperativeness of the believer. Those Christians who cooperate with the Holy Spirit in their *progressive sanctification* will receive greater rewards. Those Christians who are uncooperative will lose rewards and will suffer great anguish at the Judgment Seat of Christ because of their shame and the contempt of the Lord Jesus Christ. An excellent analogy from Scripture is Peter when he wept bitterly when the Lord Jesus Christ gave him a soul piercing look of judgment after Peter had denied the Lord three times. It has been stated that everyone's cup will be full in heaven, but the size of the cups will vary greatly.

The Firstfruits Rapture can probably best be described as a special entrance into heaven before the trials of the tribulation start. It is an exemption from the final exam for those Christians who have already demonstrated their Christian maturity during the course of this life. The following Scriptures describe this exemption:

> 2 Peter 1:10-11 (KJV) Wherefore the rather, brethren, give diligence to make your calling and election sure: for if you do these things, ye shall never fall: 11 For so an entrance shall be ministered unto you abundantly into the everlasting kingdom of our Lord and Savior Jesus Christ.
>
> Luke 21:36 (KJV) Watch ye therefore, and pray always, that ye may be accounted worthy to escape all these things that shall come to pass, and to stand before the Son of man.

In the 2 Peter 1:10-11 passage we see again a reference to an "entrance" or door offered to those mature Christians who "give diligence" as characterized by the Philadelphia Church. Luke 21:29-36 is a scripture addressed to the Church. This will be discussed in more detail in the chapter on The Olivet Discourse. This Scripture is an exhortation for believers to pray that they would be accounted worthy to escape the tribulation. The word "watch" refers specifically to a state of readiness or preparation for the Lord's return.

Christians today should be watching for the return of the Lord, and they should be praying that they will be accounted worthy to be part of the Firstfruits Rapture. It is doubtful that many Christians are following this exhortation from the Lord Himself. It is the height of arrogance to assume that one will automatically be accounted worthy to escape the tribulation. Even Paul said he was "pressing toward the mark for the prize of the high calling" in Philippians 3:14. The following Scripture describes the Firstfruits Rapture, but it is often misinterpreted as referring to a saved and an unsaved individual:

> Mat 24:40-42 (KJV) Then shall two be in the field; the one shall be taken, and the other left. 41 Two women shall be grinding at the mill; the one shall be taken, and the other left. 42 *Watch therefore: for ye know not what hour your Lord doth come.*

This Scripture is in the Christian section of the Olivet Discourse, and it is a warning to Christians that they need to be in a state of readiness if they are to participate in the Firstfruits Rapture of the Church. This Scripture is not an exhortation to get saved for the rapture. It is a warning to believers to get ready so they will be taken with the Firstfruits. Verse 42 confirms the subjects of the warning. It is absurd to think that this warning is to depraved unbelievers since it would be an exhortation to watch for someone whom they believe is dead, buried and returned to dust.

The Ten Virgins

The parable of the ten virgins in Matthew 25:1-13 is one of the clearest proof texts for the Firstfruits Rapture. The text is as follows:

Mat 25:1-13 (KJV) Then shall the kingdom of heaven be likened unto ten virgins, which took their lamps, and went forth to meet the bridegroom. 2 And five of them were wise, and five were foolish. 3 They that were foolish took their lamps, and took no oil with them: 4 But the wise took oil in their vessels with their lamps.5 While the bridegroom tarried, they all slumbered and slept. 6 And at midnight there was a cry made, Behold, the bridegroom cometh; go ye out to meet him. 7 Then all those virgins arose, and trimmed their lamps. 8 And the foolish said unto the wise, Give us of your oil; for our lamps are gone out. 9 But the wise answered, saying, Not so; lest there be not enough for us and you: but go ye rather to them that sell, and buy for yourselves. 10 And while they went to buy, the bridegroom came; and *they that were ready* went in with him to the marriage: and the door was shut. 11 Afterward came also the other virgins, saying, Lord, Lord, open to us. 12 But he answered and said, Verily I say unto you, I know you not. 13 *Watch therefore, for ye know neither the day nor the hour wherein the Son of man cometh.*

The ten virgins represent the entire Church. The number ten is the number of ordinal completion so it represents all of whatever is in question. The term virgin is in reference to the Church rather than Israel since Israel is pictured as the adulterous wife of God the Father.

See the book of Hosea, which pictures the history of the nation of Israel.

Verse 5 confirms that the entire Church "beckoned or slept," and this means that the entire Church was divided between those looking for the Return of the Lord, and those who had fallen. The doctrine of the second coming was lost to the main body of the Church during the Pergamum church age after 312 A.D., and it was not revived until the Philadelphia church age in the eighteenth century. The Laodicean or the end times church is lukewarm and indifferent to Christ's return as described in Rev. 3:14-21.

All ten virgins had oil in their lamps, which is a picture of the indwelling Holy Spirit. Unbelievers are not indwelled by the Holy Spirit. All ten virgins trimmed their lamps, and this is a picture of getting sin out of the life through confession and turning from sin (1 John 1:9). All ten virgins had their lamps burning, and this is a picture of the outward confession of faith in the Lord Jesus Christ. The Scriptures could not be any clearer that the ten virgins represent born again, blood-bought, justified Christians, but there is a division between the foolish and the wise.

The only difference between the five wise virgins and the five foolish virgins is the extra measure of oil, signifying maturity, which the wise virgins took with them. The abundance of oil represents the overflowing presence of the Holy Spirit in the lives of the five wise virgins. They are Christians who are continually filled or controlled by the Holy Spirit. The five wise virgins have matured in the faith, and they have advanced greatly in their *progressive sanctification.*

It is important to note that in the original Greek the lamps of the five foolish virgins were "going out"—not "gone out"—and the five wise virgins told the foolish virgins to "go ye rather to them that sell, and *buy for yourselves.*" This clearly teaches that the extra measure of oil is related to works since it had to be bought. Grace can not be bought. The indwelling Holy Spirit is a free gift of grace, but the filling of the Holy Spirit is clearly a work involving our submission to the Holy Spirit (Gal. 5:16-18). The five wise virgins had made preparation for the coming of the Bridegroom, and they were given the open door. The five foolish virgins had not prepared themselves, and they were turned away.

Verse 10 is a clear and concise description of the Firstfruits Rapture of those Christians who had prepared themselves for the coming of the Bridegroom. The Bridegroom came while the foolish virgins were out buying oil. The wise virgins went in with him to the marriage, *and the door was shut*.

The reference to "the door" is the same door that is promised to the Philadelphia Christians in Revelation 3:7-8 and that John saw in heaven in Revelation 4:1. The twenty-four elders and the four living creatures in Revelation 4:4-6 represent the same group of Christians as the five wise virgins and the Philadelphia church. This is the Pretribulation Rapture of mature, *progressively sanctified* believers. These are the ones who have "renewed their minds" with the mind of Christ according to Romans 12:2.

Verse 11 confirms that the five foolish virgins came to Jesus later calling Him "Lord, Lord," and asked Him to open the door to them. Jesus stated that He did not know (i.e., recognize) them. Jesus then summarizes the parable with a warning to "Watch therefore; for ye know neither the day nor the hour wherein the Son of man cometh." The lesson of this parable is for Christians to be alert and prepared for the second coming of Jesus so they will be able to go into the wedding. The necessary preparation is to be filled with or controlled by the Holy Spirit day by day and moment by moment. One of the primary signs of a maturing believer is a daily watching for the return of Jesus Christ. Worldly believers are busy with their own plans and life goals. Mature Christians need to be faithful to the Lord and consciously looking for His return.

Two Raptures Prophesied in the Feasts

Another important teaching tool from the Bible that will help explain the two phases of the rapture is the seven feasts of Leviticus 23. The type of the harvest is probably the clearest presentation of the Firstfruits Rapture, since it involves degrees of maturity and successive reapings. The seven feasts are a clear presentation of this type. The following chart provides a brief overview of the feasts that the Jewish nation celebrates to this day:

Feet	Prophetic Fulfillment	Scripture References
#1 Passover	Death of Jesus Seed Dies	John 12:24
#2 Unleavened Bread	Burial of Jesus Seed Planted	John 6:51; 1 Cor 5:7-8
#3 Firstfruits	Resurrection of Jesus Sheaf of Grain	1 Cor 15:20
#4 Pentecost-Day of Firstfruits	Firstfruits Rapture Two Loaves with Leaven	Luke 21:36, Rev 4:1, and Rev 12:5, 14:1-5
#5 Trumpets	Main Harvest Rapture All Remaining Christians	1 Thess 4:16-17; 1 Cor 15:51-52 Rev. 7:9-17
#6 Atonement	Reaping of Corners Israel Saved	Dt. 4:30-31; Zec 12:10; Jer 8:20
#7 Tabernacles	Gleaning--Gentiles in Tribulation Saved	Mt 25:32

Bible scholars have been curious as to why there are two feasts that celebrate Firstfruits. The Feast of Firstfruits (Lev. 23:10-13) was celebrated in the late spring by offering one sheaf of the firstfruits of the harvest before the Lord along with a meat (i.e., meal) offering of unleavened bread and wine. Leaven in the Bible has always been used to symbolize sin or that which is evil or corrupting. Jesus lived a sinless life, and He was resurrected from the dead on this feast day as a fulfillment of prophecy.

The next feast that the Israelites celebrated in early summer was Pentecost, also called the Day of Firstfruits. Pentecost was when the Israelites could start eating the grain from their field that had matured early. It was celebrated by offering two loaves of bread baked with leaven. "They are the Firstfruits unto the Lord" (Lev. 23:17). This feast represents the pretribulational rapture of mature believers who, though forgiven, are not sinless. These are the Philadelphia believers "clothed in white raiment" who are given the "open door" of the Firstfruits Rapture (Rev. 4:1-4).

At the end of summer, the next feast was the Feast of Trumpets to celebrate the main harvest when all believers will be raised at the last trump. Now, all the grain has matured from the heat of the summer sun. This feast represents the main harvest of all remaining believers who "have washed their robes" and have matured during the trials of the first half of the tribulation (Rev. 7:9-14).

If the reader can understand these three feasts, two firstfruits and the main harvest, then he will be able to clearly see that there is a Firstfruits Harvest of the Church in addition to the resurrection of Jesus Christ as the first of the firstfruits. Jesus is the one sheaf of grain offered *without leaven*, and the two loaves of bread baked *with leaven* are the firstfruits of the Church.

The following Scriptures are often used as arguments against the Firstfruits Rapture since they clearly refer to the entire Church being raptured. It is true that these Scriptures are referring to the entire Church still on the earth since they are describing the Main Harvest Rapture of the Church.

> 1 Th 4:13-18 (KJV) But I would not have you to be ignorant, brethren, concerning them which are asleep, that ye sorrow not, even as others which have no hope. 14 For if we believe that Jesus died and rose again, even so them also which sleep in Jesus will God bring with him. 15 For this we say unto you by the word of the Lord, that we which are alive and remain unto the coming of the Lord shall not prevent them which are asleep. 16 For the Lord himself shall descend from heaven with a shout, with the voice of the archangel, and with the trump of God: and the dead in Christ shall rise first: 17 Then we which are alive and remain shall be caught up together with them in the clouds, to meet the Lord in the air: and so shall we ever be with the Lord. 18 Wherefore comfort one another with these words.

> 1 Cor 15:51-52 (KJV) Behold, I show you a mystery; We shall not all sleep, but we shall all be changed, 52 In a moment, in the twinkling of an eye, at the last trump: for the trumpet shall sound, and the dead shall be raised incorruptible, and we shall be changed.

Paul is teaching about the Main Harvest Rapture in both of these passages. In 1 Thessalonians 4:14 Paul emphatically states that belief is all that is required for this rapture of both dead and living believers.

The faithfulness of believers is not the issue in focus here. Those that understand the Firstfruits Rapture have no problem with these verses since all believers who "remain" will be raptured regardless of faithfulness in both of these passages of Scripture.

In 1 Thessalonians 4:15 and 17 above, Paul is referring to the living believers who will be translated without seeing death. The word *alive* is sufficient to show that these believers are not dead, but Paul adds another descriptive word for these living believers. The Greek word is *perileipo* (G #4035), and it literally means to be left behind. This word is almost universally understood as referring to people who were left behind by the ones who had died, but this is a redundancy, since the word *alive* is sufficient to establish that they are not dead. Since the word is repeated in verse 17 after it has already been stated in verse 15, the word carries a special emphasis from the Holy Spirit. Not only are these Christians alive, but they have been left behind by other believers. In this Scripture, Paul even alludes to the Firstfruits Rapture when he is teaching about the Main Harvest Rapture.

Earlier in the chapter Paul writes about the Thessalonians who were faithful Christians and had the "work of faith," the "labor of love," and the "patience of hope." Many of the Thessalonians were candidates for the Firstfruits Harvest. Unfortunately, there were also Christians in the Church of Thessalonica who were caught up in the sins of the flesh (1 Thess. 4:1-12). The Thessalonians were concerned about these relatives who were believers but had fallen away to unfaithfulness and died. Paul was assuring them that every believer would be resurrected from the dead at the return of Jesus. It is a truth that every Christian will be resurrected or translated before the wrath of God falls on the earth, and faithfulness is not a criterion for this Main Harvest Rapture. Belief in Jesus Christ is the only criterion for this rapture.

The Scriptures are just as clear about the Firstfruits Rapture as they are about the Main Harvest Rapture. The book of Revelation provides a clear chronological sequence of both raptures for those Christians who are willing to understand the plain meaning of Scripture without changing literal statements into figurative language. There are also numerous types depicting a Firstfruits Rapture of faithful Christians.

Firstfruits Rapture in Revelation

The following Scripture could not express the Firstfruits Rapture any clearer than it has already been stated:

> Rev 3:8 (KJV) I know thy works: behold, I have set before thee an open door, and no man can shut it: for thou hast a little strength, and hast kept my word, and hast not denied my name.

> Rev 3:10 (KJV) Because thou hast kept the word of my patience, I also will keep thee from the hour of temptation, which shall come upon all the world, to try them that dwell upon the earth.

This Scripture is addressed to the Philadelphia church, and it clearly links works with the promise of being kept "from the hour of temptation." The other three churches in existence at the time of the return of Jesus were specifically excluded from this promise to be kept from the hour of trial. The only way to be kept from the hour of trial is to be taken to heaven. It is one thing to be protected or sealed from the persecution, but it is an entirely different matter to be kept "from the hour." Removal from the earth is the only way for this to be accomplished. After the promise in chapter 3, John sees the fulfillment of the promise of an "open door" in Revelation 4:1:

> Rev 4:1-2 (KJV) After this I looked, and, behold, a door was opened in heaven: and the first voice which I heard was as it were of a trumpet talking with me; which said, Come up hither, and I will show thee things which must be hereafter.

> 2 And immediately I was in the spirit; and, behold, a throne was set in heaven, and one sat on the throne.

It is important to note in chapters 4 & 5 of Revelation that two groups of redeemed individuals are now in heaven around the throne of God. The 24 elders are all wearing crowns and they are all seated upon thrones. The four living creatures were in the midst of the throne, demonstrating a more intimate relationship to the Lamb than even the

24 elders. These 24 elders and 4 living creatures are redeemed individuals who are in heaven around the throne worshipping God at the beginning of the seven year tribulation period. This clearly establishes a Pretribulation Rapture of Christians, but it is equally clear that all of these Christians have received crowns and thrones.

Numerous other Scriptures clearly establish that not all Christians will receive crowns and thrones. These Christians make up the churches of Thyatira, Sardis and Laodicea, and these are the churches who will go through the first three and one-half years of the tribulation. Thyatira was specifically told that she would be cast into "great tribulation" (Rev. 2:22). Sardis was told that she would not even know the hour that Jesus had come (Rev. 4:3) because she had been unwatchful. Watchfulness is the same thing that Jesus cautioned the ten virgins about, and it is not an exhortation for unbelievers. The five foolish virgins missed the opportunity of the "open door," and they faced a door that had been closed. The five wise virgins went through the open door before it was shut since they were prepared.

A careful and prayerful study of the above texts should reveal that the 24 elders and the four living creatures (i.e., Christians worthy of crowns and thrones) represent the five wise virgins and the Philadelphia church. This is the Firstfruits Harvest of faithful Christians who have prepared themselves for the return of Jesus Christ. They are the faithful Christians who have matured early before the time of the hot summer sun (i.e., the fires of the tribulation) which would ripen or mature Christians for the Main Harvest in the middle of the tribulation. This period of ripening is not a punishment for unfaithfulness, but it is an opportunity and a blessing from God to allow the remainder of the Church to be purged and purified so they will also receive rewards and positions in the Kingdom of God the Son. Three and one-half years of persecution and refinement will be nothing compared to the glory and rewards for faithfully enduring the time of testing. The period is not a purgatory where a person works out or pays for his sins so he can enter heaven. Each Christian is guaranteed entrance into heaven based strictly on his belief in the Lord Jesus Christ. The tribulation has nothing to do with earning salvation, but it has everything to do with earning rewards in the kingdom of heaven.

Jesus counseled the church of Laodicea "to buy of me gold tried in the fire" and to "repent." This is an allusion to the tribulation period since Jesus had already told them that he would reject them because they were lukewarm (Rev. 3:16). In spite of their apathy and indifference, Jesus loves the Laodiceans so He will rebuke and chasten them during the three and one-half years of the tribulation. Jesus wants them to be "rich" and to have "white raiment" (Rev. 3:18) to wear. The term rich refers to spiritual rewards, and the term white raiment refers to reigning and ruling in the kingdom because of righteous acts or righteous deeds (Rev 19:8). Once a Christian has been raptured he can no longer perform any good works for the purpose of rewards. This is why a Christian can not buy gold refined in the fire at the Judgment Seat of Christ, but he can buy this gold during the tribulation period.

Chapters 5 & 6 of Revelation describe the scene in heaven for the first three and one-half years of the tribulation. It is during this time that the four horsemen of the apocalypse wreak havoc on the earth and one-fourth of the world population dies because of war, famine and pestilence. The seven seals do not represent or pertain to the wrath of God. The first half of the tribulation is the period in which Antichrist is given complete authority over the earth without the restraining influence of the Holy Spirit (Rev. 13:5; 2 Thess. 2:7). The wrath of God is not unleashed upon the earth until the middle of the tribulation when the trumpet Judgments begin (Rev. 6:16,17; 8:1ff).

The seven-sealed scroll is little understood by the great majority of theologians. The dramatic opening of the seven-sealed scroll is analogous to a closing (i.e., the final steps of a legal transaction where property is exchanging hands) when a house has been purchased in today's economy. This has its type in the Old Testament when a person would redeem another person or a piece of property. Jesus has already paid the purchase price for redeeming the earth from Satan, but the closing has not yet taken place. After Jesus has finished opening the seven-sealed scroll—a strictly legal transaction—in the middle of the tribulation, He begins the process of taking possession of the earth. Prior to moving in and setting up His kingdom, Jesus is going to do a little housecleaning for three and one-half years in order to cleanse, disinfect, and remove some of the pests that have accumulated during the six thousand years that Satan has maintained possession. First, Jesus is going to take out the remainder of his heavenly family (i.e., the remainder of the Church), and seal and protect his earthly family (i.e., elect Jews and Gentiles) before he thoroughly fumigates his acquired property. Please excuse the slightly humorous analogy, but this is a quick way to explain a complex sequence of events.

During the opening of the seven-sealed scroll, Satan is not thrilled about his future prospects. He knows that Christians under the leadership of Jesus Christ will be moving in to take over the rule and reign of the earth. He also knows that he only has 42 months left so he takes his vengeance out on the Church. When the Church is completely removed in the middle of the tribulation, Satan then turns his vengeance upon God's earthly people, the Jews. The last half of the tribulation is called the "time of Jacob's trouble" since Satan spends his time persecuting the Jews. At the end of the tribulation, Satan gathers the armies of the earth to fight against the Lion of the tribe of Judah in his last attempt to prevent Jesus Christ from taking over the earth. The result is the battle of Armageddon, which is referred to as the winepress of the wrath of God. It should be no surprise that Jesus Christ on his white horse wins this battle. Coining a phrase from Saddam Hussein, the battle of Armageddon will truly be the mother of all battles. One-third of the world's population will die in this battle.

No Christian or member of the Church will be on the earth during the last half of the tribulation period. There will be saved people on the earth during this terrible time of judgment from the Lord, but they will be sealed and protected from the judgments of God just like Noah was sealed in the ark and protected from the judgment of the flood. All saved people on the earth during this time will have been saved during the tribulation period.

"Falling Away" in the Last Days

2 Th 2:1-4 (KJV) Now we beseech you, brethren, by the coming of our Lord Jesus Christ, and by our gathering together unto him, 2 That ye be not soon shaken in mind, or be troubled, neither by spirit, nor by word, nor by letter as from us, as that the day of Christ is at hand. 3 Let no man deceive you by any means: for that day shall not come, except there come a *falling away* (i.e., *apostasia*) first, and that man of sin be revealed, the son of perdition; 4 Who opposeth and exalteth himself above

all that is called God, or that is worshipped; so that he as God sitteth in the temple of God, showing himself that he is God.

The Greek word *apostasia* translated "falling away" is only used twice in the New Testament. Its other use is in Acts 21:21 and it is translated "to forsake." The word means departure, taking away, or separation. The best translation for *apostasia* in the context of the above Scripture is "separation". Thus, this passage of Scripture simply states that the day of the Lord cannot occur until the separation takes place and the man of sin, Antichrist, is revealed and sets himself up as god in the temple. The sequence of events is that the separation (i.e., Firstfruits Rapture) will take place, the Antichrist will be revealed, and then three and one-half years later he will set himself up in the temple as god. It is after these events that the Second Advent or the Second Coming takes place, and this is when the Main Harvest Rapture takes place.

The above sequence of events is why mature Christians should not be looking for the revealing of the Antichrist. He will not be revealed until the Firstfruits Rapture takes place, so the hope of the Christian is to be gone at the time Antichrist is revealed. This does not mean Christians cannot know the identity of Antichrist since numerous prophecies will be fulfilled about him before he is revealed. God gave a detailed description of him so Christians could identify him and prepare themselves even more for the Firstfruits Rapture. The identity of the Antichrist is so obvious that Christians stumble over it because of a lack of Bible knowledge.

Unfortunately, most Christians are not anxious for Jesus Christ to return, and they are not watchful. The Bible prophesied this condition of the Church at the time of the return of Jesus Christ for the Firstfruits. The word firstfruits means hasty fruit or that fruit which matures early. The remainder of the Church will be ready for the Main Harvest by the time it happens in the middle of the tribulation. The persecutions of the tribulation period will do wonders in the sanctification process of those members of the Church who are left on the earth for the express purpose of maturing in the faith.

The following Old Testament passage of Scripture describes how these Christians are turned over to Antichrist for three and one-half years:

The Main Harvest Rapture Prophesied in Daniel

Dan 7:25 (KJV) And he (i.e., Antichrist) shall speak great words against the most High, and shall wear out the saints of the most High, and think to change times and laws: and they shall be given into his hand until a time and times and the dividing of time (i.e., 1+2+1/2 = 3 ½ years).

Many theologians teach this is referring to Jews, but the verses that follow prove that these "saints" are Christians, since the Church is the one that will receive the kingdom of the heavens and reign with Jesus Christ:

Dan 7:27 (KJV) And the kingdom and dominion, and the greatness of the kingdom under the whole heaven, shall be given to the people of the saints of the most High, whose kingdom is an everlasting kingdom, and all dominions shall serve and obey him.

The kingdom of heaven was taken away from the Jews after they had rejected Jesus Christ according to the following Scripture:

Mat 21:43 (KJV) Therefore say I unto you, The kingdom of God shall be taken from you (i.e., the Jews), and given to a nation (i.e., the Church) bringing forth the fruits thereof.

The references to saints in the following Scriptures in Daniel are also referring to Christians for the same reason:

Dan 7:18 (KJV) But the saints of the most High shall take the kingdom, and possess the kingdom for ever, even for ever and ever.

Dan 7:21 (KJV) I beheld, and the same horn made war with the saints, and prevailed against them;

Dan 7:22 (KJV) Until the Ancient of days came, and judgment was given to the saints of the most High; and the time came that the saints possessed the kingdom.

The book of Daniel does refer to Jews, but they are referred to as "thy people" according to the following Scriptures:

Dan 9:15-16 (KJV) And now, O Lord our God, that hast brought thy people forth out of the land of Egypt with a mighty hand, and hast gotten thee renown, as at this day; we have sinned, we have done wickedly.

16 O Lord, according to all thy righteousness, I beseech thee, let thine anger and thy fury be turned away from thy city Jerusalem, thy holy mountain: because for our sins, and for the iniquities of our fathers, Jerusalem and thy people are become a reproach to all that are about us.

Dan 9:19 (KJV) O Lord, hear; O Lord, forgive; O Lord, hearken and do; defer not, for thine own sake, O my God: for thy city and thy people are called by thy name.

Dan 9:24 (KJV) Seventy weeks are determined upon thy people and upon thy holy city, to finish the transgression, and to make an end of sins, and to make reconciliation for iniquity, and to bring in everlasting righteousness, and to seal up the vision and prophecy, and to anoint the most Holy.

Dan 10:14 (KJV) Now I am come to make thee understand what shall befall thy people in the latter days: for yet the vision is for many days.

Dan 11:14 (KJV) And in those times there shall many stand up against the king of the south: also the robbers of thy people shall exalt themselves to establish the vision; but they shall fall.

Dan 12:1 (KJV) And at that time shall Michael stand up, the great prince which standeth for the children of thy people: and there shall be a time of trouble, such as never was since there was a nation even to that same time: and at that time thy people shall be delivered, every one that shall be found written in the book.

Please excuse the numerous references, but it is important for the student of Scripture to be able to distinguish between the Jews and the Church in order to rightly divide the Word of Truth. It should be clear now that Daniel 7:25 states that Christians will be turned over to Antichrist for three and one-half years during the first half of the tribulation. The Jews will be persecuted by Antichrist during the second three and one-half years, which is called the time of Jacob's trouble.

It would not be proper to conclude this first section without addressing the primary Scripture describing the Main Harvest Rapture of the Church. The following passage of Scripture is the most detailed in regard to this phase of the rapture:

Rev 7:9-17 (KJV) After this I beheld, and, lo, a great multitude, which no man could number, of all nations, and kindreds, and people, and tongues, stood before the throne, and before the Lamb, clothed with white robes, and palms in their hands; 10 And cried with a loud voice, saying, Salvation to our God which sitteth upon the throne, and unto the Lamb. 11 And all the angels stood round about the throne, and about the elders and the four beasts, and fell before the throne on their faces, and worshipped God, 12 Saying, Amen: Blessing, and glory, and wisdom, and thanksgiving, and honour, and power, and might, be unto our God for ever and ever. Amen. 13 And one of the elders answered, saying unto me, What are these which are arrayed in white robes? and whence came they? 14 And I said unto him, Sir, thou knowest. And he said to me, *These are they which came out of great tribulation, and have washed their robes, and made them white in the blood of the Lamb.* 15 Therefore are they before the throne of God, and serve him day and night in his temple: and he that sitteth on the throne shall dwell among them. 16 They shall hunger no more, neither thirst any more; neither shall the sun light on them, nor any heat. 17 For the Lamb which is in the midst of the throne shall feed them, and shall lead them unto living fountains of waters: and God shall wipe away all tears from their eyes.

According to Revelation 7:14 these "came out of great tribulation" but they have now "washed their robes." Salvation in the evangelical sense is referred to in the Bible as taking a bath but not as washing defiled garments. In Revelation 3:4 the church of Sardis (i.e., Christians) had defiled their garments, but they washed their garments in the blood of the lamb before the Main Harvest Rapture.

Revelation 7:9-17 is clearly taking place in the middle of the tribulation, and the judgments of Jews and Gentiles do not take place until the end of the tribulation. The sheep and goat judgment is the judgment of the Gentiles and it takes place on the earth and not in heaven which is the location of the events in this passage of Scripture. The 144,000 Jews do not even preach the gospel of the kingdom until the last half of the tribulation.

The description of the saints in Rev. 7:15 as being before the throne of God and serving him night and day in his temple (i.e., priestly service) is a picture of the Church and not Israel as a nation or a group called the tribulation saints saved during the tribulation. The entire section of Revelation 7:9-17 is a picture of a "great multitude," the churches of Thyatira, Sardis and Laodicea, cleansed and sanctified by the blood of the Lamb. They were already saved at the time the tribulation began, but they had not yet matured to the point of being ripe for harvest.

Section II—The Firstfruits Rapture in Typology

The study of typology is extremely helpful in understanding prophecy by providing pictures that help the student see more clearly the meaning of some of the more obscure doctrinal statements. This is also true in regard to the Firstfruits Rapture. In addition to clear doctrinal statements about the Firstfruits Rapture in the New Testament, the Old Testament contains teachings about the Firstfruits Rapture in types such as Enoch and Elijah.

Philip, the man who disappears with the spirit (Acts 8:39), is a type of the individual raptured as he was seeking the lost. Elijah is a type of the individual raptured as he was busy establishing the saints. Both were about the Lord's business exercising their gifts in using the talents given them by the Holy Spirit. Philip and Elijah were side by side with saved individuals who were yet immature believers, but only

Philip and Elijah were taken leaving the immature believers behind. These are clear types of the Firstfruits Rapture of mature believers.

Elijah and Elisha

The primary Old Testament type for the Firstfruits Rapture is Elijah and Elisha walking along together when a fiery chariot—a picture of judgment—separated them and Elijah was taken up by a whirlwind into heaven. It is important to note that Elisha immediately rent (i.e., tore) his clothes which is a symbol of repentance. It is also highly significant that Elisha refused to talk about the coming rapture of his mentor, Elijah. This is like a great majority of the Church today who refuse to talk about the fulfillment of prophecies and the soon-coming rapture. Thus, they are failing to watch for the return of Jesus, and they will be left behind just like Elisha.

The details of Elijah's translation contain very important truths about which Christians will be taken and which will be left at the Firstfruits Rapture. In Elijah, we have a model of readiness for the Lord's return. Step by step he walked with God: "the Lord hath sent me to Bethel"; "the Lord hath sent me to Jericho"; "the Lord hath sent me to Jordan" (2 Kings 2:2). In the midst of apostasy, Elijah was creating nurseries of devotion and study in the schools of the prophets. He was boldly witnessing for God without fear, and he was waiting for God without fainting. Suddenly, in a moment of time, Elijah was separated from Elisha, the fledgling prophet, and he was carried into heaven by a whirlwind. In the miracle of translation and the holiness that made that miracle possible, Elijah did more for the maturation of Elisha and the sons of the prophets than he had done in his whole life.

It is important to note that the Lord told Elijah to anoint Elisha as his successor before Elijah was raptured. When Elijah found Elisha, he was plowing with twelve yoke of oxen. Thus, Elisha was a very rich man which is an indication of where his heart was at the time of his commission as a prophet. It is also significant that the sons of the prophets at both Bethel and Jericho attempted to talk to Elisha about the coming rapture of Elijah, but Elisha said "Yea, I know it; hold ye your peace" (2 Kings 2:3,5). Elisha is telling them not to speak about it. Both of these facts about Elisha give a picture of the Christian who will be left behind after the Firstfruits Rapture. Numerous Christians have spent their lives seeking after wealth and material possessions instead of the things of God. They are uncomfortable about studying or talking about Bible prophecy, and especially the soon return of our Lord Jesus Christ.

The refusal to speak about the rapture is the norm in the Church today. Christians do not want to hear about Bible prophecy and the return of Jesus Christ. Three and one-half years in great tribulation will likely change this attitude among the majority of Christians. The hot summer sun will cause the wheat left for the main harvest to die from the roots up, and the golden pods of grain will mature rapidly. Numerous Christians still have their roots sunk deeply into the earth, and no pods of grain have yet appeared. The fires of the tribulation will mature those Christians who are still babes in Christ, with the result that many will reign and rule with Jesus Christ in His kingdom.

When Elijah was raptured, he and Elisha were walking along two together when "there appeared a chariot of fire, and horses of fire, and parted them both asunder; and Elijah went up by a whirlwind into heaven" (2 Kings 2:11). It is not coincidental that the "evil servant" in the Olivet discourse who was not interested in nor concerned about the coming of the Lord was also "cut asunder" at the time of the Lord's return (Matt 24:50-51). The following verses describe the difference between watchful Christians and unwatchful Christians at the time of the Firstfruits Rapture. The unwatchful Christians do not want to speak about the Firstfruits Rapture just like Elisha did not want to speak about it:

> Mat 24:40-42 (KJV) Then shall two be in the field; the one shall be taken, and the other left. 41 Two women shall be grinding at the mill; the one shall be taken, and the other left. 42 Watch therefore: for ye know not what hour your Lord doth come.

> Mat 24:48 (KJV) But and if that evil servant shall say in his heart, My lord delayeth his coming;

It is important to know that wheat dies from the roots up as it becomes mature. As the roots die, the heads become ripe with grain (i.e., fruit) and bow as though in prayer to the heavenly Father. The tares remain stiffly erect, and they are easily distinguished from the wheat. Scripture confirms that harvest takes place when the grain is ripe and not before according to the following Scripture:

> Mark 4:29 (KJV) But when the fruit is brought forth, immediately he putteth in the sickle, because the harvest is come.

The Scriptures also confirm that Israel is not saved (i.e., harvested) until after the main harvest is over as shown in the following Scripture:

> Jer 8:20 (KJV) The harvest is past, the summer is ended, and we are not saved.

Numerous Scriptures compare the redemption of mankind to the agricultural harvest in Israel established and ordained by God as to the order and methods of harvesting. Much can be learned from a study of the type of the harvest.

Enoch

Enoch is another great type of the Firstfruits Rapture. In the firstfruits feast called Pentecost, it was celebrated by offering two wave-loaves of bread baked with leaven as a firstfruits offering to the Lord. The two loaves symbolized both Jews and Gentiles who would make up the Church. Therefore, Elijah is the type of Jewish Firstfruits while Enoch is a type of the Gentile Firstfruits who will be offered to the Lord at the time of the Firstfruits Harvest of the Church.

A study of Enoch reveals the characteristics of the Christian Gentile who will be accounted worthy to participate in the Firstfruits Rapture. It is significant that we know absolutely none of the physical facts of his life. There is not one single outstanding event recorded in the life of Enoch. He was raptured out of profound obscurity into heaven. The following Scripture says it best:

> James 2:5 (KJV) Hearken, my beloved brethren, Hath not God chosen the poor of this world rich in faith, and heirs of the kingdom which he hath promised to them that love him?

It is those who are unimportant in this life who will be the greatest in the kingdom. Many of those Christians who are in positions of power and authority in the Church now are going to be greatly disappointed in the coming kingdom. D. M. Panton stated it this way, "The Church knows nothing of her brightest stars, for she moves beneath the range of their heavenly orbits."

Enoch's one testimony was that he preached about the second coming of the Lord to execute judgment upon all people (Jude 14-15). The only other recorded characteristic of Enoch was that he walked with God (Gen 5:22, 24), and this was recorded twice for special emphasis by the Holy Spirit. Thus, the type of Enoch is in agreement with the numerous Scriptures that confirm that looking for the coming of the Lord Jesus Christ is the *single most important factor* to guarantee a participation in the Firstfruits Rapture. In many verses God admonishes the faithful believer to watch. The constant expectation of the Lord's return is the greatest incentive to insure a close walk with the Lord. It was true at the time of Enoch, and it is true today. Thus, the Firstfruits Rapture is peculiarly linked with testimony to the Lord's return.

Enoch is listed in the great hall of fame chapter on faith in the book of Hebrews. The following Scripture clearly states that Enoch was translated long before the judgment of the flood because he pleased God. It also confirms that his translation was a reward for diligently seeking the Lord:

> Heb 11:5-6 (KJV) By faith Enoch was translated that he should not see death; and was not found, because God had translated him: *for before his translation he had this testimony, that he pleased God.*
> 6 But without faith it is impossible to please him: for he that cometh to God must believe that he is, and that *he is a rewarder of them that diligently seek him.*

Paul Striving for the Prize

This faith in Hebrews chapter 11 is not the one point in time saving faith that all Christians have when they believe on the Lord Jesus Christ, but it is the daily living faith that bears fruit for the kingdom and earns an important position in the coming millennial kingdom of our Lord and Savior Jesus Christ. Paul talks about this daily fellowship faith of progressive sanctification. It is a mature faith that will attain to a special out-resurrection that Paul worked hard to achieve as stated in the following Scripture:

> Phil 3:7-14 (KJV) But what things were gain to me, those I counted loss for Christ. 8 Yea doubtless, and I count all things but loss for the excellency of the knowledge of Christ Jesus my Lord: for whom I have suffered the loss of all things, and do count them but dung, *that I may win Christ*, 9 And be found in him, not having mine own righteousness, which is of the law, but that which is through the faith of Christ, the righteousness which is of God by faith: 10 That I may know him, and the power of his resurrection, and the fellowship of his sufferings, being made conformable unto his death; 11 *If* by any means I might *attain unto the resurrection of the dead*. 12 Not as though I had already attained, either were already perfect: but I follow after, if that I may apprehend that for which also I am apprehended of Christ Jesus. 13 Brethren, I count not myself to have apprehended: but this one thing I do, forgetting those things which are behind, and reaching forth unto those things which are before, 14 I press toward the mark for the *prize* of the high calling of God in Christ Jesus.

The Greek word for "resurrection" in verse 11 above is the word *exanastasis* and it means *out-resurrection* or resurrection out from among the dead. This is the only place in the Bible this word is used. It is clearly a resurrection that Paul was attempting to attain by works. This is the Firstfruits Rapture that will occur pretribulational, and all who participate in this resurrection will have crowns and sit on thrones as shown in Revelation chapter 4. Verse 12 above confirms that the requirement for this out-resurrection is to be "perfect," which is a word in the King James Version meaning mature in the faith.

The Firstfruits Rapture is more than an escape for saints from the tribulation period. It is a guarantee of great reward and entrance into the kingdom with a position of authority in the reign and rule of Jesus Christ. Thus, participation in the Firstfruits Rapture is clearly related to works and rewards for faithful service to the Lord Jesus Christ. Consequently, all Christians should be striving for this goal in accordance with the following Scripture, which is repeated for emphasis:

> Luke 21:36 (KJV) Watch ye therefore, and pray always, that ye may be accounted worthy to escape all these things that shall come to pass, and to stand before the Son of man.

Section III—The Firstfruits Rapture-Criticisms Rebuttal

All criticisms of the doctrine of the Firstfruits Rapture stem from a failure of theologians to distinguish between the doctrines of grace and works or between justification and sanctification as explained earlier. Therefore, the main criticism of the Firstfruits Rapture is that Christians who hold this view are guilty of legalism or Galatianism, which is a mingling of works and grace to accomplish salvation. This criticism is completely unjustified since Galatianism adds works to grace for the purpose of spiritual rebirth or the legal term for spirit salvation, which is called justification.

The Firstfruits Rapture is not related to the justification of the believer, but it is related to the progressive sanctification of the believer. Attainment of spiritual maturity is not a prerequisite for or direct result of spiritual rebirth. Failure to attain to the Firstfruits Rapture does not affect the fact of spiritual rebirth in any way. Consequently, it is unjustified and even absurd to think that the Firstfruits Rapture is a legalistic doctrine. It is simply a reward for faithful service in the Lord's work. Numerous Christians will lose all of their rewards, but they can not lose their salvation since it is a gift from God and not related to works in any form or fashion.

Salvation is by grace, but rewards are according to works. This is a fundamental division in the Bible since works have nothing to do with spirit salvation. It is only by faith in the Lord Jesus Christ that a person is saved. However, after an individual is born again, he is admonished to walk, seek, strive, follow, obey, serve, labor, learn, do, etc. to earn rewards.

The Firstfruits Rapture also should not be explained as the reward of resurrection since all believers, unbelievers too for that matter, will experience resurrection. The fact of resurrection before the millennium is for all believers, and no one will be left behind in their graves. Thus, the fact of resurrection is directly related to grace and the salvation experience. However, the timing of resurrection is definitely related to works and progressive sanctification. As stated above, Paul was working very hard in order to attain unto the out-resurrection.

All Christians will be raptured in either the Firstfruits Rapture or the Main Harvest Rapture. The Firstfruits Rapture will take only those Christians who are mature in the faith. The Main Harvest Rapture will include numerous Christians who have matured during the tribulation, but it will include all Christians whether they are mature or not.

Another common criticism is that the phased rapture rends or divides the body of Christ, which is the Church. If this criticism is valid, then the Church is already in deep trouble since the Head has been severed, and He is currently in heaven. In addition, the body has already been divided since more than half of the body of Christ is already in heaven with the Head while the remainder of the Church is still on the earth. It only takes a moment of reflection and common sense to see the shallowness of this criticism. The Firstfruits Rapture does not divide the Church any more than the fact that the Head is currently in heaven along with the great majority of the Church. The fact that some of the Church will receive their resurrection bodies sooner than others is also applicable in this argument since the Head already has His resurrection body.

The Church is a unit and will not be divided. However, God the Father uniquely works in the life of every Christian to bring them to maturity in the faith. Some mature earlier than others, and unfortunately, some never mature in this life. Therefore, the doctrine of rewards assures that faithful Christians will be richly recognized for their efforts to cooperate in the sanctification process. Many Christians' lives will have been a total waste when they arrive in heaven, and they will have earned no rewards or a position in the kingdom of God the Son. Other Christians will receive rich rewards for their lives that they have lived, and they will have important positions in the kingdom of God the Son.

Christians are left on earth after salvation so that they might grow and follow the example of Jesus Christ. Christians are to serve now so that they might reign later (Matt 25:21; John 12:26). All Christians are members of God's heavenly family, and all will see (i.e., be present in) the kingdom of God the Son. Unfortunately, numerous Christians will be subject to an enforced sanctification process at the Judgment Seat of Christ, and they will be saved according to the following Scripture:

> 1 Cor 3:11-15 (KJV) For other foundation can no man lay than that is laid, which is Jesus Christ. 12 Now if any man build upon this foundation gold, silver, precious stones, wood, hay, stubble; 13 Every man's work shall be made manifest: for the day shall declare it, because it shall be revealed by fire; and the fire shall try every man's work of what sort it is. 14 If any man's work abide which he hath built thereupon, he shall receive a reward. 15 If any man's work shall be burned, he shall suffer loss: *but he himself shall be saved; yet so as by fire.*

After this enforced sanctification, the lives, personalities and character of these Christians will be totally different since they will then be perfect. Their lives (i.e., souls) will have been lost in the judgment fires of the Judgment Seat of Christ. In their new lives, personalities and character, they will be greatly ashamed for their failures to live faithful lives while on the earth, and there will be weeping and gnashing of teeth. It is a common belief that these Christians will experience this shame intermittently throughout the millennium. At the end of the millennium when Jesus turns the kingdom back over to God the Father, all shame and tears will be wiped away as all Christians enter into the eternal bliss of a sinless perfect life with Jesus Christ in the New Jerusalem.

An understanding of the Firstfruits Rapture will explain passages of Scripture that are typically avoided by both pretribulation rapturists and midtribulation rapturists. The Firstfruits Rapture also reconciles the arguments between these two opposing camps of prophetic scholars.

Both groups are correct in that there is both a pretribulation and a midtribulation rapture. It will be a great honor to be able to participate in the pretribulational Firstfruits Rapture. For those faithful Christians whom the Lord finds watching, He has promised an "open door."

Chapter 2

THE JUDGMENT SEAT OF CHRIST

A Just Recompense of Reward

...So that what our eyes looked on, what our ears listened to; what our hearts loved, what our minds believed, what our lips said, what our hands wrought, where our feet walked: –these are the unimpeachable evidences of the Judgment Seat. The evidence wholly decides the award: "whether it [the award] be good or bad." The Greek points to the award: "that each may receive according to the *things done*, whether *"it"* –i.e., what he receives– "be good or bad." Reward is strictly defined by works. So somewhere there exists a draft by the hand of God of what our life might have been, and still can be; some have lived wonderfully near God's thought for them: let us find and follow that Divine original.

D.M. Panton – *The Judgment Seat of Christ*

2 Cor 5:10 (KJV) For we must all appear before the judgment seat of Christ; that every one may receive the things done in his body, according to that he hath done, whether it be good or bad.

One of the greatest incentives for Christians to live Godly lives is a knowledge and understanding of the Judgment Seat of Christ. The Judgment Seat of Christ is probably one of the least understood topics in Scripture. Numerous Christians have the vague idea that they will appear at this judgment in order to determine if they have been saved. This is incorrect since the only people who will appear at this judgment are saved people. Every Christian's salvation will have already been determined or he would not be at this judgment.

The Judgment Seat of Christ will be a judgment of the works of Christians for the purpose of determining rewards and chastisements that will be distributed by Jesus Christ. There will be chastisements for unfaithful believers at the Judgment Seat of Christ. This is a difficult truth for Christians to accept, but numerous Scriptures confirm it to be true.

Please understand, 2 Corinthians 5:10 is talking about Christians. Again, only Christians will stand before the Judgment Seat of Christ. The Greek word for bad in this verse is *kakos*, and it is translated *evil* 43 times in the New Testament. This is the only place where it is translated *bad*. The word is the antonym of *agathos*, which means good. The Scripture means exactly what it says. Christians will be recompensed for the good things that they have done, and they shall also be recompensed for the evil things that they have done, if they have not been forgiven according to 1 John 1:9. The faithful Christian confesses his sins daily.

Another Scripture that is directed specifically to Christians is Colossians 3:25, "But he that doeth wrong shall receive for the wrong which he hath done; and there is no respect of persons." Paul is writing "To the saints and faithful brethren in Christ which are at Colosse..." It would be foolish for Paul to be warning them of something that could not possibly apply to them. Paul is telling them that they will be rewarded for their good works, but that they will also be recompensed for the evil that they do.

NOTE: All sin that has been confessed by the believer has been forgiven by the Lord Jesus Christ in his current function as our High Priest. Only unconfessed sin will be recompensed at the Judgment Seat of Christ (1 John 1:9).

Grace and Works

The primary reason that so many Christians do not understand the Judgment Seat of Christ and the just recompense of reward is their failure to understand the relationship between grace and works. God has made a covenant of grace with man.

> Eph. 2:8-9 (KJV) For by grace are ye saved (i.e., you have been saved) through faith; and that not of yourselves: it is the gift of God: 9 Not of works, lest any man should boast.

These verses describe the covenant of faith that deals with the past aspect of salvation apart from any of man's works. This includes works before faith and works after faith. Works do not procure salvation by grace, add to salvation by faith, or make salvation by grace any more sure. This salvation pertains to the spirit of man and it is called spiritual rebirth.

This is a salvation that was accomplished in the past, and it is the present possession of every believer. It is an active, continuing, ever-abiding salvation, and it is eternally secure for every believer. There is nothing man can do to annul this salvation. This includes adultery, homosexuality, drunkenness, lying, covetousness, gossip, gluttony, discord, jealousy, selfish ambition, dissension, factions, and envy. Christians will never stand before God to be judged in regard to this salvation since this judgment took place at Calvary. It is a work of God. Man did nothing to earn it, and he can do nothing to lose it. It is the gift of God.

The next verse in Ephesians describes present aspect of our salvation:

> Eph 2:10 (KJV) For we are his workmanship, created in Christ Jesus unto good works, which God hath before ordained that we should walk in them.

Good works should occur after spiritual rebirth, since this is how Christians grow and mature. Many Christians do not grow and mature in the faith. This growing and maturing in obedience and good works is frequently referred to as "salvation" in the Bible. The Christian should be careful not to confuse his daily walking, or progressive salvation with his past salvation of spiritual rebirth. They are very different, but Christians often confuse them.

Salvation: Past, Present and Future

The soul is what we are as a person. It is our mind, emotions, intellect, personality, will, heart (i.e., in a metaphorical sense), and character. Thus, our soul is our life. The Greek word for *soul* is *psuche*, and it is alternately translated as *soul* or *life* throughout the New Testament. The word refers to the natural life of an individual, since the soul is the seat of a person's emotions, feelings and desires pertaining to his man-conscious existence.

The spirit is different from the soul. The spirit determines our God-conscious existence, and the body determines our world-conscious existence. In simpler terminology, our spirit puts us in contact with God; our soul puts us in contact with ourselves; and our body puts us in contact with the physical realm.

In addition to the salvation that Christians currently possess (i.e., spirit salvation), the Scriptures are replete with two other phases of salvation that are both present and future. The present salvation pertains to our growing and maturing as a Christian. The Bible calls this the salvation of the soul (i.e., life). Our future salvation pertains to the salvation of the body when we are given resurrection bodies.

Most Christians have no difficulty understanding that their bodies have not yet been redeemed, but few Christians understand that the salvation of the soul (i.e., life) is a salvation that is being affected now, and this salvation is directly related to the Covenant of Works. Most Christians confuse soul salvation with spiritual rebirth because tradition has used the terms *soul* and *spirit* interchangeably. Careful exegesis (i.e., interpretation) of Scripture reveals that soul and spirit are not synonymous in Scripture, and numerous Scriptural passages have been grossly misunderstood because of this traditional error. It is because of this misunderstanding that Galatianism (i.e., Lordship Salvation) and Balaamism (i.e., the Doctrine of Worldly Compromise) are rampant in the Church today.

It is at the Judgment Seat of Christ that the salvation of the soul (i.e., life) will be determined. Numerous Scriptures exhort believers not to neglect this salvation and to seek it with all of their strength. Jesus exhorted believers to save their souls (i.e., *psuche, life*) and even described how in the following passage of Scripture:

> Mat 16:24-27 (KJV) Then said Jesus unto his disciples, If any man (i.e., if any of you) will come after me, let him deny himself, and take up his cross, and follow me. 25 For whosoever will save his life (i.e., psuche) shall lose it: and whosoever will lose his life (i.e., psuche) for my sake shall find it. 26 For what is a man profited, if he shall gain the whole world, and lose his own soul (i.e., psuche)? or what shall a man give in exchange for his soul (i.e., psuche)? 27 For the Son of

man shall come in the glory of his Father with his angels; *and then he shall reward every man according to his works.*

The above Scripture is clear that the present salvation of the soul is a salvation that believers seek, and the last sentence confirms that the salvation of the soul (i.e., *psuche*) is directly related to this present aspect of salvation and future rewards.

Paul was exhorting the "saints in Christ Jesus at Philippi" to save their souls in the following Scripture:

Phil 2:12 (KJV) Wherefore, my beloved, as ye have always obeyed, not as in my presence only, but now much more in my absence, *work out your own salvation with fear and trembling.*

Innumerable preachers and teachers have pulled this Scripture from its context and attempted to explain that it really does not mean that believers work out their salvation. Their error is failure to rightly divide the Word of Truth and understand that Paul is not talking about spiritual rebirth. Paul is talking about the salvation of the soul (i.e., life), and this is a salvation that is directly related to rewards and to our works.

Jesus bids his disciples to "lose their soul," not to "save it"! The Christian loses his soul (i.e., life) when he surrenders the control of his life to the Holy Spirit. A life lived under the control and power of the Holy Spirit will be saved and will result in rewards and a position of honor and trust in the millennial kingdom. A selfish life that is lived for the pleasures and wants of the flesh is carnal and will earn no rewards or honors.

The loss of the soul is not eternal condemnation but the loss of rewards, position and honor in the millennial kingdom. It is a life wasted in the pursuit of earthly things under the power and control of the soulical nature (i.e., flesh nature).

The failure to understand the salvation of the soul as different from spiritual rebirth is the reason for the misunderstandings between Calvinists and Arminians. The Calvinists emphasize the Scriptures that deal with spiritual rebirth and teach the eternal security of the believer. They neglect, twist or ignore the Scriptures dealing with a salvation that can be lost. The Arminians emphasize the Scriptures dealing with the salvation of the soul, which can be lost, and erroneously equate them with spiritual rebirth. Scriptural truth falls between the two extremes.

Spiritual rebirth **is** eternally secure, since it is based upon grace and the work performed by Jesus on Calvary. The righteousness of God is imputed—a legal term—to all believers and nothing can alter the believer's standing in Christ. The salvation of the soul is conditional upon obedience to God, and it is a salvation that can be lost by the unfaithfulness of the believer. Numerous Scriptures pertain to the salvation of the soul, while only a few deal with spiritual rebirth. A further understanding of soul salvation requires one to have knowledge of the tripartite (i.e., three-part) nature of man.

Tripartite Nature of Man

Man is a tripartite (i.e., three-part) being created in the image of the triune God. He is composed of body, soul and spirit, and there is a salvation connected to each part.

> 1 Th 5:23 (KJV) And the very God of peace sanctify you wholly; and I pray God your whole spirit and soul and body be preserved blameless unto the coming of our Lord Jesus Christ.

The animal kingdom is dichotomous (i.e., two-part) and possesses only soul and body. Animals have soul life, but they do not have spirit life. Since man is trichotomous (i.e., three-part), his *complete* redemption must encompass spirit, soul and body. The great majority of Christians have traditionally confused the spirit and soul of man by making them synonymous.

The spirit of man is the immaterial part of man that links him directly with God. Man's sin in the Garden of Eden resulted in death, and it was man's spirit that died in the Garden of Eden. With an unredeemed, inanimate spirit, man is alienated from God (Eph. 2:12). Once a person has been saved spiritually, he has been quickened or made spiritually alive, and nothing can ever change that condition (Eph. 2:1). This aspect of man's salvation is a spiritual rebirth and it is accomplished when man's spirit is regenerated (i.e., made alive) by the Holy Spirit.

Spiritual rebirth is a supernatural work of God, and it is not something that man attains to in any way. The result of spiritual rebirth is faith—a gift from God—and man's response of believing that the death of Jesus Christ atoned for his sin. There are not as many Scriptures directed at this aspect of salvation as most Christians think. Acts 16:31 describes this salvation succinctly, "Believe on the Lord Jesus Christ, and thou shalt be saved, and thy house." This salvation is both free and apart from the works of man. This includes works before faith and works after faith. The Scriptures always speak of this salvation in regard to Christians in the past tense. It was accomplished in the past, and it is the current possession of every believer.

The salvation of the soul is entirely different from spirit salvation, and it must not be associated with the passive aspect of salvation. Careful exegesis of Scripture reveals that *soul* and *spirit* are never used interchangeably (cf. 1 Thessalonians 5:23, Hebrews 4:12). Scripture carefully differentiates between the past, completed work of spirit salvation, and the present work of soul salvation, which is to be completed in the future. The book of James was written to *believers* exhorting them to save their souls:

> James 1:21 (KJV) Wherefore lay apart all filthiness and superfluity of naughtiness, and receive with meekness the engrafted word, which is able to save your souls.

Christians are to put off sin and study their Bibles. This is work. It is through a knowledge of, and obedience to the Word of God that Christians mature and save their souls. The Epistles of 1 and 2 Peter were also written to believers regarding the salvation of the soul, and Peter carefully depicts soul salvation as occurring in the future:

> 1 Pet 1:7 (KJV) That the trial of your faith, being much more precious than of gold that perisheth, though it be tried with fire, might be found unto praise and honour and glory at the appearing of Jesus Christ:
> 1 Pet 1:9 (KJV) Receiving the end of your faith, even the salvation of your souls.

The Epistle to the Hebrews was also written to believers in regard to soul salvation, and the writer warns them about the consequences of neglecting this salvation. The writer even includes himself as someone who could neglect this salvation, and no one doubts that the writer—probably Paul—was born again spiritually:

> Heb 2:2-3 (KJV) For if the word spoken by angels was stedfast, and every transgression and disobedience received a just recompense of reward; 3 How shall we escape, if we *neglect so great salvation*; which at the first began to be spoken by the Lord, and was confirmed unto us by them that heard him;

The above Scripture also confirms that "a just recompense of reward" can be negative as well as positive, and this ties in with 2 Corinthians 5:10 where evil deeds will also be recompensed for those who have not received cleansing according to 1 John 1:9.

The third part of man is his body, which brings him into contact with the physical world. Man is not complete without all three parts. The salvation of the believer's body is guaranteed and it is entirely future. This salvation will occur at the resurrection. Few Christians err by believing that our bodies have already been redeemed (Rom. 8:23).

The reader should now be able to comprehend that the Christian's salvation involves spirit, soul and body, and all three are important. Thus, the faithful Christian can state in all truth, "I have been saved; I am being saved; and, I shall be saved." Unfortunately, there will be many Christians who will lose their souls, and this prospect is difficult for most Christians to comprehend and accept. The Christian who understands this truth will see numerous Scriptures open up that were previously closed to the understanding. It will also mean a greater maturity in the faith and great reward at the Judgment Seat of Christ.

According to Scripture man can be categorized as soulical, spiritual or carnal. The soulical man is a non-Christian, and Christians can be classified as either spiritual or carnal. The soulical man is dominated by his soul, which does not and can not relate to God. The soulical man is alienated from God, and he is unable to grasp spiritual truth. His spirit must be regenerated (i.e., born from above) in order for him to discern spiritual truth.

The spirit of man is the seat of the higher divine life. The indwelling Holy Spirit controls the Christian who lives his life controlled by the spirit nature, and this makes him a spiritual Christian. The spiritual Christian is able to control his emotions, feelings, and desires pertaining to his still-present man-conscious existence. This results in the subjection of his unredeemed body and his soulical man (i.e., flesh nature) to the Holy Spirit. This is commonly called walking in the spirit, being filled with the spirit, living the exchanged life, or crucifying the flesh. <u>The Christian who lives this way will live a life that is pleasing to God.</u> He will be rewarded with crowns and a responsible position in the millennial reign of Jesus Christ. The position of authority will be directly related to the faithfulness exhibited in this present life that Christians live.

The Christian who lives his life according to the spirit will not only receive rewards and a position in the kingdom of heaven, but the person he is at the resurrection will pass through the testing fire and transfer over into the kingdom (1 Peter 1:7). In simple terminology, this is the salvation of the soul (i.e., life). The Christian who lives according to his flesh nature will have his soul (i.e., life) destroyed in the testing fire. The following Scripture states this very clearly:

> Rom 8:12-13 (KJV) Therefore, **brethren**, we are debtors, not to the flesh, to live after the flesh. 13 For if ye (i.e., Christians) live after the flesh, ye (i.e., Christians) shall die: but if ye (i.e., Christians) through the Spirit do mortify the deeds of the body, ye (i.e., Christians) shall live.

This Scripture is not talking about spiritual death or bodily death but the loss of the soul. The destruction of the souls of Christians is not a popular subject in Sunday Schools across the nation, but it is a Scriptural truth. There are several Scriptures that talk about the perdition (i.e., destruction) of Christians, but the great majority of believers relegate these passages of Scripture to the unsaved, even though the passages are addressed to "the elect," "believers," "brethren," etc.

> Heb 10:39 (KJV) But we are not of them who draw back unto **perdition**; but of them that believe (i.e., are faithful) to the saving of the soul.

This Scripture is talking about Christians (Heb. 10:19) going on into perfection (i.e., maturity) or drawing back unto perdition (i.e., destruction of the soul). This brings us to the very hard truth about the method God will use to destroy the souls of those believers who have lived a life of sin and unfaithfulness. It is clear from Scripture that the believer's works will be tried by fire according to the following Scripture:

> 1 Cor 3:12-13 (KJV) Now if any man build upon this foundation gold, silver, precious stones, wood, hay, stubble; 13 Every man's work shall be made manifest: for the day shall declare it, *because it shall be revealed by fire; and the fire shall try every man's work of what sort it is.*

John the Baptist also preached that the Messiah would baptize believers with the Holy Spirit *and with fire* according to the following Scripture:

> Mat 3:11 (KJV) I indeed baptize you with water unto repentance: but he that cometh after me is mightier than I, whose shoes I am not worthy to bear: he shall baptize you with the Holy Ghost, *and with fire*:

Clearly the works (i.e., lives) of Christians will be tried by fire, but few Christians seek to understand more of this trial by fire that will take place at the Judgment Seat of Christ. The following Scripture reveals that the baptism of fire will take place in the lake of fire (i.e., Gehenna), which is called the second death. This is the same place where the Antichrist, the False Prophet, and unbelievers will be cast for all eternity:

> Rev 2:11 (KJV) He that hath an ear, let him hear what the Spirit saith unto the churches; He that overcometh shall not be *hurt of the second death.*

The Scriptures are clear that not all Christians are overcomers, and this Scripture confirms that those who are not overcomers will be *hurt by the second death*, which is the lake of fire. Therefore, it becomes clear that the baptism of fire that John the Baptist was warning believers about and the trial by fire that Paul was talking about will take place in the lake of fire.

Jesus himself also confirms in the following Scripture that believers should not fear those who are able to kill the body, but they should fear him (i.e., God) who is able to kill the soul in the lake of fire. One thing that Jesus never did was to give idle warnings. It would be foolish for Jesus to warn disciples to fear the loss of their souls in the lake of fire if it were not a real possibility. Jesus in talking to his disciples (Matt 10:5) warns them that they will be hated of all men (Matt 10:22) and then He gives a warning for all believers:

> Mat 10:28 (KJV) And fear not them which kill the body, but are not able to kill the soul: but rather fear him (i.e., God) which is able to destroy both soul and body in hell (i.e., Gehenna or the lake of fire).

There is one other primary Scripture that warns believers about the negative side of God's Righteous Judgment. Few Christians are able to understand that this Scripture is referring to unfaithful believers.

Judgments: For the Lost and Saved

Revelation 20:11-15 concerns itself with the great white throne judgment. This judgment is only for the lost, and it gives the final destiny of the unsaved as follows:

> Rev 20:14-15 (KJV) And death and hell were cast into the lake of fire. This is the second death. 15 And whosoever was not found written in the book of life was *cast into* the lake of fire.

Chapter 21 of Revelation is about believers and verses 7 and 8 distinguish the difference between faithful and unfaithful believers. Again, unfaithful believers will have their *part* in the lake of fire. This is a judgment by fire of the believer's works (1 Cor. 3:15). This is analogous to Shadrach, Meshach, and Abednego being cast into the fiery furnace (Dan 3). They were not hurt since they had remained faithful. All they lost were the bonds on their hands and feet. Their end result is in contrast to the carnal Christian whose life will be lost since his life's works consisted of wood, hay and stubble (1 Cor 3:12). It is easier to confess our sins now than to wait for God to purge us by fire. Carnal Christians will suffer loss at the Judgment Seat of Christ.

The references clearly differentiate between being "cast into the lake of fire" and having a "*part* in the lake of fire." It is difficult for most Christians to understand how one reference can be talking about the unsaved while the other reference is talking about the saved when both are referring to the lake of fire. The primary difference is the context in which each Scripture is found, but an in-depth study of the Greek words involved also reveals much about the Scriptures involved. One clear distinction is the fact that the unsaved will not have just a *part or portion* in the lake of fire, but they will be cast there for all eternity. This is a very important distinction. The two verses in question are as follows:

> Rev 21:7-8 (KJV) He that overcometh shall inherit all things; and I will be his God, and he shall be my son. 8 But the fearful, and unbelieving (i.e., unfaithful), and the abominable, and murderers, and whoremongers, and sorcerers, and idolaters, and all liars, shall have their *part* in the lake which burneth with fire and brimstone: which is the second death.

Verses 1-5 of chapter 21 are referring to the end of the millennium. Verse 6 depicts salvation as a free gift (i.e., salvation by grace) while verse 7 pertains to overcoming believers who will have an inheritance in the kingdom of heaven (rewards according to works). Verse 8 pertains to believers who have lost their inheritance in the kingdom because of unconfessed sin and disobedience. These carnal Christians who have not submitted to progressive sanctification will be forcefully sanctified by fire. They will suffer loss (1 Cor 3:15).

The Greek word for fearful is *deilos* and means believers who are timid or afraid to exercise their faith. The Greek word for unbelieving is *apistos* and it refers to believers who are unfaithful, not worthy of confidence or untrustworthy. The Greek word for abominable is *bdelusso* and means believers who have defiled themselves without the cleansing provided by Jesus according to 1 John 1:9. The Greek word for murderer is *phoneus* and it means believers who have committed murder physically or in their hearts by hating fellow Christians. The Greek word for whoremongers is *pornos* and it means believers who are fornicators or who are unclean and impure. The Greek word for sorcerer is *pharmakeus* and means believers who are drug users or drug dealers. The Greek word for idolaters is *eidololatres* and it means believers who are covetous. The Greek word for liars is *pseudes* and it refers to believers who are deceitful by lying.

All of the above Greek words define sins committed by Christians in day to day life, and these Christians are not receiving the cleansing that Jesus provides in his current function as our High Priest. If these Christians do not repent and confess their sins (1 John 1:9) before the main harvest rapture in the middle of the tribulation, they will be cleansed by fire. They will have a part in the lake of fire. Their souls (i.e., lives) will be lost (i.e., destroyed) and they will lose their inheritance in the kingdom of heaven. This is not the traditional interpretation of the above Scripture, but the interpretation is correct. Christians need to wake up to some of the hard truths of Scripture.

> Gal 6:7-9 (KJV) Be not deceived; God is not mocked: for whatsoever a man soweth, that shall he also reap. 8 For he that soweth to his flesh shall of the flesh reap corruption; but he that soweth to the Spirit shall of the Spirit reap life everlasting (i.e., life for the age). 9 And let us not be weary in well doing: for in due season we shall reap, if we faint not.

This Scripture pertains to works, and it is directed to Christians. Paul is warning the Galatians about the lives they are living. The Judgment Seat of Christ is not called the Awards Banquet of Christ. Judgment is just that. It will be good or bad depending on obedience to the Word of God.

Only a believer has the choice of sowing to the flesh or sowing to the Spirit, and "life everlasting" means the blessed life that faithful overcomers will inherit in the kingdom. It does not mean spiritual rebirth in the context in which it is located. Sowing is working and working does not attain spiritual rebirth. "Corruption" is the Greek word *phthora* and it means *perish* or *destroy*. Christians who sow to their flesh nature will have their souls destroyed in the lake of fire. Christians who sow to the spirit nature that was received when they were saved will save their souls from being destroyed in the lake of fire. This test of fire is only for the believer's life. The spirits of believers are saved forever and can not be lost (1 Cor. 5:5)!

All believers will have a soul in Heaven. The only question is how much change will occur at the Judgment Seat of Christ. Unfaithful Christians will experience a great change in their person and will have little or no rewards. These are the Christians who will lose their souls in the lake of fire.

The Christian who loses his soul for Jesus' sake will end up saving his soul (Mat. 16:24-27). This is related to works and it is accomplished by crucifying the soulical nature and allowing the spirit nature controlled by the Holy Spirit to control the life. The spirit is saved when one believes in the atonement of Jesus on the cross. The soul is saved when one takes up his cross and follows Jesus. Spirit salvation is by grace and occurs at some point in time. Soul salvation is by works and is only accomplished after the believer has endured or persevered until the end. The end is either death or rapture.

There are numerous Scriptures that pertain to the salvation of the soul, and they are traditionally interpreted as pertaining to evangelical or spiritual salvation. They are usually associated with sanctification and righteous living. This is the reason that the teachings of Lordship Salvation have permeated the Church. Numerous Christians are pointing their fingers at other Christians and consigning them to the ranks of the lost because their lives do not measure up to preconceived notions of how a Christian should live.

> Mat 24:45-51 (KJV) Who then is a faithful and wise servant, whom his lord hath made ruler over his household, to give them meat in due season? 46 Blessed is that servant, whom his lord when he cometh shall find so doing. 47 Verily I say unto you, That he shall make him ruler over all his goods. 48 But and if that evil servant shall say in his heart, My lord delayeth his coming; 49 And shall begin to smite his fellow servants, and to eat and drink with the drunken; 50 The lord of that servant shall come in a day when he looketh not for him, and in an hour that he is not aware of, 51 And shall cut him asunder, and appoint him his portion with the hypocrites: there shall be weeping and gnashing of teeth.

The above Scripture is routinely interpreted as depicting a saved and an unsaved individual. A careful reading of this Scripture reveals two saved individuals who differ only in their faithfulness to their Lord and Master Jesus Christ. The first servant is faithful in performing the duties that were assigned to him by the Master. When his Master returns the faithful servant will be richly blessed and assigned a position in the kingdom.

The second servant failed to watch for the return of his Master and he allowed himself to be controlled by his soulical or flesh nature. He will be "cut asunder" (i.e., separated from the faithful servant), and he will receive a *portion* with the hypocrites where there will be weeping and gnashing of teeth. "Weeping" is deep regret and "gnashing of teeth" is deep anguish because of unfaithfulness. The Greek word for portion means a measured amount of suffering with other unfaithful servants during the first half of the tribulation for the purpose of purification and cleansing. A hypocrite can be an unsaved person who pretends to be saved, or it can be a saved person who pretends to be more spiritual than he is. The great majority of the Church today falls into this category.

The parable of the talents in Matthew 25:14-30 is in the Church portion of the Olivet discourse (also described in chapter 6), and it depicts the current Age of Grace with the Judgment Seat of Christ at the end of this age. The man in the parable is Jesus Christ and the servants represent all Christians. Each servant received a portion of the Lord's goods and was expected to work for the Lord according to the abilities that he received. Every Christian has at least one spiritual gift that he is to use in the Lord's work. This is in addition to the natural talents and abilities that are God-given. The Judgment Seat of Christ will be a place where all Christians will give an account of themselves and show how they have used these spiritual gifts and abilities in the Lord's work. In the parable all three servants are saved spiritually, but all are not faithful to their calling.

The first two servants are faithful, and they receive as a reward a position in the kingdom. The unfaithful servant lost his inheritance, and he did not receive a position in the kingdom. He was unprofitable to the Lord, and he was "cast into outer darkness." "Outer darkness" is not the same as hell (i.e. Gehenna or the lake of fire). "Cast into outer darkness" is an ancient idiom that means to receive the displeasure of the master. The three Scriptural references to "outer darkness" are found in Matthew 8:12, 22:13, and 25:30 and all refer to children of God.

The parable of the pounds in Luke 19:13-27 runs parallel with the parable of the talents. Jesus is the nobleman and the ten servants represent the entire Church. Ten is the number of ordinal completion so the complete Church is in view. The one pound represents the life that each Christian is given in order to live for the Lord. Some Christians grow and mature in the faith and their lives bear much fruit in proportion to their faithfulness. The servant who gained ten pounds depicts the Christian who has matured in the faith to the maximum. Remember that ten is the number of ordinal completion. The servant who gained five pounds represents the Christian who matures enough in the faith to warrant a position in the kingdom. Five is the number of Grace in Scripture and it pictures the Christian who works in the power of the Spirit (i.e., his is Spirit led).

The servant who had gained zero pounds represents Christians who do not work for the Lord. These Christians will lose their inheritance in the kingdom even though they will **not** lose their salvation in the evangelical sense. The unfaithful servant had his pound (i.e., his life or soul) taken away from him. This is analogous to the Christian who loses his life (soul) because he has lived according to his flesh nature. This is the Christian who is saved according to the following:

> 1 Cor 3:15 (KJV) If any man's work shall be burned, he shall suffer loss: but he himself shall be saved; yet so as by fire.

The "citizens" in Luke 19:14 refer to the Jews who rejected Jesus as their King. They lost their inheritance in the kingdom of the heavens. The nation of Israel will receive their earthly inheritance and dwell in the land of Israel as the premier nation in the world during the millennium. The Church received the inheritance of the kingdom of the heavens according to the following Scripture:

> Mat 21:43 (KJV) Therefore say I unto you, The kingdom of God shall be taken from you (i.e., the nation of Israel) and given to a nation (i.e., the Church) bringing forth the fruits thereof.

Even though the Church as an entity received the kingdom of the heavens, there will be many Christians who will lose this inheritance just like Israel did because of unfaithfulness and disobedience. Scripture distinguishes between Christians who are able to "*see* the kingdom of heaven" and Christians who will "*enter* the kingdom of heaven." "Enter the kingdom" literally means to enter into the King's dominion and refers to being assigned a responsible position in our Lord's kingdom.

"See the kingdom" means to be physically present in the coming millennial kingdom but having no position of authority. All Christians will "see the kingdom" but not all Christians will "enter the kingdom." The failure of Bible students to see this difference has resulted in the rapid growth of the false doctrine of Lordship Salvation. Numerous Christians equate "enter the kingdom" with salvation in the evangelical sense, but it is actually related to the ongoing present aspect of our salvation as described earlier in the chapter.

> John 3:3 (KJV) Jesus answered and said unto him, Verily, verily, I say unto thee, Except a man be born again, he cannot *see the kingdom of God*.

The above Scripture confirms that spiritual rebirth is necessary for a person to understand or comprehend the kingdom of God.

> John 3:5 (KJV) Jesus answered, Verily, verily, I say unto thee, Except a man be born of water and [of] the Spirit, he cannot *enter into the kingdom of God*.

This Scripture adds the criterion that one must be "born of water" in order to "enter the kingdom." The phrase "born of water" has puzzled numerous students of the Bible, and there is much debate over exactly what it means. Many think it means physical birth with the water referring to the amniotic fluid. Others think it means water baptism. The Church of Christ and several other denominations think that water baptism is necessary for salvation in the evangelical sense. Some believe that it means the cleansing that Christ provides by "the washing of water by the word,..."

The correct interpretation has to be the cleansing that Christ provides since the grammatical construction only allows for a figurative interpretation of "born of water." Physical birth and water baptism are both literal acts. The second "of" in the verse is not in the original autograph so the first "of" governs the words water and spirit. This means that both objects of the same preposition must either be literal or figurative. Since "born of Spirit" has a figurative meaning, "born of water" must also have a figurative meaning. Thus, Ephesians 5:25-27 delineates the meaning of the phrase "born of water," and it definitely refers to the sanctification process that faithful Christians are passing through as they mature in the faith.

Progressive sanctification is the process whereby Christians become Christ-like in character, and this means that Christians actually take on the character of God. This can not be accomplished by improving the soulical nature (i.e., the old man) in Christians. It necessitates the difficult process of killing the old nature (i.e., losing the soul) so that the new spirit nature born of God can control.

Progressive sanctification does not occur instantaneously as does the new birth experience (positional sanctification), but it takes a lifetime of faithful obedience to the Word of God. This is the "renewing of the mind" in Romans 12:2 and the "perfecting holiness" in 2 Corinthians 7:1. All Christians experience the new birth (i.e., they are justified), but all Christians are not being sanctified in the current pilgrim walk through the wilderness. It is a fact that all Christians will be finally cleansed and sanctified by the Lord Jesus Christ, but it will be an enforced sanctification for numerous Christians. Believers who voluntarily submit to sanctification in this life will be rewarded with responsible positions in the kingdom.

Christians who allow the old nature to control their lives will lose rewards at the Judgment Seat of Christ, and they will lose their lives (i.e., souls). In simpler terms, their lives will have been a total waste. When they arrive in the kingdom in their new bodies, their lives will be totally different in regard to their character, behavior, attitudes and interest. It is then that they will realize the wasted life that they lived in the current pilgrim walk, and there will be much weeping and anguish expressed for their failure to appropriate the promises of God. These "children of the kingdom" will have lost their inheritance, and there will be much sorrow and grief for their unfaithfulness to the Lord Jesus Christ.

> Mat 8:12 (KJV) But the children of the kingdom shall be cast out into outer darkness: there shall be weeping and gnashing of teeth.

The Scriptural term son or sons has a much deeper meaning than most Bible students understand. The Greek word is *huios* and the primary meaning is male offspring of a parent. It is often used metaphorically in Scripture to describe those who manifest a certain character, whether evil or good. Matthew 5:9,45 use the word *huios* and it refers to those who reflect the character of God. The Greek word for child or children is *teknon*. In contrast to *huios*, it means the fact of birth whereas *huios* stresses the dignity and character of the relationship. All Christians are children (i.e., *teknon*) of God, but not all Christians will be sons (i.e., *huios*) of God. Unfortunately, the King James Version of the Bible does not discriminate between the mature *huios* and the immature *teknon*.

The following Scripture reveals the difference between children of God (i.e., heirs of God), and sons of God (i.e., joint-heirs with Christ):

> Rom 8:14-17 (KJV) For as many as are led by the Spirit of God, they are the sons (i.e., *huios*) of God. 15 For ye have not received the spirit of bondage again to fear; but ye have received the Spirit of adoption, whereby we cry, Abba, Father. 16 The Spirit itself beareth witness with our spirit, that we are the children (i.e., *teknon*) of God: 17 And if children (i.e., *teknon*), then heirs; heirs of God, and joint-heirs with Christ; if so be that we suffer with him, that we may be also glorified together.

The sons (i.e., huios) of God are those Christians who are led by the Spirit and not their soulical or flesh nature. All Christians have received the Spirit of adoption, which means we are children of God and, therefore, heirs of God. We also shall be "joint-heirs with Christ; *if so be that we suffer with him...*" This Scripture plainly states that Christians who are led by the Spirit of God and who suffer with Christ will not lose their inheritance as a child of God. Maturity is the requirement.

The Roman noble in New Testament times would choose one of his boys thought to be the most suitable to be his son and heir. This child was adopted as distinct from the other children, and he was made head of the house under the father. His relationship to the father was the same as the other children, but his position in the family was superior to the others. Those who refuse to distinguish between simple heir-ship to God and joint heir-ship with Jesus make the former conditional upon suffering with Christ. This makes works (i.e., suffering with Christ) a condition for salvation. Believers should not fall into this trap. Salvation is by grace, but rewards are according to works.

Heirs are those who are born of the Spirit. Joint-heirs are those who are "born of water and [of] the Spirit." Sanctification is just as critical for being a son of God as justification is for being a child of God. The receiving of the inheritance is just as dependent upon sanctification as it is upon justification. The atoning blood and the sanctifying Word and Spirit are required for Christians to receive the inheritance.

It is foolish for Christians to neglect the water of cleansing because of an alleged sufficiency in the blood. The brazen laver of cleansing (1 John 1:9, Ex. 38:8) is just as indispensable for its purpose as the altar is for its office. The great majority of Christians stop at the altar (i.e., the Cross) without proceeding to the laver and the tent of meeting where fellowship, close communion, and the adoption as son awaits. It is by faith in Christ that Christians are sanctified as well as justified, but the sanctifying faith is the mature fruit bearing faith and not the dead faith spoken of in James 2:17.

Summary

The end of the Age of Grace is rapidly approaching and the Church will be completely removed from the earth before the wrath of God falls on the earth in the middle of the tribulation. The Antichrist will be given authority for 42 months during the tribulation. Those Christians who have matured in the faith will be taken out before Antichrist is revealed, but much of the Church who have been indifferent to spiritual things will be left to endure the tribulation of Antichrist for the purpose of refining and maturing.

All Christians will appear before Jesus at the Judgment Seat of Christ where there will be execution of perfect justice and righteousness. Every Christian will be judged according to his works. Rewards will be given where merited, and punishment will be rendered where merited. Rewards will consist of positions of authority in the millennial kingdom according to the Christian's faithfulness in the current wilderness trek. Punishment will be the loss of the inheritance or the failure to be a co-heir with Christ in His millennial kingdom.

There will also be some type of punishment described in the Scriptures as being analogous to being flogged or receiving many stripes for being unfaithful to the Lord. This description of the punishment is metaphorical rather than corporal, but the Scriptures are clear that it will be extremely unpleasant for those Christians receiving this punishment. 2 Corinthians 5:11 describes the Judgment Seat of Christ as a place where the "terror of the Lord" will be manifested. In regard to the Judgment Seat of Christ, Hebrews 10:31 says, "It is a fearful thing to fall into the hands of the living God." Hebrews 10:30 also refers to the Judgment Seat of Christ and states, "Vengeance belongeth unto me, I will recompense, saith the Lord. And again, *The Lord shall judge his people.*"

The purpose of this chapter is not to frighten or intimidate Christians but to awaken them to the truths of Scripture. The time for the return of the Lord and Master Jesus Christ is extremely close, and the great majority of Christians are not prepared. A large number of God's people do not even bother to worship Him one day out of the week. Many are alcoholics, homosexuals, drug users, adulterers, and liars. They are saved by Grace, but they will suffer the vengeance of Almighty God unless they repent of their sins and receive the cleansing that Jesus is now providing as our High Priest.

Jesus will be our Judge at the Judgment Seat of Christ, and it will be a time of terror for many Christians. Those who refuse to "walk in the light" now will "fall into the hands of the living God," and they will find it to be a "fearful," "terrible" experience since the "terror of the Lord" will be manifested, and a just "recompense" will be meted out. Conversely, it will be a most joyful experience for Christians who have served the Lord faithfully in this life. Christians who have been virtually unknown in the Church while on the earth will be accorded the most important positions in the millennial kingdom. They will also be honored by their presentation as the Bride of Christ. Salvation is by grace, but rewards, both good and bad, are according to works.

> 1 Pet 1:14-17 (KJV) As obedient children, not fashioning yourselves according to the former lusts in your ignorance: 15 But as he which hath called you is holy, so be ye holy in all manner of conversation; 16 Because it is written, Be ye holy; for I am holy. 17 And if ye call on the Father, who without respect of persons judgeth according to every man's work, ***pass the time of your sojourning here in fear***:

Chapter 3

THE SEVEN FEASTS

God's Plan for the Ages

Has the Church swallowed a blunder? Is the Feast of Trumpets too obvious, thereby being a roadblock? If so, where did we go wrong? And what feast is correct? What does it mean, "the last trump?" Pentecost started in Acts 2. The first trump announced the opening of this feast on the day of Pentecost. When the time comes to fulfill or complete this feast, the second trump will announce that day by calling up the saints to be with Jesus…Pentecost is the Jubilee Feast for the church. Jubilee Day for the church is spiritual and is announced with a silver trumpet. The first trump announced the start of this glorious dispensation by filling believers with the Holy Ghost, that same Spirit that will quicken us when the last trumpet blows completing this feast and taking us to Jesus…completely fulfilling this feast.

Peggy J. Flowers – ***Will The Real Rapture Feast Stand UP?***

The seven feasts ordained by God for Israel to celebrate are located in the 23rd chapter of Leviticus. These feasts were a teaching tool for the children of Israel. They promised a coming Messiah and an ultimate salvation for the nation.

The Hebrew word for feast (Lev 23:2) means appointment (i.e., a fixed time or season). The Hebrew word for convocation (Lev. 23:3) means an assembly of people, but the word carries a deeper connotation of assembling for the purpose of a rehearsal for something. Thus, the seven feasts of God were given as a pattern or rehearsal of future events that will occur at the appointed times, but God first gave Israel the Sabbath as a sign of a perpetual covenant, a great hope for a future millennial rest. This is confirmed in Lev 23:3 and in the following:

Exo 31:13-17 (KJV)   Speak thou also unto the children of Israel, saying, Verily my sabbaths ye shall keep: for it is a sign between me and you throughout your generations; that ye may know that I am the LORD that doth sanctify you. 14 Ye shall keep the sabbath therefore; for it is holy unto you: every one that defileth it shall surely be put to death: for whosoever doeth any work therein, that soul shall be cut off from among his people. 15 Six days may work be done; but in the seventh is the sabbath of rest, holy to the LORD: whosoever doeth any work in the sabbath day, he shall surely be put to death. 16 Wherefore the children of Israel shall keep the sabbath, to observe the sabbath throughout their generations, for a perpetual covenant. 17 It is a sign between me and the children of Israel for ever: for in six days the LORD made heaven and earth, and on the seventh day he rested, and was refreshed.

Every time Israel celebrated the Sabbath they were to remember that God created the heaven and earth in six days and rested on the seventh. The Sabbath was also a sign of another pattern of God's seven thousand year plan for man. A sign is something that portends something beyond itself, and the Sabbath as a sign taken in conjunction with other Scriptures points to the terminus in God's plan for the ages. This terminus is the seventh thousand-year period, and it is commonly called the millennium or rest (Heb 4). All of creation groans in travail awaiting the millennium when God will remove his curse from the earth, and Jesus Christ will reign over the earth as the Head of a perfect government. The Scriptures confirm this seven thousand year plan, and there is much historical evidence to confirm it.

The following Scripture verse provides the figurative meaning of the word day when the literal meaning does not make any sense:

2 Pet 3:8 (KJV) But, beloved, be not ignorant of this one thing, that one day is with the Lord as a thousand years, and a thousand years as one day.

One must be careful not to apply the day-equals-a-year interpretation to all of the prophetic Scriptures since this is a violation of basic hermeneutical principles. It is appropriate to take the word *day* figuratively when it makes no sense when taken literally. A primary example of when day should be taken figuratively (i.e., one thousand years) is the following Scripture:

> Hosea 6:1-2 (KJV) Come, and let us return unto the LORD: for he hath torn, and he will heal us; he hath smitten, and he will bind us up. 2 *After two days* will he revive us: i*n the third day* he will raise us up, and we shall live in his sight.

The word *day* used in the plural and singular in this Scripture clearly makes no sense when taken literally, so the figurative interpretation must be sought. The above Scripture is a prophecy about Israel who rejected their Lord and Savior (i.e., the Messiah). Because of this rejection Israel was torn and smitten, and they will remain this way for two days or two thousand years. It is "in the third day" that Jesus will revive Israel. It is not a coincidence that almost two thousand years have elapsed since Israel's Messiah came to earth. The third day is only a short time away. The time for Israel's restoration is very near.

The third and fourth chapters of the book of Hebrews describes a rest [lit. 'a Sabbath keeping,' 'a Sabbath rest'] that is yet future and designed for the people of God. When understood in connection with the prophetic Scriptures about the millennium, it becomes clear that this "Sabbath rest" is the millennial kingdom that is to last for a literal one thousand years. This means that man is given six days or six thousand years to work, but the seventh thousand-year period is the millennial rest that equates with the Sabbath. According to most chronologies taken from Scripture, the earth is very close to the end of six thousand years. For example, Ussher's chronology places creation at 4004 B.C. Since the millennial rest will be ushered in by Jesus Christ, and there is a seven year tribulation period before it begins, the return of Jesus for the Church must be very close.

In addition to the Sabbath day, the seven feasts also gave a pattern of prophetic events that were future, and Jesus Christ was to fulfill each one. The following Scripture confirms this:

> Col 2:16-17 (KJV) Let no man therefore judge you in meat, or in drink, or in respect of an holyday (i.e., feast day), or of the

new moon, or of the sabbath days: 17 Which are a shadow (i.e., type or picture) of things to come; but the body (i.e., substance or fulfillment) is of Christ.

Basically, this Scripture states that Christians are free from observing the legalistic requirements of the Law, but it also states that these feast dates are important as types of future events that will be fulfilled by Jesus Christ. These feasts are landmarks for God's plan for the age.

Three Interpretations of the Bible

The number three in Scripture represents divine perfection. It is the first of four perfect numbers in Scripture. Seven denotes spiritual perfection. Ten denotes ordinal perfection, and twelve denotes governmental perfection. All things that are specially complete are stamped with the number three. God is Father, Son and Holy Spirit. He is omniscient, omnipresent, and omnipotent. Time is past, present and future. The kingdom of God has three aspects. Man was created as body, soul and spirit. Thus, the divine stamp on Scripture includes three interpretations.

The literal-historical includes the literal events that took place, and it is the primary basic interpretation. The second interpretation is often called the spiritual, and it includes the devotional or personal applications that are to be made from Scripture. It is the job of pastors to present the spiritual applications that are to be made from Scripture.

The third interpretation of Scripture is called the prophetic or doctrinal interpretation of Scripture. The prophetic interpretation is the most neglected of the three interpretations since it requires a great deal of Bible study and a close intimate walk with the Lord. It is the job of teachers to present the prophetic interpretation of the Scriptures to Christians.

The Prophetic Significance of the Feasts

#1 Passover

The first feast commanded by God was Passover. This was celebrated on the 14th day of the first month of Nisan (i.e., Abib) in the evening

(Lev 23:5). This feast was instituted in Egypt on the night before the exodus from Egypt. The Passover lamb was killed on the evening of the 14th of Nisan and the blood was sprinkled on the doorposts and lintel as a security against the death angel who was to pass over that night.

The New Testament fulfillment of this feast was the death of Christ on Calvary. Jesus celebrated the Passover with his disciples on the evening of the 14th. The lamb was slain and they celebrated Passover according to the Pharisees who were the conservatives of Jesus' day. The Jewish day always began at sundown according to God's pattern in Genesis so the 14th of Nisan began at sundown on a Tuesday evening. Jesus was crucified Wednesday morning—still the 14th of Nisan—at 9:00 (i.e., the 3rd hour) and He died at 3:00 in the afternoon.

The Sadducees were in control of the Sanhedrin, and they celebrated the Passover according to the Greek reckoning of time, which began the day at midnight instead of sundown. This is the reason that Jesus was able to eat the Passover and also die at the precise time (i.e., 3:00 p.m.) that the lamb was traditionally slain by the Sadducees at that time. Caiaphas was the high priest and he was a Sadducee. The Sadducees ate the Passover meal on Wednesday night after Jesus was crucified that day. It was still the day of Passover to them since their day did not end until midnight. An understanding of the Jewish and Greek reckonings of when the day started resolves the apparent discrepancies in the four gospels concerning the crucifixion, the resurrection of Jesus, and the differences in the times that the Passover meal was celebrated.

#2 Unleavened Bread

The feast of Unleavened Bread (Lev 23:7,8) was celebrated for seven days and it began on the evening of the 15th of Nisan. It is significant that the first and seventh days of the feast of Unleavened Bread are annual Sabbaths or High Days. The seven feasts ordained by God for Israel contain seven days that are to be celebrated as Sabbath days (Lev 23:8, 21, 25, 28, 30, 31, 32, 35, 36, 38, & 39). These Sabbath days along with an outline of the seven feasts are presented in chart form at the end of this chapter.

The reason that tradition holds that Jesus was crucified on Friday stems from a misunderstanding of the annual Sabbaths ordained by God. Preparation Day was the day before the Sabbath so the name Preparation Day became synonymous with Friday. This was true 52 times during the year, but there were seven Preparation Days during the Jewish year that occurred on other days during the week. This was the case during the week that Jesus was crucified. Wednesday was the day of Passover, but it was also Preparation Day for the first day of Unleavened Bread which was an annual Sabbath or High Day as described in the following verse:

> John 19:31 (KJV) The Jews therefore, because it was the preparation, that the bodies should not remain upon the cross on the Sabbath day, (*for that Sabbath day was an high day*,) besought Pilate that their legs might be broken, and that they might be taken away.

The piece of bread (i.e., matzo) used by the Jews to observe this feast today is clearly typical of our Lord since it is striped (1 Peter 2:24) and pierced (John 19:37). The feast lasted seven days since it was customary to mourn for the dead for three days which are called *days of weeping*, and then followed by four *days of lamentation* making a total of seven days.

According to rabbinical tradition, the spirit wandered about the tomb for three days hoping to re-enter the body since it took this long for corruption to take place. This is why Jesus had to lie in the tomb for a full three days and three nights to prove that he had gained the keys to hell and death (Rev. 1:18). Thus, Jesus fulfilled the feast of Unleavened Bread precisely at the correct time by being placed in the tomb on the first moments of the first day of Unleavened Bread and remaining there for the full three *days of weeping*.

The Jews also had a practice of calling the entire eight-day celebration by the name Passover even though only the first day was actually Passover. The remaining seven days were the feast of Unleavened Bread, and the feast of Firstfruits also occurred during this eight-day celebration.

Leaven in the Scriptures always refers to evil or that which corrupts. This is why the Jews were to spend seven days purging out all leaven from within the house. This is a picture of the believer purging out the evil from within himself. Paul expressed the fulfillment of this as follows:

> 1 Cor 5:7-8 (KJV) Purge out therefore the old leaven, that ye may be a new lump, as ye are unleavened. For even Christ our Passover is sacrificed for us: 8 Therefore let us keep the feast, not with old leaven, neither with the leaven of malice and wickedness; but with the unleavened bread of sincerity and truth.

The prophetic fulfillment of the feast of unleavened bread was the burial of Christ. He was placed in the tomb on the first moments of the first day of Unleavened Bread. The Jews were to feed on unleavened bread for a period of seven days. The body of Jesus was the unleavened bread according to the following Scripture:

> John 6:51 (KJV) I am the living bread which came down from heaven: if any man eat of this bread, he shall live for ever: and the bread that I will give is my flesh, which I will give for the life of the world.

#3 Firstfruits

The next feast day was the feast of Firstfruits, and it occurred during the same eight days as Passover and Unleavened Bread. The day of its celebration was the day after the weekly Sabbath, and it was celebrated by waving one sheaf of the Firstfruits before the Lord (Vs. 10, 11). There was also a burnt offering of a male lamb without blemish (Vs 12), and a meat (i.e., meal) offering of unleavened bread and wine (Vs 13). It is not coincidence that this feast day occurred on the same Sunday that Jesus was resurrected from the dead, ascended into heaven with his blood, sprinkled his own blood on the mercy seat in the tabernacle in heaven, and returned to earth to teach his disciples for forty days.

It should be clear that the feast of Firstfruits was fulfilled by the resurrection of Jesus and the placing of his blood on the mercy seat in heaven. Jesus is the spotless lamb, the unleavened bread, and the single sheaf of grain waved before God.

It is at this point in the seven feasts that confusion sets in since the fourth feast is also called Firstfruits, but it is more commonly called Pentecost, the feast of Harvest, or the feast of Weeks.

Even more confusing is the Old Testament referral to three feasts that are to be celebrated by the Jews in the following Scripture:

> Exo 23:14-17 (KJV) Three times thou shalt keep a feast unto me in the year. 15 Thou shalt keep the feast of unleavened bread: (thou shalt eat unleavened bread seven days, as I commanded thee, in the time appointed of the month Abib; for in it thou camest out from Egypt: and none shall appear before me empty:) 16 And the feast of harvest, the firstfruits of thy labours, which thou hast sown in the field: and the feast of ingathering, which is in the end of the year, when thou hast gathered in thy labours out of the field. 17 Three times in the year all thy males shall appear before the Lord GOD.

The three feasts were three separate gathering times during the year in the spring, summer and fall. The feast of Passover, the feast of Unleavened Bread and the feast of Firstfruits were celebrated in the spring gathering. The feast of Firstfruits (Lev 23:10-14) and the day of Firstfruits (Lev 23:15-21 & Num. 28:26) are often confused, and this has presented a problem in understanding the order of the resurrection. Jesus was resurrected on the feast of Firstfruits. There will also be a rapture of the Firstfruits of the Church as a fulfillment of the day of Firstfruits, which is more commonly called Pentecost.

The transliterated Hebrew word for Firstfruits which points to the resurrection of Christ is *re'shiyth* (i.e., ray-sheeth) and it means the very first in time, place, order or rank. This was the first mature sheaf of grain and was waved before the Lord to celebrate the feast (Lev 23:10-11).

The transliterated Hebrew word for Firstfruits which points to the Firstfruits rapture of the church is *bikkuwr* (i.e., bik-koor'). This word means the Firstfruits of the crop which mature early, but it does not refer to the very first one in order. Both of these Hebrew words are used together in the following passage of Scripture:

Exo 23:19a (KJV)   The first (i.e., re'shiyth) of the firstfruits (i.e., bikkuwr) of thy land thou shalt bring into the house of the LORD thy God.

In other passages these two words are both translated "firstfruits." Jesus is the firstfruits (i.e., re'shiyth). He is the fulfillment of the #3 Feast of Firstfruits. As we shall see next, mature Christians are the firstfruits (i.e., bikkuwr) of the #4 Feast of Pentecost - Day of Firstfruits.

Jesus was the Firstfruits and the fulfillment of this third feast. Jesus is the first of the Firstfruits, and those mature Christians who are prepared for the return of Jesus and are looking forward to it are the Firstfruits. Both of the above Hebrew words are translated Firstfruits in Scripture, but there is a clear distinction between them. There are even two separate feasts to celebrate each one.

#4 Pentecost—Day of Firstfruits

Pentecost is also called the feast of Weeks because it takes place seven weeks after the feast of Firstfruits. It always occurs on the "morrow after the seventh sabbath" so it always occurs on Sunday. Pentecost in 2022 will occur on June 5th. It would behoove the reader to be well aware of the date of Pentecost each year since it is conceivable that the Firstfruits rapture may take place on this date. The date of Pentecost for the next several years is as follows:

2023	May 28	2024	May 19	2025	June 8
2026	May 24	2027	May 16	2028	June 4
2029	May 20	2030	June 9	2031	June 1

There are numerous prophetic scholars who are especially interested in the dates of the celebration of Rosh Hashanah (i.e., feast of Trumpets) each year. The reason for this interest is the belief that the rapture at the last trump will take place on Rosh Hashanah, and this belief is probably accurate. Unfortunately, these prophetic scholars overlook the fact that #4 Pentecost must be fulfilled before #5 Rosh Hashanah is fulfilled.

Many think that Pentecost was fulfilled when the Church was instituted on Pentecost, however this was only the beginning of the fulfillment of Pentecost. It seems appropriate that the Church Age will begin and end on Pentecost with the rapture of the Firstfruits of the Church.

The celebration of Pentecost is described in Lev. 23:15-21. The offering to the Lord includes two loaves of bread baked with leaven (Vs 17). "They are the Firstfruits unto the Lord" (Vs 17). It should be clear that this Firstfruits cannot refer to Jesus since the loaves were baked with leaven, a symbol of sin and corruption in the Bible. There are two loaves baked with fine flour that came from the sheaves of grain that matured early.

The two loaves of bread represent both Jews and Gentiles which make up the faithful remnant of the Church. They will be raptured at the beginning of the seven year tribulation period. This is the same group of Christians referred to as the Philadelphia Church in Revelation 3:7-13. These are the Christians who are kept from the "hour of temptation" (Rev. 3:10) because of their faithfulness. There are quite a few Scriptures that confirm both a Firstfruits and a main harvest rapture of the Church. Both of these are in addition to the Firstfruits resurrection of Jesus (Vss 10-14).

Pentecost is the fourth feast and the third of the seven annual Sabbaths or High Days (Vs 21).

#5 Rosh Hashanah—Feast of Trumpets

The feast of Trumpets (i.e., Rosh Hashanah) is the first of the three feasts that occur in the fall of the year. It is described in verses 23-25, and it is celebrated by the blowing of trumpets. The feast day occurs on the first day of the seventh month called Tishri so it is a New Moon celebration. The Jews followed a Lunar calendar that is based on the movements of the moon rather that the sun. The day of the feast could not be known ahead of time since it depended on the appearance of the New Moon. As soon as the New Moon appeared the shofer (i.e., ram's horn) would be blown to signify that the feast day had arrived (Psalm 81:3). Since the New Moon could not be calculated precisely, it became the custom to celebrate two days instead of one. Thus, Rosh Hashanah is now celebrated on the first and second of Tishri to be certain the New Moon appears.

Rosh Hashanah is a memorial of the grace extended by God to Abraham when God substituted a ram to be sacrificed in place of Abraham's son, Isaac. This is the reason the feast is celebrated by blowing a ram's horn. The day is also considered by some Bible scholars to be the birthday of Abraham, Isaac, Jacob and Samuel. It is also considered by many to be the birthday of Jesus Christ. This is the reason that Joseph and Mary were unable to find a room for the night. Jerusalem and the surrounding towns (i.e., Bethlehem) were filled with Jews who had come to Jerusalem to celebrate the fall feasts. It would also have been the appropriate time for a census since the work of the harvest was past and winter had not yet arrived. The shepherds would still be abiding in the fields at night since the rainy and cold season was still future.

The New Testament fulfillment of the feast of Trumpets is clearly the Main Harvest Rapture of the Church according to the following Scriptures:

> 1 Th 4:16-17 (KJV) For the Lord himself shall descend from heaven with a shout, with the voice of the archangel, and with the trump of God: and the dead in Christ shall rise first: 17 Then we which are alive and remain shall be caught up together with them in the clouds, to meet the Lord in the air: and so shall we ever be with the Lord.

> 1 Cor 15:51-52 (KJV) Behold, I show you a mystery; We shall not all sleep, but we shall all be changed, 52 In a moment, in the twinkling of an eye, at the last trump: for the trumpet shall sound, and the dead shall be raised incorruptible, and we shall be changed.

The big question in the above Scripture is the meaning of "the last trump." Rosh Hashanah and Yom Kippur are such High Holy Days that preparation for them begins a month earlier on the first day of the Jewish month Elul. Each day throughout the month of Elul the ram's horn trumpet is blown. On the day before Rosh Hashanah no trumpets are blown. Then trumpets are blown throughout the day on Rosh Hashanah in varying sequences and differing blasts (i.e., short and long blasts).

Sometime on the second day of Rosh Hashanah the last trumpet blast is sounded, and this trumpet blast is called the Great Tekiah. The Great Tekiah is "the last trump" that Paul was referring to and it will signal the Main Harvest Rapture of the Church on some future feast of trumpets, which will take place somewhere in the middle of the tribulation. This is the reason that numerous Bible scholars pay so much attention to the celebration of Rosh Hashanah each year.

The Main Harvest Rapture of the Church will be the final harvest of all Christians who "remain." It is the prophetic fulfillment of the fifth feast, Rosh Hashanah. It will happen in the middle of the tribulation. Mature Christians are watching to "be accounted worth to escape all these things."

> Luke 21:36 (KJV) Watch ye therefore, and pray always, that ye may be accounted worthy to escape all these things that shall come to pass, and to stand before the Son of man.

The catching up of John in Revelation 4:1-2 is a picture of the Firstfruits Rapture and not the Main Harvest Rapture. The Firstfruits Rapture occurs at the beginning of the seven year tribulation. The "open door" in heaven (Rev. 4:1) is the same "open door" that was promised to the church of Philadelphia for being faithful (Rev. 3:8). The main harvest rapture is described in Revelation 7:9-17. The 24 elders (Rev. 4:4) are those who are accounted worthy to participate in Firstfruits. They are overcomers, and they have earned for themselves crowns to signify that they will reign and rule with Jesus Christ during the millennial kingdom.

The elder in Revelation 7:13 asks John a rhetorical question about where all these other Christians came from, and John answers the question by saying that they came out of great tribulation (See Rev. 2:22). Please note that they washed their robes and not themselves (Rev. 7:14). They were already saved (i.e., spiritually reborn) when the tribulation began, but they were unfaithful Christians who had defiled their garments by sin and disobedience (See Rev. 3:4). They have now been cleansed according to 1 John 1:9.

It is at the end of chapter 7 of Revelation that all Christians are in heaven and God is about to release his wrath upon the earth. No Christian will ever have to go through the wrath of God on the earth.

The Firstfruits rapture has fulfilled the day of Firstfruits (i.e., Pentecost), and the main rapture of the Church has fulfilled the feast of Trumpets (i.e., Rosh Hashanah). At this point there are two remaining feasts that must and will be fulfilled by Jesus Christ. The remaining feasts are the day of Atonement (i.e., Yom Kippur) and the feast of Tabernacles (i.e., Succoth).

The feast of Trumpets is the fifth feast and the fourth of the seven annual Sabbaths or High Days (Vs 25).

#6 Yom Kippur—Atonement

The day of Atonement, Yom Kippur, is the most revered of Israel's holy days. Yom Kippur is celebrated on the 10th day of Tishri, and the Jewish people start preparing their hearts for it during the previous month of Elul. The feast of Rosh Hashanah begins on the 1st of Tishri, and this begins the sober countdown to Yom Kippur. The first ten days of Tishri are called the Ten Days of Awe, and they are for the purpose of repentance by Israel.

The weekly Sabbath that falls in these ten days is even called Shabbat Shuvah, the "Sabbath of Repentance." It is a Sabbath of turning away from sin and preparation for the coming judgment. Yom Kippur means a day of covering and it is a day observed as Israel's annual cleansing from sin. It is a day of fasting and the most holy of all Jewish feasts. Traditionally, Yom Kippur is the day that Moses came down from Mount Sinai with the second set of stone tablets. Israel had received forgiveness for the sin of idolatry with the golden calf.

The New Testament fulfillment of the day of Atonement will be the day that Jesus is revealed from heaven and sets his feet down on the Mount of Olives (Zech. 14:4). This is often called the Revelation of Jesus Christ, and the Scriptures refer to it as his "coming in the clouds with great power and glory" (Mk 13:26).

His appearing will take place at the height of the battle of Armageddon, and it is the day that Israel will be saved as a nation. Two-thirds of the Jews shall die but one-third will be brought through the fire, and they will call upon the name of the Lord and be saved (Zech. 13:8,9). This is the day that Israel will receive her atonement for her sins, and she will be reconciled to God. The day that this occurs will almost certainly take place on some future day of Atonement at the end of the tribulation period.

The period in between the fulfillment of the feast of Trumpets (i.e., the main harvest rapture) and the fulfillment of the day of Atonement (i.e., the salvation of Israel as a nation) is known as the time of Jacob's trouble (Jeremiah 30:7). This is the last three and one-half years of the seven year tribulation, and it will be a time of terrible affliction and sorrow for Israel.

Before the Jews can be annihilated, Jesus will return to save them. This will likely be on the day of Atonement. The Jews will see Jesus, recognize him as their true Messiah, and acknowledge him as Lord and Savior. The nation will be saved in a day (Rom. 11-26).

Moses confirms in the following Scripture that Israel receives her Atonement in the tribulation period:

> Deu 4:30-31 (KJV) When thou art in tribulation, and all these things are come upon thee, even in the latter days, if thou turn to the LORD thy God, and shalt be obedient unto his voice; 31 (For the LORD thy God is a merciful God;) he will not forsake thee, neither destroy thee, nor forget the covenant of thy fathers which he sware unto them.

The following Scripture celebrates the glorious salvation of Israel when they look upon Jesus and realize the one they crucified is their true Messiah:

> Zec 12:10 (KJV) And I will pour upon the house of David, and upon the inhabitants of Jerusalem, the spirit of grace and of supplications: and they shall look upon me whom they have pierced, and they shall mourn for him, as one mourneth for his only son, and shall be in bitterness for him, as one that is in bitterness for his firstborn.

The day of Atonement is the sixth feast and the fifth of the seven annual Sabbaths or High Days (Vs 28).

#7 Tabernacles

The feast of Tabernacles is the seventh and final feast ordained by God for Israel to celebrate (Vss 33-36). This feast is known in Jewry today as Succoth, and it is celebrated in the third gathering in the fall of the year after the harvest. It is celebrated on the 15th day of the seventh month Tishri and the feast continues for seven days. During these seven days the people were to dwell in booths (i.e., small shelters called sukkah) that were made from the branches of palm trees and willows from the brook. This was to remind them of the Palm trees of Elim (See Ex. 15:27-16:1) and the willows of Babylon (Psalm 137). It was also to remind them of their fathers who lived in tents during the forty years in the wilderness.

In contrast to Rosh Hashanah and Yom Kippur, the feast of Tabernacles (i.e., Succoth) was a time of rejoicing and thanksgiving for the harvest that had been gathered and the forgiveness that God had extended to the people. The feast even became known as "The Season of Our Joy." Other names for the feast are the *Feast of Booths*, the *Feast of In gathering*, and simply *The Feast*. It is highly significant that the feast is observed after the final gathering of the harvest.

The number *seven* is very prominent in the feast of Tabernacles. It is the seventh feast in the seventh month, and it is celebrated for seven days. The New Testament fulfillment of this feast is clearly the establishment of the millennial kingdom of Jesus Christ at the end of the seven year tribulation period. The last day of the feast is called the *Day of the Great Hosanna*. This is the day that all the inhabitants of the earth will literally worship the Great Hosanna. The prophets referred to it as the Great Day of the Lord.

The following Scripture details the celebration of the feast of Tabernacles:

> Deu 16:13-15 (KJV)   Thou shalt observe the feast of tabernacles seven days, after that thou hast gathered in thy corn and thy wine: 14 And thou shalt rejoice in thy feast, thou, and thy son, and thy daughter, and thy manservant, and thy maidservant, and the Levite, the stranger, and the fatherless, and the widow, that are within thy gates. 15 Seven days shalt thou keep a solemn feast unto the LORD thy God in the place which the LORD shall choose: because the LORD thy God shall bless thee in all thine increase, and in all the works of thine hands, therefore thou shalt surely rejoice.

Even the land will rejoice when the millennial kingdom is established in fulfillment of the feast of Tabernacles. The following Scripture describes this event:

Isa 35:1-2 (KJV) The wilderness and the solitary place shall be glad for them; and the desert shall rejoice, and blossom as the rose. 2 It shall blossom abundantly, and rejoice even with joy and singing: the glory of Lebanon shall be given unto it, the excellency of Carmel and Sharon, they shall see the glory of the LORD, and the excellency of our God.

The first and eighth days of Tabernacles are the sixth and seventh annual Sabbaths or High Days (Vs 39) that are celebrated by Israel.

Summary

God ordained that Israel celebrate seven feasts at three seasonal gatherings during the year in the spring, summer, and fall. These feasts served as pictures or rehearsals for prophetic events that were yet future. The first gathering in the spring was the celebration of the feasts of Passover, Unleavened Bread, and Firstfruits. These three feasts pointed to the death, burial, and resurrection of Jesus Christ, the Redeemer and Messiah of Israel. It is no coincidence that the fulfillment of these prophetic pictures occurred at the precise time set by God. Jesus died on Passover, was buried on Unleavened Bread, and was resurrected on Firstfruits.

The second gathering in early summer was the feast of Pentecost. It is no coincidence that the initial prophetic fulfillment of Pentecost occurred when the Church was instituted on this date and 3,000 people were saved. Israel has been set aside for 2,000 years as the fulfillment continues throughout the Church Age.

The final fulfillment or end of this feast will occur when the Church age ends and the Firstfruits of the Church are raptured and caught up to heaven. These Firstfruits are the faithful members of the Church who have reached maturity in the current Church Age and they are given the "open door" They are the 24 elders who are seated on thrones, and they are all wearing crowns at the beginning of the seven year tribulation period.

Pentecost is also called the Day of Firstfruits since it is the day that the Firstfruits of the Church are harvested. Not all Christians will have crowns and not all Christians will be in this first harvest. The great majority of the Church will be rejected by Jesus because of unfaithfulness (i.e., immaturity). The hot summer sun (i.e., the fires of the tribulation under Antichrist) will cause many Christians to reach maturity before the main harvest of the Church. This will be the fulfillment of the feast of Trumpets which occurs in the fall.

The third gathering season occurs in the fall with the celebration of the feasts of Trumpets, Atonement, and Tabernacles. The rapture of the remainder of the Church will be the fulfillment of the feast of Trumpets, and it will occur before the wrath of God is unleashed upon the earth. The Revelation of Jesus Christ and the salvation of the nation of Israel in one day will be the prophetic fulfillment of the Day of Atonement. The establishment and completion of the millennial kingdom of Jesus Christ will be the prophetic fulfillment of the feast of Tabernacles.

Since the fulfillment of the first four feasts occurred on exactly the days that the feasts were to be celebrated, it seems wise to speculate that the fulfillment of the remainder of these feasts will occur on their respective feasts dates also.

Jesus rebuked the spiritual leaders of his day for not seeing the season of Christ's first advent (Luke 12:54-56). Christians today are doing the same thing. The study of the feasts should sound the alarm and send a wake-up call to all Christians who have fallen asleep and are lukewarm and indifferent to the prophetic Scriptures.

The Antichrist is almost ready to be revealed, but the Firstfruits rapture will occur before this takes place. Some Christians have stated that they are waiting for Antichrist to be revealed before they believe the prophetic truths of the Bible. If these Christians are still here when Antichrist is revealed, it will be too late to escape the persecution under Antichrist.

Christians are already seeing a transition in attitudes toward believers. This is most evident on television talk shows where Christians are mocked and scorned. The surge in the homosexual rights movement, the right to abortion movement, the women's rights movement, and the ethnic cleansing movement is only the beginning of a depraved society gone mad with selfishness and self-centeredness.

It will become intolerable for Christians who are left for the main harvest in the tribulation period. It is a time of maturing fire when many will fall to a martyr's death (Rev 6:9).

There is an "open door," an abundant entrance, waiting for those who diligently seek Him.

2 Pet 1:10-11 (KJV)   Wherefore the rather, brethren, give diligence to *make your calling and election sure*: for *if ye do these things*, ye shall never fall:11 For so an entrance shall be ministered unto you abundantly into the everlasting kingdom of our Lord and Saviour Jesus Christ.

CHART OF SEVEN FEASTS

Feast Name	Prophetic Fulfillment	Days Celebreated	Sabbath Day(s)
SPRING FEASTS			
#1. Passover	Death of Jesus	One	None
#2. Unleavened Bread	Burial of Jesus	Seven	First & Seventh
#3. Firstfruits	Resurrection of Jesus	One	None
SUMMER FEAST			
#4. Pentecost (Day of Firstfruits)	Church Age (Beginning & End) Rapture of Church (Firstfruits)	One	Yes
FALL FEASTS			
#5. Trumpets	Rapture of Church (Main Harvert)	Two	First
#6. Atonement	Revelation of Jesus / Salvation of Israel	One	Yes
#7. Tabernacles	Millennium Begins	Seven	First & Eighth

THREE BIBLICAL INTERPRETATIONS
OF THE SEVEN FEASTS

Feast	Literal Historical Event	Figurative Application for the Church	Prophetic Fulfillment
#1. Passover	Passover in Egypt	Salvation of Spirit by Faith Alone, Christian Applies Blood, Justification	Jesus Dies on Calvary (Seed dies)
#2. Unleavened Bread	Exodus from Egypt	Repentance, Purging of Evil Out of the Life, Sanctification	Jesus Buried in Tomb (Seed Planted)
#3. Firstfruits	Red Sea Passage	Water Baptism, Dying to Self, Living for Christ, Living the Exchanged Life	Resurrection of Jesus (1st Sheaf)
#4. Pentecost (Day of Firstfruits)	Israel at Mount Sinai	Filing of Spirit, Christian's Empowerment for Service	New Testament Pentecost (Rapture of Firstfruits)
#5. Rosh Hashanah (Feast of Trumpets)	Tabernacle Built	Gathering Together for Worship, Witnessing, Christian Fellowship	Rapture of Church (Main Harvest)
#6. Atonement	Construction of Ark of Covenant	Communion, Cleansing from Sin, Bible Study, Fellowship with the Lord	Return of Jesus in Power and Glory (Gleaning)
#7. Tabernacles	Israel Crossing Jordan	Living Victorius Christian Life	Millennial Kingdom (Reaping of corners)

Chapter 4

THE FIVE CROWNS

Rewards for the Faithful

Paul therefore reveals the conditions of the coronation to which he summons the whole Church. (1) Self-mastery is an essential for crown-winning. "Let us also …lay aside every *weight*, and the sin which doth so easily beset us, and let us run with patience the race." (2) The glory of the crown is to be the conscious incentive of the soul. (3) Disobedience forfeits the crown. "Hold fast that which thou hast, that no one take *thy* crown." Thus it is certain that all crowns are conditional on works done after faith, and all are attainable by achievement…For crowns are rewards, not given unless the conditions are fulfilled. A crown is given, not at the beginning of a race, but at the end; it is a circlet of glory granted only to the successful runner.

D.M. Panton – *The Judgment Seat of Christ*

The doctrine of rewards at the Judgment Seat of Christ is sadly a neglected topic in our pulpits today, but it is one of the most important for the Christian. This doctrine pertains to the future inheritance of the Christian, and it is a central theme of the Bible. Yet, the great majority of churches rarely preach or teach on this doctrine. It is incorrectly assumed that all Christians will be co-heirs with Christ in his coming kingdom and all crowns and rewards are automatic. While it is true that all Christians will have God as their inheritance, there is an inheritance from the Lord that is not automatic.

There are several aspects of the doctrine of rewards such as the prize for the overcomers, treasures in heaven, praise and honor from Christ, co-reigning with Christ, participation in the wedding banquet, and a special class of resurrection. All of these aspects seem to be directly linked to the five crowns that are to be awarded to the faithful overcomers at the Judgment Seat of Christ. They are earned rewards.

Only those Christians who have earned all five crowns will qualify for "the prize" that Paul talked about (Phil 3:14). The prize is the "full reward," and those believers who obtain it will be selected as the Bride of Christ. This is the highest level of the three levels of service in the kingdom. A chart is given at the end of this chapter to help the reader understand the importance of faithful service to the Lord Jesus Christ in the current age.

There will be many positions of service in the kingdom of God the Son, and the rank of each Christian who qualifies to enter the kingdom will be determined by faithfulness while on earth. Contrary to popular opinion, the phrase "enter the kingdom" does not refer to a person's spirit salvation in the evangelical sense (i.e., the kingdom of God the Holy Spirit). The phrase literally means to enter into the king's dominion, and it refers to Christians who qualify to reign and rule with Jesus Christ in his millennial kingdom (i.e., the kingdom of God the Son). This privilege is directly related to the doctrine of rewards which depends upon the manner in which the Christian lives his life during the current age. As explained earlier, this is the salvation of a person's soul.

The current age is a time when God is taking a people out of the Gentiles "for his name" (Acts 15:14) so they can be tested for the purpose of filling positions in the kingdom of God the Son. There will apparently be three levels of service in the kingdom, and these levels of service appear to be linked to the five crowns. Clearly those who enter the kingdom will have won "stephanos crowns" at the Judgment Seat of Christ, but it is not absolutely clear about the ranks of the crowns. However, some delineation of ranking order is suggested as the crowns appear to be related to the three levels of service in the kingdom.

The chart at the end of the chapter may be helpful in understanding the crowns as they are related to the ranks in the kingdom.

The Crown of Life

The first and basic crown that is required for entrance into the kingdom of God the Son is the "crown of life." It must be remembered that the crowns are earned rewards and do not pertain to the new birth experience which is entrance into the kingdom of God the Holy Spirit. Salvation of a person's spirit through faith in Jesus Christ can never be lost. Crowns can be lost and the Scriptures attest to this fact. The crown of life is referred to in the following Scriptures:

> James 1:12 (KJV) Blessed is the man that endureth temptation: for when he is tried, he shall receive *the crown of life*, which the Lord hath promised to them that love him.
> Rev 2:10 (KJV) Fear none of those things which thou shalt suffer: behold, the devil shall cast some of you into prison, that ye may be tried; and ye shall have tribulation ten days: be thou faithful unto death, and I will give thee *a crown of life.*
> Rev 3:11 (KJV) Behold, I come quickly: hold that fast which thou hast, that no man take thy crown.

The crown of life will be awarded at the Judgment Seat of Christ to those Christians who are "faithful," "love him," and "hold fast." These are Christians who lose their lives to Christ that they might gain them in eternity. This is the salvation of the soul.

> Luke 9:23-24 (KJV) And he said to them all, If any man will come after me, let him deny himself, and take up his cross daily, and follow me. 24 For whosoever will save his *life* shall lose it: but whosoever will lose his *life* for my sake, the same shall save it.

The crown of life will be awarded to those Christians who have their souls saved at the Judgment Seat of Christ. It is a salvation based on works. (*This is very different from the salvation of the spirit which is by grace, through faith in Jesus Christ, without any works of any kind).* The salvation of the soul, represented by receiving the crown of life, is a reward to those Christians who seek the Lord and overcome the flesh through confession of sin and filling of the Holy Spirit. (1 John 1:9)

> Rev 3:5 (KJV) He that overcometh, the same shall be clothed in white raiment; and I will not blot out his name out of the

book of life, but I will confess his name before my Father, and before his angels.

The book of life is greatly misunderstood by the majority of preachers and teachers. The book of life is the basis for rewards in heaven, not entrance into heaven. Every believer's name was written in the book of life "from the foundation of the world" (Rev 17:8). These are all the ones chosen by God for salvation. Everyone who has his name in this book has the potential for living a life under the control of the Holy Spirit resulting in the crown of life or a reward for good works.

Having one's name blotted out of the book of life does not mean the loss of salvation in the evangelical sense, but the loss of the crown of life or the loss of reward. This crown is a basic requirement for entrance into the kingdom of Jesus Christ and for earning one or more of the other four crowns. Jesus personally described how this crown is earned in the following Scriptures:

> Mat 10:39 (KJV) He that findeth his life (i.e., soul) shall lose it: and he that loseth his life (i.e., soul) for my sake shall find it. Mat 16:27 (KJV) For the Son of man shall come in the glory of his Father with his angels; and *then he shall reward every man according to his works.*

Verse 27 above clearly establishes that the salvation of the soul is a result of works, and it is directly related to the crown of life. Thus, the loss of the crown of life is the loss of the soul and the loss of reward and not the loss of the salvation of the spirit which is a free gift from God. If man must maintain good works in order to keep this salvation, then it would not be a free gift nor would it be by grace. Salvation is by grace, but rewards are according to works.

Numerous Christians will be in heaven whose names were blotted out of the book of life. These are the Christians who lost all of their reward by living a life controlled by the soulical or flesh nature. Their lives will have been a waste, but their spirits will be saved. There are many examples of this in the Bible.

Saul is a primary type of the Christian who loses his life and his crown by disobedience. Other Old Testament types who had lost their inheritance by disobedience are Reuben who lost his double portion because of sin, Esau who sold his birthright for a meal of red stew, and Lot who lost his reward because he loved the things of the world. All of these men were saved spiritually, but they lost their rewards in the coming messianic kingdom.

Every Christian who wins the crown of life is an overcomer and will reign and rule with Jesus Christ in the millennial kingdom. Those Christians winning only this crown will be ruling from the third level in the kingdom, and they will reign over the cities of the earth.

The parable of the pounds in Luke 19:11-27 is a picture of the "good servant" who has been faithful "in a very little." He will reign over the cities of the earth. This servant is in contrast to the "good *and faithful* servant" who will be made "ruler over *many things*" in the parable of the talents in Matthew 25:14-25:30. The "good and faithful servant" will be reigning from the second level in the kingdom. The *incorruptible crown* and the *crown of righteousness* appear to be linked to the "good and faithful servant." The reader may want to refer to the chart at this point in order to grasp the subtle differences in the degrees of faithfulness and the degrees of responsibility in the millennial kingdom.

The Incorruptible Crown

1 Cor 9:24-27 (KJV) Know ye not that they which run in a race run all, but one receiveth the prize? So run, that ye may obtain. 25 And every man that striveth for the mastery is temperate in all things. Now they do it to obtain a corruptible crown; but we *an incorruptible*. 26 I therefore so run, not as uncertainly; so fight I, not as one that beateth the air: 27 But I keep under my body, and bring it into subjection: lest that by any means, when I have preached to others, I myself should be a castaway.

The incorruptible crown is awarded on the basis of winning a spiritual race that is marked out by God for each believer. It is a daily race of "putting off" the sins of the flesh which then allows the believer to "put on" the fruits of the spirit (Col 3). This requires self-discipline of the body which is used by the Holy Spirit to manifest the life of Christ. This life is dependent on the filling of the Holy Spirit through confession of sin and a sensitivity to the leading of the Lord.

There is a difference in being "in Christ" and having "Christ in us." All Christians are in Christ, but Christians winning this Crown have Christ in them. The winner of this crown has been successful in denying the fleshly desires and appetites of the body. He has been successful in "crucifying the flesh" (Gal 5:22-24).

This crown is tied in with the "good and faithful servant" who will be "ruler over much" (Matt. 25:21). According to the following Scripture, it is also apparently a prerequisite for winning the crown of righteousness:

Crown of Righteousness

2 Tim 4:7-8 (KJV) I have fought a good fight, I have finished my course, I have kept the faith: 8 Henceforth there is laid up for me a crown of righteousness, which the Lord, the righteous judge, shall give me at that day: and not to me only, but unto all them also that love his appearing.

In order to summarize and place these crowns in perspective up to this point, it is important to understand that the crown of life pertains to the soul while the incorruptible crown is connected to the body. Thus, the believer who fights a good fight and finishes the course (i.e., he overcomes sin that affects body, soul, and spirit) will have won the crown of life and the incorruptible crown. It is now possible to win the crown of righteousness which is a higher award in the second level of the kingdom. In order to win this crown, the believer must not only "fight a good fight" and "finish his course," but he must also "keep the faith."

The keeping or guarding of the faith is required for winning the Crown of Righteousness. This is not the common faith connected to salvation in the evangelical sense but the faith that speaks of Christ's coming kingdom and produces good works through those who hope in Him. This is why verse 8 above says this crown will go to those Christians who "*love his appearing*." Thus, those Christians who are alert to and anxiously looking for the return of Jesus are the ones who are keeping the faith. These are Christians who are daily occupied with Jesus Christ through his Word and anticipate his return.

Many Christians perform "good works," but they do them in the power of the flesh. To the observer who sees only the "outward appearance," these works do not appear any different than good works in the power of the Holy Spirit. Even the Christians performing these works do not realize that they are merely wood, hay, and stubble. These works will perish in the fire at the Judgment Seat of Christ. Even Peter resorted to the arm of flesh when he cut off the soldier's ear in the Garden of Gethsemene.

The primary test for determining the quality of these works is the motive behind the works, for God "looketh on the heart." Many works are performed by Christians for the purpose of exalting and glorifying self. They are performed in order to receive praise and honor from men and not from God. The parable in Luke 19:12-27 pictures the outcome of a servant who performs works in the power of his own flesh. This servant kept his pound laid up in a napkin (i.e., sweat cloth). This servant is called wicked—not slothful—and he loses all reward the same as the servant who hid his talent in the ground (Mat. 25:14-30). The servant who hid his talent in the ground was called wicked and slothful (i.e., he did not even work in the power of the flesh).

Many Christians who work hard in the Church and occupy positions of leadership are going to be surprised when they appear at the Judgment Seat of Christ and learn that they were hiding their pounds in the sweat cloths of self-effort.

Christians often get caught up in works that are to be seen by men rather than God. Sometimes it is even hard for Christians to know their own true motives. That is why David prayed for God to search his heart and show him any evil ways. Many Christians find it hard to say "no" when asked to help. They are afraid of what people think. They get caught up in pleasing a pastor or friends rather than God. We are told to fear God and not men. It should be remembered that God's yoke is light and not heavy. If one's yoke feels heavy or burdensome, then it may be the yoke of man rather than God.

Many of these hard working believers are Laodicean Christians who do not realize that they are "wretched, miserable, poor, blind and naked" (Rev. 3:17). They are too busy to study their Bibles. The common thread for these Christians is a lack of knowledge about the deeper things in Scripture. They relate everything to basic evangelical salvation and think all rewards are automatic. They lack understanding of the deeper truths of God's Word pertaining to the salvation of the soul and the doctrine of rewards.

Crown of Rejoicing

The Crown of Rejoicing and the Crown of Glory are the two highest crowns awarded to Christians for their faithfulness in seeking the Kingdom of Heaven.   It is commonly thought that seeking the Kingdom of Heaven is seeking to be born again, but this is incorrect. Only believers are able to seek the Kingdom of Heaven, and it should be the ambition of every Christian.

The Crown of Rejoicing will be awarded on the basis of soul winning and not spirit winning as is commonly thought among Christians. Evangelism (i.e., witnessing to the unsaved) is a very important work, and there will be rewards for those Christians who evangelize with the correct motives. Unfortunately, much witnessing about Jesus is done out of guilt, coercion by pastors, self-exaltation, and various other reasons, but the true motive should be love for the Lord Jesus Christ and a desire to please our Lord and Savior by being obedient to the leading of the Holy Spirit. A strong desire to obey the prompting of the Holy Spirit will give the believer boldness in witnessing.

The true soul winner is the Christian who wins saved people to a life of obedience by teaching them the deeper truths (i.e., epignosis) of Scripture. Soul winning involves teaching and motivating Christians to be overcomers. Spirit winning saves man from the penalty of sin, but soul winning saves man from the power of sin.

Spirit winning gets the believer into heaven, but soul winning gets the believer into the kingdom of heaven. Spirit winning involves a salvation that can not be lost, but soul winning involves a salvation that can only be attained by persevering in good works until the end. Spirit winning involves a gift that is without cost, but soul winning involves a prize that is worked for, and it is very costly. The rewards, however, are very great and far surpass the costs involved.

The highest or first level of rule in the kingdom belongs to the Bride of Christ, and this level will be composed of Christians who have won the soul winning crown which is called the Crown of Rejoicing. This crown is described in the following Scripture:

> 1 Th 2:19 (KJV) For what is our hope, or joy, or crown of rejoicing? Are not even ye in the presence of our Lord Jesus Christ at his coming?

The Thessalonians were very faithful Christians—unlike the Corinthians—and Paul had high hopes of them entering the Kingdom of God the Son. The following Scripture is only one that confirms this to be true:

> 2 Th 1:5 (KJV) Which is a manifest token of the righteous judgment of God, that ye may be counted worthy of the kingdom of God, for which ye also suffer:

Paul was greatly pleased that the Thessalonians had a mature faith, and they persevered under persecutions and trials. Paul was confident that their souls (i.e., lives) would be saved because of their faithfulness and that they would be part of the Kingdom of God the Son.

Paul was also confident about the Philippians and their perseverance unto the saving of the soul according to the following Scripture:

Phil 4:1-3 (KJV) Therefore, my brethren, dearly beloved and longed for, *my joy and crown*, so stand fast in the Lord, my dearly beloved. 2 I beseech Euodias, and beseech Syntyche, that they be of the same mind in the Lord. 3 And I entreat thee also, true yokefellow, help those women which laboured with me in the gospel, with Clement also, and with other my fellow labourers, *whose names are in the book of life*.

The above Scripture confirms that Paul is confident that their names will not be blotted out of the book of life. Note again that the book of life is clearly linked with works and not grace.

It is important to understand that soul winning involves a great deal more than memorizing a few Scriptures and an opening line to determine if someone has been spiritually reborn (i.e., they have entered the Kingdom of God the Holy Spirit). Soul winning involves knowing God by knowing the Scriptures and meditating upon them night and day. It involves being filled with the Holy Spirit and leading other Christians into the spirit-filled life. It involves Bible study, prayer, praise and worship, and it entails more than showing up at visitation on Monday nights. Soul winning requires a daily walk with Christ and an abiding in Christ so that He can work through the believer.

Crown of Glory

1 Pet 5:1-4 (KJV) The elders which are among you I exhort, who am also an elder, and a witness of the sufferings of Christ, and also a partaker of the glory that shall be revealed: 2 Feed the flock of God which is among you, taking the oversight thereof, not by constraint, but willingly; not for filthy lucre, but of a ready mind; 3 Neither as being lords over God's heritage, but being ensamples to the flock. 4 And when the chief Shepherd shall appear, ye shall receive a *crown of glory* that fadeth not away.

The second crown in the highest level of rule is the Crown of Glory, and it is possibly the highest ranking crown of all. This crown will go to those faithful under shepherds over a flock. The elders are those who are spiritually mature in the Church. It is thought that they represent pastors and teachers who are responsible for feeding the flock, but it is any Christian who has matured in the faith and who exercises his spiritual gift in serving the body of Christ. These are the Christians whom God has placed in charge over the other servants according to Matthew 24:25.

All Christians are responsible for feeding and edifying the body of Christ by utilizing their spiritual gifts. Those Christians who exercise their gifts will be assigned positions of responsibility in feeding other Christians at the appropriate time. In addition, it seems inconsistent that God would offer a crown to only those Christians who have the gifts of prophecy and teaching or to ordained pastors of local churches. Certainly all pastors should win this crown, but this seems doubtful in the current Laodicean Church Age.

It seems certain that only a small percentage of those in the Church will qualify to win this crown. Indeed, most of those in the Church are spiritual babes in Christ and never even give it a thought that they will stand before Jesus Christ at the Judgment Seat of Christ to give an accounting of their lives. Numerous Christians will have their names blotted out of the book of life because they will not be accounted worthy of the Kingdom of God the Son. There are numerous Scriptures that warn of this possibility, but pastors and teachers relegate these warnings to the unsaved (i.e., reprobates). It is necessary to grossly twist the plain teaching of the Scriptures to arrive at this conclusion. The Bible was written to believers, and the warnings in the Bible are meant for believers.

The Crown of Rejoicing and the Crown of Glory seem to be tied in with the "faithful and wise servant" of Matthew 24:45 who will be made "ruler over all his goods" as shown in Matthew 24:47. Christians who win these crowns will have won all five crowns. They will be chosen as the Bride of Christ, and they will rule from the highest level in the kingdom. They will receive a full reward according to the following Scripture:

> 2 John 1:8 (KJV) Look to yourselves, that we lose not those things which we have wrought, but that we receive a full reward.

SUMMARY

The Scriptures are clear that not all Christians will be overcomers at the Judgment Seat of Christ. It is important for the reader to strive to enter in the kingdom of God. This involves a great deal more than simple salvation according to the free grace of God. So many preachers are caught up in the grace of God and salvation by faith that they completely ignore the plain teaching of Scripture on the rewards that God has for those Christians who are willing to go on into maturity. Once a Christian has been born of the Spirit, he has the freedom to become a disciple of Jesus Christ or to continue as a slave to his own soulical nature, the old man (Eph. 4:22-24).

Numerous preachers today get caught up in judging whether a person is saved or not by how he lives. It has become a common practice for pastors to cause Christians to doubt their salvation by attempting to describe what a real Christian is like. Using the criteria established by many pastors today, Jesus Himself would have failed the tests so common in Christian circles. He drank wine, which contained alcohol, and He was friend to prostitutes and those in the lower socioeconomic levels of society. He was highly critical of the religious establishment. It is inappropriate for Christians to attempt to judge another person's salvation experience by that person's behavior. We are admonished not to judge (Mat. 7:1). The Bible tells us that some Christians in the current Laodicean church age will live just like unsaved people.

No one except God knows who belongs to him. The only criterion for whether a person is a Christian is his belief in the Lord Jesus Christ. Contrary to popular teaching, the Bible teaches "easy believism," and there is no additional criteria needed to prove that faith is real and valid. The person who believes on the Lord Jesus Christ receives his assurance of salvation the moment he believes (Rom. 8:16). He knows within his heart that he believes, and it is wrong for anyone to rob him of his assurance of salvation by pointing to his works. Salvation is a free gift and no works are required either before or after to either gain salvation or prove that salvation is real. It is the Judaizers who tie works into salvation by faith by making works a necessary consequence of faith. This is the heresy of Lordship Salvation.

It is God's desire that every Christian come to repentance after he has been saved spiritually. Repentance is a continual work of a Godly Christian. The gospel of John was written so that men would believe and be saved (John 20:31). It is significant that the word repentance is not found even once in the book.

God does not desire for any Christian to lose his soul. The following Scripture is one of the most misunderstood verses in all of Scripture:

> 2 Pet 3:9 (KJV) The Lord is not slack concerning his promise, as some men count slackness; but is longsuffering to us-ward, not willing that any should perish, but that all should come to repentance.

This Scripture is written "to them that have obtained like precious faith with us through the righteousness of God and our Saviour Jesus Christ" (2 Peter 1:1). Thus, the recipients of this exhortation are born again, blood-bought, justified Christians. The "us-ward" are Christians and not unsaved people whom God is desperately trying to save. God saves whomever he wishes and whenever he wishes, and then he calls them to repentance. It is only after we have been born again that we can truly repent of our sins and save our souls. God is long-suffering to us-ward (i.e., Christians) and does not want any of us to perish (i.e., lose our soul). This is confirmed in the following Scripture which is also written by Peter:

> 1 Pet 1:9 (KJV) Receiving the end of your faith, even the salvation of your souls.

If the Christian attains the end of his faith which is the salvation of his soul, then he will be awarded the Crown of Life, and he will enter the Kingdom of God the Son and reign and rule with Jesus Christ in the coming messianic kingdom. Many Christians will not receive the end of their faith which is the salvation of their souls. Their names will be blotted out of the book of life and their lives will perish in the judgment fires of the Judgment Seat of Christ. They will have lost their souls and their inheritance as co-heirs with Christ. Numerous Scriptures attest to this fact, but Christians refuse to apply these Scriptures to themselves.

Numerous pastors attempt to use these Scriptures to show that many Christians have not truly been born again spiritually, but spiritual rebirth is not the issue in these Scriptures. The salvation of the soul is the issue, and this salvation pertains to works, and rewards for these works at the Judgment Seat of Christ. Thus, the Crown of Life is the basic crown for being a part of the Kingdom of God. The following Scriptures are usually misinterpreted as pertaining to the salvation of the spirit, but they are referring to entrance into the kingdom of God the Son:

> Luke 13:24 (KJV) *Strive* to enter in at the strait gate: for many, I say unto you, will seek to enter in, and shall not be able.
> Luke 13:28 (KJV) There shall be weeping and gnashing of teeth, when ye shall see Abraham, and Isaac, and Jacob, and all the prophets, in the *kingdom of God*, and you yourselves thrust out.

A person does not strive to get saved. It is only when he ceases to strive and he trusts in the finished work of Jesus Christ on Calvary that he is saved spiritually. However, one does save his soul by striving in the power of the spirit, and this salvation gains one entrance into the Kingdom of God. Many Christians strive to enter in by the works of the flesh, but they will not be able to enter the kingdom because their lives will be lost. The following Scripture pertains to the salvation of the soul and the crown of life that is so crucial for every believer to win:

> Heb 2:2-3 (KJV) For if the word spoken by angels was stedfast, and every transgression and disobedience received a just *recompense of reward*; 3 How shall we escape, if we neglect *so great salvation*; which at the first began to be spoken by the Lord, and was confirmed unto us by them that heard him;

Please note the highlighted phrases to understand that this is a salvation accomplished for the purpose of reward. The implication is that Christians will not escape destruction if they neglect this salvation. This destruction is not eternal damnation but the loss of the soul and the Crown of Life.

One final Scripture exhorting Christians to save their souls and win the Crown of Life is the following:

Phil 2:12-13 (KJV) Wherefore, my beloved, as ye have always obeyed, not as in my presence only, but now much more in my absence, **work out your own salvation** with fear and trembling. 13 For it is God which worketh in you both to will and to do of his good pleasure.

The Incorruptible Crown and the Crown of Righteousness are the crowns awarded those Christians who reign from the second highest level of rule in the Kingdom of God the Son. They are most likely represented by the 24 elders in Revelation 4 and 5. The 24 elders are analogous to the 12 disciples who were administrators with Jesus when he was on the earth. The number 12 is the number of earthly government while the number 24 is the number of heavenly government. Thus, the 12 disciples were the earthly equivalent of the 24 elders who will be crowned sovereigns in the Kingdom of God the Son.

The Crown of Rejoicing and the Crown of Glory are the crowns awarded to those who will reign from the highest level of rule in the kingdom These Christians make up the Bride of Christ and they are most likely represented by the four living creatures in Revelation 4 and 5. The number four is the number of creation and represents all things created. The Bride of Christ will be reigning over all the Lord has which is all created things.

The four living creatures of Revelation look like a lion, an ox, a man, and an eagle. Clearly they are the praise and worship leaders in John's vision of heaven since the 24 elders follow their lead in praise and worship. It is interesting that these four creatures symbolize the different aspects of Jesus Christ presented in the four gospels. The lion represents Jesus as the King of Israel since He is the Lion of the tribe of Judah, and the book of Matthew depicts this side of Jesus. The ox (i.e., calf) represents Jesus Christ as the suffering servant presented in the book of Mark. The man represents the human nature of Jesus Christ as presented in the gospel of Luke. The eagle represents the divine nature of Jesus Christ as presented in the gospel of John.

Thus, the four living creatures reflect the character of Jesus Christ in his different roles. They cannot represent Jesus Christ in the book of Revelation since they participate in worship, and they clearly depict redeemed individuals. Therefore, they represent a class of Christians who most closely resemble the image and character of Jesus Christ. They have the very mind of Christ. This group, in all probability, represents none one other than the Bride of Christ.

It is significant that Lucifer was the praise and worship leader in heaven before his fall and he was the most powerful being created by God. It may very well be that the Bride of Christ will take the place of Lucifer. Clearly the Bride of Christ will be co-heirs with Christ so their authority will be over all creatures. This was also the position of Lucifer before his fall. He was the most powerful creature in the universe.

It is a beautiful plan of God to replace the rebellious Lucifer with lowly man whose only qualification is that he learned to be a servant. Those Christians that follow Jesus' example, as a servant now, will reign and rule with Him in the coming Kingdom.

The book of Esther presents in typology the fall and exclusion of Lucifer from the kingdom in Queen Vashti who was disobedient to King Ahasuerus when he was showing the riches of his glorious kingdom. Lucifer was also very beautiful, but he became proud, disobedient and resentful of his position in second place. Hence, the criterion for reigning and ruling is humility in place of pride.

The Christian's position in the kingdom is determined by faithfulness in performing the Lord's work in the power of the spirit and in obedience to Him in this life. There will be many Christians who will be ashamed at the appearing of the Lord Jesus Christ because of their selfishness and their love of the things of this world. The things of the world will pass away, but the things done for the Lord will be greatly rewarded (1 John 2:17).

The Kingdom of God the Son is a literal kingdom occupying time and space. It is one thing to be a subject in this kingdom (i.e., all Christians). It is an honorable thing to be an officer in the king's service and be an administrator over a portion of his kingdom (i.e., Christians who enter the kingdom and rule over cities). It is quite another matter to be among the king's court and take part in governing the kingdom and live in the palace in close proximity to the king (i.e.,

Christians who enter the kingdom and rule over many things). It is still a more prestigious honor to be the wife of the king and co-reign with him from his throne (i.e., the Bride of Christ). This is a simplified analogy of the Kingdom of God the Son with the three levels of rule and those unfortunate ones who will have no position of authority in the kingdom.

The five crowns addressed in Scripture represent the goals that every Christian should strive to attain in his Christian walk with the Lord. Every wise Christian should set about earning all five crowns so that he can receive a full reward and reign and rule as the Bride of Christ. Only those Christians who have kept themselves clean and pure and who have lived in close communion and fellowship with the Lord Jesus Christ will be rewarded with the "prize" of the high calling of God. These servant Christians will be gloriously presented as the Bride of Christ. The honor will be unparalleled in all of history.

CHARTS OF FIVE CROWNS

CROWN	SCOPE OF AUTHORITY	KIND OF SERVANT	DESCRIPTION
Crown of Life	"Ruler over cities" Luke 19;17	"Good" Luke 19:17	"The Chosen"
Incorruptible Crown and Crown of Righteousness	"Ruler over many things" Matt 25:21	"Good and Faithful"	"The Faithful"
Crown of Rejoicing and Crown of Glory	"Ruler over all His goods" Matt 24:47	"Faithful and Wise" Matt 24:45	"The Wise"

CROWN	HOW EARNED
Crown of Life	Repent and be baptized, patiently endure the present trials and testing of life. Baptism is via water and pictures the death of the self. Spirit baptism occurs the moment of one's salvation (i.e., spiritual rebirth)
Incorruptible Crown	Be filled with the Holy Spirit. Put off fleshly desires and appetites of the body. Turn from the things of the world.
Crown of Righteousness	Mature in the Word. Put on the fruits of the Spirit consistently. Keep the faith. Love His appearing.
Crown of Rejoicing	Be a soul winner (i.e., Motivate other Christians to win the Crown of Life by saving their souls).
Crown of Glory	Tend, lead and nourish the flock (i.e., Exercise spiritual gifts in building up and edifying the body of Christ). Know the Scriptures.

Chapter 5

THE BRIDE OF CHRIST

The Ultimate Reward

God forbid that we should narrow down the blessed company of those who shall sit with Christ upon His throne to any little exclusive circle of our own electing. God give us the largest-hearted Christian love and unity. Does it not speak to all the instincts of our being that it would somehow be impossible for the self-indulgent, time-serving professor of religion – saved perhaps, but saved by the skin of his teeth, wanting only enough of Christ to keep him out of danger, and sacrificing as little as he can for his faith and his Lord – that he should share the place and the same reward with the martyr who lays down his life at the stake or the equally faithful soldier of the cross who lives out a life of self-denial and loving service for Jesus? There is a difference here and there will be an awful difference there. But beloved, let us take no risks, let our watchword be:

> 'I want to stand when Christ appears
> In spotless raiment dressed;
> Numbered among His hidden ones
> His holiest and best.
> Give me, oh Lord, Thy highest choice,
> Let others take the rest.
> Their good things have no charm for me,
> For I have got Thy best.'

A.B. Simpson – ***Christ In The Bible Commentary***, V.6, p. 500.

Rev 21:9 And there came unto me one of the seven angels which had the seven vials full of the seven last plagues, and talked with me, saying, Come hither, I will show thee the bride, the Lamb's wife.

It is a widespread and common misconception among Christians that the bride of Christ and the Church are synonymous. The Church and the body of Christ are one and the same (Eph. 1:22-23), but no Scripture equates one of these groups of Christians with the bride of Christ. Tradition is responsible for this doctrinal error, and tradition is a worthy opponent for anyone attempting to replace it with Scriptural truth.

The Church consists of all spiritually reborn people from Pentecost to the end of the age of Grace which will end with the Firstfruits Rapture of the Church. As an illustration, John the Baptist was not a member of the Church since he died before Pentecost. Therefore, he could not be a member of the bride, and he even referred to himself as a "friend of the bridegroom" (John 3:29).

In 2 Corinthians 11:2 Paul tells the Corinthians that he has "espoused" them to Christ. Espoused means betrothed or engaged, and Paul clarifies his statement by saying that he desires to present them as a chaste (i.e., pure) virgin, *but he is afraid* that their minds would be led astray from sincere and pure devotion to Christ. This Scripture clearly indicates that sincere and pure devotion to Christ is a prerequisite for being presented as the bride of Christ. Matthew 1:18 also uses the word espoused to show Mary's relationship to Joseph and his intent was to "put her away" when he thought she had been unfaithful. There will be numerous Christians who will be "put away" or disqualified as the bride of Christ.

Paul compared the Christian life to a race where all run but only one receives the "prize" (1 Cor. 9:24-27). Paul was fearful that he would become a "castaway" so he worked diligently to keep his body in subjection. In chapter three of Philippians, Paul talks about losing all things so that he might "gain Christ." He also says that he wants to "know Christ and the power of his resurrection and the fellowship of sharing in his sufferings, becoming like him in his death, and so, somehow, to *attain to the resurrection* from the dead."

The resurrection Paul is talking about in this passage of Scripture is something that is earned. The usual transliterated Greek word for resurrection is *anastasis*. The Greek word used in Philippians 3:11 is *exanastasis*. The word literally means the *out-resurrection* from among the dead. This is the only place this Greek word is found in the Bible. It refers to a partial resurrection of Christians who have attained to a certain standard. Hebrews 11:35 calls it the "better resurrection," and it is also related to works.

In this passage of Scripture Paul emphasizes that he is working very hard to win the "prize" which is in Christ Jesus. The prize is clearly the highest reward that a believer can receive for faithful, spirit-filled service in the Lord's work. The Scriptures are replete with types, parables and doctrinal statements which express the honor and blessing attached to those who attend the wedding of the Lord Jesus Christ.

The Scriptures also attach shame and reproof to those Christians who have not prepared for themselves a wedding garment (Mat. 22:1-14). The wedding garment represents the good works that pass through the judgment fire at the Judgment Seat of Christ. It is clear from these Scriptures that being selected as the bride of Christ was Paul's goal for himself and for as many Christians as Paul could persuade to make the supreme sacrifice of self.

The Church and the bride are not the same. The Scriptures confirm that the bride of Christ comes out of the body of Christ. They also give the Biblical criteria for being a member of the bride of Christ. As stated above, pure and sincere devotion to Christ is one of the criteria.

In order to comprehend the truths about the bride of Christ, it must first be understood that the Church is one and will never be divided. Everyone in the Church is there by the grace of God, and works do not enter in at all. The rapture of the firstfruits of the Church does not divide the Church any more than the death of Church members or the fact that the Head of the Church is currently in heaven while many of its members are still on the earth. The home of the Church will be the New Jerusalem. All Church members will be totally cleansed by the Lord Jesus Christ, and the sin nature that plagues Christians in this age will be eradicated in the coming age (i.e., the millennium). Those in their earthly bodies of flesh and blood will still have their sin nature during the millennium, but they will not be tempted by Satan and his group of fallen angels who will be consigned to the "bottomless pit" during the kingdom age.

> 1 Cor 10:11 (KJV) Now all these things happened unto them for *ensamples*: and they are written for our admonition, upon whom the ends of the world are come.

The things written in the Old Testament are written as types and examples for our learning. A student of Scripture must consider all of

Scripture and not just selected verses. One of the primary hermeneutical principles (i.e., rules for Bible interpretation) is called the first mention principle. This principle is well-known and it states that the first time a subject is broached in Scripture gives the meaning that is attached to it all through the Word of God.

Eve, a Type of the Bride

The first bride in Scripture was Eve and her origin (Gen. 2:22-23) is well-known among Christians, but few understand the prophetic significance of her origin. The different methods for the creation of Adam and Eve were for a reason. Adam is a type of Christ and just as Adam's bride was taken out of his body, Christ's bride will be taken out of his body, the Church. Eve was made from a small portion of Adam's body. She was made out of one rib and the flesh attached to that rib. The type is accurate for the bride of Christ. Adam was put to sleep before his side was opened. Christ was also put to sleep before his side was pierced and blood and water poured out. The blood represents the salvation of the spirit which is by grace. The water represents the salvation of the life which is a work and which is attained by the washing of water by the Word (Eph. 5:25-27). Thus, the bride of Christ must "be born of water and the spirit." Many in the Church are not "born of water" since they do not avail themselves of the cleansing that Jesus is now providing as our High Priest (I John 1:9), and they do not study the Bible.

The bride of Christ will come out of those who not only see the kingdom (John 3:3) but those who **enter** the kingdom (John 3:5). Briefly, entering the kingdom literally means to enter into the King's dominion and refers to reigning and ruling with Jesus Christ. Seeing the kingdom means to enter heaven and applies to all Christians. All Christians will see the kingdom, but not all Christians will enter the kingdom. Seeing the kingdom is of grace only. Entering the kingdom is contingent upon works which can be summarized by one word, **obedience**.

Continuing with the type of Adam and Eve as Christ and his bride, God told Adam to cleave to his wife. When Eve sinned, Adam remained with her, but in order to do so he had to take her sin upon himself. The typical teaching is that Christ had to lay aside his glory in heaven and take upon himself the sin of his bride in order to reconcile her to God. Of course, Jesus died for the whole Church which is his body, but he also died to redeem the Jews and the Gentiles which are not part of the Church. The typical teaching clearly establishes that the bride is only a small portion of his body.

At this point it is necessary to address the relationships of Jesus during his three and one-half years of ministry. Jesus had many disciples during his ministry, but he chose twelve to assist him in the administration of his ministry. It is significant that twelve is the number of governmental perfection in Scripture. Out of this twelve Jesus chose three disciples with whom He was much more intimate, and they went places with him that the other disciples did not go. These three disciples were Peter, James and John, and John was described as the disciple "whom Jesus loved." The relationships of Jesus on the earth clearly establish differing degrees of intimacy, and these relationships are a preview of the millennial kingdom.

All believers will be in the millennial kingdom, but like the disciples, some Christians will be closer and more intimate with Christ. The twelve disciples represent those who will "enter the kingdom," or more specifically those who will reign and rule with Jesus Christ. The three disciples represent those selected as the bride of Christ. These are the faithful Christians who have won all five crowns and will be the closest to Christ. The number three in Scripture represents divine perfection. All things that are specifically complete in Scripture are stamped with the number three.

Only those who win the Crown of Life offered by Jesus will "enter the kingdom." Additional criteria will be used to select the bride. Love for Christ accompanied by pure and sincere devotion is one of the selecting factors according to Scripture. Winning the other four crowns will be a natural outcome for spirit-filled Christians that love Jesus Christ with pure and sincere devotion.

Ruth, a Type of the Bride

Ruth is one of the primary types in the Old Testament which represents the bride of Christ. A book could be written on this one type, but a few of the basic analogies will have to suffice. The love story between Ruth and Boaz can be found in the book of Ruth.

Boaz, a rich and powerful Jew, is a type of our Kinsman-Redeemer, Jesus Christ. Naomi, a poor, helpless widow in exile from the land of Israel is a type of the nation of Israel. Ruth and Orpah are a type of the Church. Both are Gentiles barred from the covenant nation by the law. By the grace of God both became members of the family of God while Naomi (i.e., Israel) was in exile. Ruth is a type of the bride of Christ who remained faithful to Naomi (i.e., Israel) and Boaz (i.e., Jesus).

It is significant that Orpah did not cross over the Jordan River and enter into Israel. Crossing the Jordan River is a picture of the spirit-filled life in the current age, and a prophetic type of entrance into the millennial kingdom. Orpah went back to Moab, a type of the world. This is exactly what numerous Christians do after they are saved. They live in sin because they love the world and the things of the world. They do not enter into the spirit-filled life which requires daily confession of sin (1 John 1:9). Orpah did not lose her status as a member of the family of God even though she did not remain faithful. Neither do Christians lose their salvation when they become unfaithful and carnal (2 Tim. 2:11-13).

The reader should take careful note of what Ruth did in qualifying as the bride of Boaz. First, it must be remembered that Ruth represents the helpless, hopeless sinner, alienated from God, stranger to the covenants of promise, condemned by the law, and doomed to eternal darkness before she became a member of the family of God. Her salvation was by grace and grace alone. After her salvation she entered the spirit-filled life (i.e., crossed over Jordan) and gleaned in the field of Boaz. This is a picture of witnessing for Jesus in the world, and it is a trademark of the faithful Christian.

The book of Ruth contains numerous spiritual lessons for the faithful Christian, but the primary lesson is her actions before she appeared at the threshing floor where she spent the long night of threshing and winnowing at the feet of Boaz. The bride of Christ (i.e., Philadelphia Christians) will spend the long night of threshing and winnowing at the feet of Jesus while Israel (i.e., Naomi) and the remainder of the Church (i.e., Orpah) spend this long night (i.e., 42 months each in tribulation) in the world.

Threshing and winnowing is not the separation of the saved from the unsaved but represents a separation of the chaff from the wheat or a separation of the bad from the good. It is a picture of the purging of the Church during the first three and one-half of the tribulation and the purging of Israel during the last three and one-half years of the tribulation. The last three and one-half years is called the "time of Jacob's trouble."

Ruth did three highly significant things before she appeared on the threshing floor and lay down at the feet of Boaz. She washed herself, anointed herself with perfumed oil, and put on her finest clothes. Washing herself is a picture of confession of sin and being cleansed of all unrighteousness (1 John 1:9). Thus, the bride of Christ must have availed herself of Jesus' current function as High Priest. Anointing herself with perfumed oil is a picture of being filled with the Holy Spirit. Those making up the bride of Christ will be spirit-filled Christians who bear fruit. The fruit of the spirit is love, joy, peace, patience, kindness, goodness, faithfulness, gentleness, and self-control (Gal. 5:22-23). All Christians are not fruit-bearers and those branches which do not bear fruit will be purged (John 15:5-7; Rom. 11:19-22). They will be rejected by Jesus as his bride for their unfaithfulness.

Ruth also dressed herself in her finest clothes. This is a picture of the wedding garment, a type of good works (i.e., righteous acts) of the saints. Revelation 19:7 confirms that the bride makes herself ready by providing for herself a wedding garment of good works. Only those Christians who have the "wedding garment" of "works of righteousness" will be invited to the wedding and make up the bride of Christ.

> Mat 22:11-14 (KJV) And when the king came in to see the guests, he saw there a man which had not on a wedding garment: 12 And he saith unto him, Friend, how camest thou in hither not having a wedding garment? And he was speechless. 13 Then said the king to the servants, Bind him hand and foot, and take him away, and cast him into outer darkness; there shall be weeping and gnashing of teeth. 14 For many are called, but few are chosen.

> Rev 19:7-8 (KJV) Let us be glad and rejoice, and give honour to him: for the marriage of the Lamb is come, and his wife hath made herself ready. 8 And to her was granted that she should be arrayed in fine linen, clean and white: for the fine linen is the righteousness of saints (NIV – righteous acts).

Matthew 22 confirms the rejection of one who has not prepared for himself a wedding garment. "Outer darkness" in verse 13 is not hell as is commonly thought. The phrase is an ancient oriental idiom that means to receive the displeasure of the master. It is a picture of the chastisement for unfaithfulness that Christians will receive at the Judgment Seat of Christ.

The phrase "outer darkness" is used three times in Matthew and all refer to children of God who are not allowed to enter the kingdom. Matthew 8:12 refers to the Israelites who lost their inheritance when the kingdom was taken from them and given to the Church. Matthew 22:13 refers to those in the Church who did not prepare for themselves a wedding garment of good works. Matthew 25:30 also refers to the unfaithful in the Church who did not work for the Lord in the power of the Holy Spirit.

Rebekah, a Type of the Bride

Genesis 24 is a prophetic picture (i.e., type) of God choosing a bride for his Son, Jesus. Abraham typifies God the Father, and Isaac is a type of Jesus Christ. Eliezer is analogous to the Holy Spirit, and Rebekah represents the bride of Christ. Abraham made a covenant with Eliezer for him to go to Abraham's own people to find a bride for Isaac. Abraham clearly specified that Eliezer was not to go to the Canaanites (i.e., the lost) to choose a bride for Isaac. This is a clear picture of the Holy Spirit choosing a bride for Christ from God's own people, the Church. The bride of Christ is to be chosen from the family of God and not the world. Abraham did not seek a bride for Isaac until after Isaac had been placed on the altar as a burnt offering. The selection of Christ's bride was after his death, burial and resurrection.

Eliezer met Rebekah by a well of water, a type of sanctification (Isaiah 12:3). The water typifies the Word (Isaiah 55:1,2). The bride will consist of saved people who are interested in and guided by the Word of God. Eliezer spoke not of himself or drew attention to himself, but he spoke of and magnified Isaac. The Holy Spirit acts in the same way in regard to Jesus Christ. Eliezer opened his storehouse of treasure and showed it to Rebekah and her family. The Holy Spirit also reveals the treasures and gifts of God the Father. Laban, a type of the carnal Christian, was enamored with and interested in the gifts.

Rebekah was interested in Isaac, a type of the Bridegroom. Rebekah was asked to leave everything and be guided by Eliezer through the wilderness. Christians who make up the bride are guided through the current wilderness by the Holy Spirit. Rebekah had to choose to be the bride of Isaac. Christians have this same choice, but they must be willing to leave their current home (i.e., the world) in order to go and be with Jesus. When Rebekah saw Isaac coming from a distance, she took her veil and covered herself. This is typical of Christians putting on the wedding garment as they prepare to meet the Bridegroom.

There are numerous other analogies in this passage of Scripture such as the old age of Abraham and Eliezer typifying the eternality of God the Father and the Holy Spirit. Rebekah drew much water from the well for herself and others, and this typifies the faithful Christian who is filled with the spirit and leads others into the spirit-filled life. Rebekah was willing to leave all to go and be with Isaac whom she had never seen. Her only knowledge of Isaac was the witness of Eliezer who testified about Isaac. This is identical to faithful Christians who are anxious for the Bridegroom to return based on the testimony of the Holy Spirit to the spirits of these Christians. It pertains to those who are looking for the return of the Bridegroom. Many in the Church today are enamored with spiritual gifts and indifferent to the Bridegroom and are not watching for him.

The Ten Virgins

The Olivet discourse in Matthew 24 and 25 is little understood by Christians, and this includes pastors and teachers. In verse 3 the disciples of Jesus asked him to tell them about the signs that would signal his return and the end of the age. Jesus answered the question in regard to the Jews, the Church and the Gentiles since each group is dealt with separately by God. The Olivet discourse will not be understood until this is understood.

Matthew 24:4-31 pertains strictly to the Jews and all takes place during Daniel's seventieth week. Matthew 24:32-25:30 pertains strictly to the Church and all takes place during the Church age from Pentecost until the beginning of Daniel's seventieth week. Matthew 25:31-46 pertains to the Gentiles during the tribulation, and all takes place during the tribulation.

The parable of the ten virgins is in the section addressed to the Church and the ten virgins symbolize the entire Church since ten is the number of ordinal completion in the Bible. The five wise virgins represent those in the Church who are called out because of their readiness (i.e., maturity), and they enter into the wedding. The five foolish virgins represent those in the Church who are rejected because of their unfaithfulness. The Scriptures never refer to an unsaved person (i.e., reprobate) as a virgin. The five wise virgins had one thing that the foolish did not have, and that was the extra measure of oil. This is a clear picture of being filled with the spirit. All ten virgins had oil because all of their lamps were burning. This is a clear picture of being indwelled by the Holy Spirit. The indwelling of the Holy Spirit is a free gift by the grace of God, and it occurs the moment a person believes on the Lord Jesus Christ.

It is important to note that the extra measure of oil had to be bought which is a clear reference to works. The cost is dear and each person has to work for it himself. The cost is life itself with the service, surrender, fellowship, purity of life, love and sincere devotion that are implied in the word "bride." It is also important to note that the virgins who were ready went into the wedding, and the door was shut (Mat. 25:10). The faithful Philadelphia church was also provided an open door and they were kept from the hour of trial (i.e., tribulation) coming upon the whole earth. Also, the Apostle John was provided with an open door (Rev. 4:1) and he went directly to heaven at the beginning of the tribulation. The five foolish virgins do not show up in heaven until later (Mat. 25:11), and the main body of the Church does not show up in heaven until it is taken out of the tribulation (Rev. 7:9-17). This great multitude in white robes can not be those saved during the tribulation since they are the saved Gentiles, and their judgment takes place on the earth at the end of the tribulation. Their judgment is the sheep and goat judgment described in Matthew 25:31-46.

The main point of this explanation is that the bride of Christ will be chosen out of the five wise virgins, and works are critical to being identified with the bride. Paul was willing to lose all things to "gain Christ," and so must all Christians who do not wish to be among the "castaways." *Castaways do not go to hell.* When the Apostle Paul said this he was not worried about going to hell, but he was concerned about being disqualified for the "Prize." Castaways are simply rejected for intimate communion with Christ during his reign and rule in the kingdom. They are "put away" because of unfaithfulness.

There are several other lesser types in Scripture that reveal other characteristics of the bride of Christ, but these types reveal much more information about Christ and his millennial kingdom than they do about the bride. The following are brief references to these types:

1.   Joseph and Asenath are types of Christ and his bride.
2.   Moses and Zipporah are types of Christ and his bride.
3.   Jacob and Rachael are types of Christ and his bride.
4.   David and Abigail are types of Christ and his bride.

The relationship between grace and works in the Scriptures is the most misunderstood theological concern in all of Scripture. Many make salvation a works related achievement and totally disregard the grace of God. Others make salvation a gift of grace, but they require works to prove the salvation. These are the Judaizers or those caught up in the error of Lordship Salvation.

Others make salvation a gift of grace and rewards are automatic. They totally disregard works as a prerequisite for rewards. Salvation is a gift of God, and works do not enter in at all either before or after spiritual rebirth. However, works do enter in to realize many of the promises of God that are directly related to the millennial kingdom.

A correct understanding of the relationship between grace and works is necessary to understand the Word of the kingdom since works are necessary for an abundant entrance into this kingdom. All Christians will enter heaven and see the kingdom. All Christians will not enter the kingdom, and fewer still will enter the bridal chamber of Christ.

The twelve disciples represent those who will enter the Kingdom. Only Peter, James and John went with Christ to the Mount of Transfiguration. These closest disciples knew Jesus in a more intimate way. They represent the bride

Knowing Christ intimately now is the requirement for knowing him as his bride in the coming Kingdom.

ARE YOU READY FOR THE WEDDING?

"The Spirit and the Bride say, Come..."

(Revelation 22:17)

Chapter 6

THE OLIVET DISCOURSE

The Signs of Christ's Return

This most important utterance of the Lord shows exactly what we see elsewhere. [In the Olivet Discourse] the Speaker has passed to the very close of this age, for, though the expectant mother is liable to more or less distress throughout the period she carries the child, yet "travail" is only the brief, though most acute time immediately before the birth. If but the force of this one figure had been grasped, the church of God might have been spared from books innumerable and bulky, written on the futile plan of trying to make the details of nineteen centuries fit the details of prophetic scriptures, especially the book of Revelation. Thus in this major prophecy the whole gospel age is summarized briefly, especially while its closing days are elaborated fully.

G.H. Lang – *The Revelation of Jesus Christ*, p. 63

The Olivet Discourse is found in chapters 24 and 25 of the book of Matthew. A common error among prophetic scholars is the failure to see the Church in the book of Matthew and, especially, in the Olivet Discourse. It is routinely stated that the Olivet Discourse is all Jewish and does not pertain to the Church. This very serious exegetical error conveniently applies all the promises to the Church and all the threats to the Jews. The commands of God are also dispensed to the Jew by those in the Church while the privileges are retained without any precepts or responsibilities being applied to the Church. This is an incorrect division of Scripture. The result is failure to correctly interpret the Olivet Discourse and present a logical, consistent picture of the signs that will accompany the return of Jesus Christ to planet earth to set up his kingdom.

The Gospel of Matthew does portray Jesus Christ as King of the Jews, and it also speaks much about "the kingdom of heaven." Many theologians also err in this respect by setting aside "the kingdom of heaven" as being Jewish or earthly only. The kingdom of heaven has two compartments with one being earthly and one being heavenly. The Jews were promised an earthly Jerusalem and Christians were promised a new heavenly Jerusalem.

The Son of Man as the ladder of Jacob unites the earthly aspect with the heavenly aspect. Jesus as the Son of God is the point of the ladder that touches heaven while Jesus as King of the Jews is the foot of the ladder that touches the earth. Thus, the Church is found in the Gospel of Matthew and even in the Olivet discourse, contrary to the traditional teaching by seminaries.

The Olivet Discourse actually addresses all three classes of people who are part of God's overall plan. Every human being belongs to one of these three classes of Jews, Christians, or Gentiles. The Jews and the Gentiles who are God's people (i.e., they were saved outside of the Church age) are attached to the earthly portion of the kingdom while the Church belongs to the heavenly portion.

It is important for the reader to first understand the term kingdom of heaven before the Olivet Discourse is explained. The kingdom of God and the kingdom of heaven are sometimes synonymous in Scripture but not always. The Scriptures teach us that the kingdom of God has three different aspects that correspond with the Trinity of God.

The first aspect is the kingdom of God the Father, and it is the rule of God over all creation. This means everything created including planets, angels, animals, lost men, saved men, and even the insects. Every molecule in the universe comes under God's dominion in this aspect of His kingdom. Daniel 4:34-35 refers to this aspect of the kingdom. When a person is born physically he enters the Kingdom of God the Father.

The second aspect is the kingdom of God the Holy Spirit, and it rules over the believer's heart and life but only by permission from the believer. This kingdom is entered by faith in the Lord Jesus Christ. Romans 14:17-19 refers to this aspect of the kingdom. The spiritually reborn person after entering this aspect of the kingdom has two ways that he can live his life. If he allows his depraved flesh nature to dominate, then this aspect of the kingdom will not be operating within the believer. This believer is referred to as a carnal Christian.

However, if the believer allows the Holy Spirit to dominate, this kingdom will be in operation, and He will experience righteousness, peace and joy in the Holy Spirit while being a faithful servant to Christ and acceptable to God the Father. This Christian is called the spiritual Christian, and he will qualify to enter the third aspect of the kingdom that is described next.

The kingdom of God the Son is a visible, literal, corporal, and future kingdom that has boundaries of time and space. The Old Testament calls it the "messianic kingdom," while the New Testament refers to it as the millennium or the kingdom of heaven. This kingdom is still future, and it is the one that Jesus Christ commanded his disciples to pray for when he instructed them to pray, "Thy kingdom come." This kingdom is entered by works, and numerous Christians will fail to enter because of sin, disobedience and a love of this world. Numerous Scriptures refer to this kingdom in the New Testament. It is commonly believed that all Christians will enter this kingdom, but this is not true. The following Scriptures are just a few that confirm that only a relatively few Christians will enter this kingdom:

Luke 18:17 (KJV) Verily I say unto you, Whosoever shall not receive the kingdom of God as a little child shall in no wise enter therein.

Luke 18:24-25 (KJV) And when Jesus saw that he was very sorrowful, he said, How hardly shall they that have riches enter into the kingdom of God! 25 For it is easier for a camel to go through a needle's eye, than for a rich man to enter into the kingdom of God.

Acts 14:22 (KJV) Confirming the souls of the disciples, and exhorting them to continue in the faith, and that we must through much tribulation enter into the kingdom of God.

John 3:5 (KJV) Jesus answered, Verily, verily, I say unto thee, Except a man be born of water and of the Spirit, he cannot enter into the kingdom of God.

Mat 22:14 (KJV) For many are called (i.e., saved), but few are chosen (i.e., to enter the kingdom).

2 Th 1:5 (KJV) Which is a manifest token of the righteous judgment of God, that ye may be counted worthy of the kingdom of God, for which ye also suffer:

Entrance into this kingdom is by works. It is a privilege that will be granted to those believers who have earned rewards. Those who lose their rewards will not be granted this privilege. The following Scripture warns Christians not to lose their crown:

> Rev 3:11 (KJV) Behold, I come quickly: hold that fast which thou hast, that no man take thy crown.

In summary, the three aspects of the kingdom of God operate in different spheres. The first is entered by creation or physical birth. The second is entered by the new creation or the new birth. The third must be entered by re-creation by the washing of water by the Word. This is through confession of sin and growing in knowledge and thus earning rewards.

The majority of preachers and teachers in the Church today teach only the second aspect of the kingdom, and they believe that one only needs to be saved to receive rewards and enter the third aspect of the kingdom. Numerous Christians will be surprised and even shocked when they are not allowed to enter the kingdom of God the Son. These Christians who do not "study to show thyself approved unto God" will not be invited to reign and rule with Jesus Christ.

The nation of Israel spurned the offer of the kingdom of heaven when they rejected Jesus Christ as their king. The reason for this rejection may be directly attributed to the actions of the Scribes and Pharisees during the time of the earthly ministry of Christ.

The Scribes and Pharisees were regenerate Jews who had fallen into pride and sin, and they had become barren. This is why Jesus' message to them was not, "Believe and be saved," but, "Repent for the Kingdom is at hand." They had no fruit in their lives and had stopped watching for the coming Messiah. The carnality of the Jews caused them to reject Jesus as the Messiah prophesied in the Old Testament. It was because of this rejection that the offer of the kingdom of heaven was taken away from the nation of Israel and offered to a new nation that would bring forth fruit (Mat. 21:43). This new nation was the Church, and the criterion for receiving the kingdom was still the bearing of fruit. It was not automatic upon salvation.

It was because of Israel's rejection of Jesus that the house of Israel would become a desolation and remain so for approximately two thousand years (Hos. 5:15-6:2). The offer of the kingdom remained open to Israel for 40 years, and if the Jews had repented as a nation, Jesus would have set up his kingdom then. The failure of the nation to repent resulted in the desolation of the house of Israel by the armies of Titus in 70 A.D. The term *house of Israel* included the people, the temple, the city of Jerusalem, and the land of Israel. This desolation will extend through the Great Tribulation (i.e., the time of Jacob's trouble), but Israel will be restored at the beginning of the third millennium. This restoration was what Jesus' disciples were inquiring about when Jesus gave his discourse about the signs that would accompany his second coming at the end of the age. Jesus gave this discourse to his disciples while He sat on the Mount of Olives so it has become known as the Olivet Discourse.

The Olivet Discourse is a three-part, connected discourse dealing with the Jews, the Christians, and the Gentiles. The first part pertains to the Jews (Mat. 24:4-31) while the second part deals exclusively with the Christians (Mat. 24:32-25:30). The third part concerns the Gentiles (Mat. 25:31-46).

The first part deals exclusively with events pertaining to Israel during Daniel's seventieth week (i.e., the seven year tribulation) and with the return of Israel's Messiah at the end of the tribulation. Israel had rejected the Messiah so they must now pass through the Great Tribulation and await her Messiah. The second part concerns the new recipients of the offer of the kingdom of heaven. The emphasis in this section is on present faithfulness during the current age in view of the return of Jesus Christ to judge the Church and assign positions in the millennial kingdom. The third part concerns the judgment of the Gentiles at the return of Christ in power and glory at the conclusion of the tribulation.

The Jewish section is restricted to the seven year tribulation since Israel has been set aside during the present time while God removes from the Gentiles "a people for his name." The time for God to deal once again with Israel is awaiting the completion of the present dispensation which has been called the Church Age or the Age of Grace.

The Christian section pertains to the Church so it deals with people during the present time (i.e., the Church Age) who are the recipients of the offer of the kingdom after Israel's rejection of the offer. Events during this section occur during the time of Israel's desolation. The common belief that this section concerns Israel cannot be true since God is not directly dealing with the nation of Israel at this time. The kingdom of heaven has been taken from Israel, and it is being offered to those in the Church who are "bringing forth the fruits thereof" (Mat. 21:43).

The Gentile section only has Gentiles in view since God will have completed his dealings with both the Church and the nation of Israel. "Judgment must begin at the house of God" (1 Peter 4:17). The Christians and the nation of Israel must be judged first, and then God will judge the Gentiles at the end of the tribulation and immediately before the millennial kingdom is established.

There are several distinctions among the three sections that separate them. Parables are found in the Christian section alone, and this is in accordance with Matthew's gospel leading up to the discourse. Parables appear in the Gospel of Matthew in chapter thirteen, and it was at this point in the ministry of Jesus that He left the house, went down by the seaside, and began to speak in parables. The house refers specifically to Israel, and the sea is peculiarly related to the Gentiles. Thus, the teaching in Matthew 13:1 is that Jesus departed from the group to which he came (i.e., Israel), went to an entirely separate group (i.e., the Gentiles), and began to speak in parables. Thus, the first mention of parables in Matthew's gospel is peculiarly related to the Gentiles and the taking out of the Church.

Another distinguishing mark among the three sections pertains to salvation and judgment. Salvation in the Jewish section is concerned with physical deliverance, and the judgment associated with it is the Great Tribulation here upon the earth. The salvation in the Christian section pertains to the believers' soul/life, and the judgment is the Judgment Seat of Christ in the heavens. Salvation in the Gentile section pertains to entrance into the kingdom, and the judgment takes place with the Son of Man seated on "the throne of his glory" down here on the earth at the end of the Tribulation.

Each of the three sections of the Olivet Discourse must be understood separately from the other two sections, or there will be confusion and gross misinterpretation of Scripture. This is the reason the parable of the ten virgins is so grossly misinterpreted, and so few Christians actually understand what it means.

In summary, the kingdom of heaven (i.e., the millennium) is the focus of God's plan since the creation of Adam, and the Olivet Discourse describes God's final dealings with the three divisions of mankind—Jew, Christian, and Gentile—just prior to the end of this age and leading into the millennial kingdom. It is important to note that entrance into this kingdom—both earthly and heavenly spheres—is dependent upon works that pass through the judgments of Jesus Christ. The sad truth is that the majority of the Church is completely oblivious to these kingdom truths, and they have no idea about what lies just ahead at the Judgment Seat of Christ. The Judgment Seat of Christ will be a traumatic time for numerous Christians

Jewish Section (Mat. 24:4-31)

The Jewish section of the Olivet Discourse begins at Matthew 24:4 where Jesus answers his disciples' question about the desolation of Israel until the nation of Israel shall see Jesus and say, "Blessed is he that cometh in the name of the Lord." The larger scope of the question that the disciples asked included the desolation of the "house of Israel" as well as the destruction of the temple. Luke 21:20-24 describes the initial desolation of the house of Israel by Titus in 70 A. D. This was when the temple was destroyed and the Diaspora took place. Jesus said nothing about his coming in connection with the destruction of the temple.

Matthew 24:4-31 deals exclusively with events pertaining to Israel during the seven weeks (i.e., the 49 years) of Daniel, and Daniel's seventieth week (i.e., the seven year tribulation), and with the return of Israel's Messiah at the end of the tribulation. The disciples asked Jesus about the desolation of Israel and what would be the sign of his coming to restore Israel. Since the sign for the coming of Jesus depended upon whether a person was a Jew, Christian, or Gentile at the time, Jesus answered the question for each of these three classes of people. The response to the Jew is in Matthew 24:4-31 and the description is that of seven year tribulation period called the seventieth week of Daniel.

The first sixty-two weeks of Daniel ended when Messiah was "cut-off" (i.e., crucified), and we are currently in a parenthesis called the Church Age, or Age of Grace, when God is no longer directly dealing with the nation of Israel. God will not resume His direct dealing with the nation of Israel until the removal of the Church. This is the reason that all of the Jewish section of the Olivet Discourse in the Gospel of Matthew must take place during the tribulation before Jesus returns in power and glory.

The first warning that Jesus gives to the Jew is in verse 4 and it tells them not to be deceived by any "man." This warning is highly appropriate since Israel will be deceived by the Antichrist at his first coming as leader of Babylon the Great. He is the white horseman in the four horsemen of the apocalypse, and he will deceive Israel into thinking that he is the Messiah.

Verse 5 states that many will come and claim to be Christ. This verse will be fulfilled in the tribulation when the followers of Antichrist will claim to have reached Christ consciousness through the powers of transcendental meditation. Antichrist will claim to be the incarnation of the true Christ who has come as the great teacher or avatar of mankind. The realization of Christ consciousness is supposedly available to everyone through the powers of the mind. This is the original lie of attaining godhead through self-effort that Satan used to deceive Eve in the Garden of Eden. Large numbers of people are still being duped by this ancient lie of Satan that appeals to a person's pride.

Verse 6 is parallel with the red horseman of the apocalypse, and verse 7 is parallel with the black and pale horsemen of the apocalypse in Revelation 6. The red horseman is war, and the black horseman is famine and pestilence. War, famine and pestilence will result in the pale horseman or death and Hades for one-fourth of the world population.

Verse 8 is a transition from the first three and one-half years of Daniel's seventieth week to the last three and one-half years which is called the "time of Jacob's trouble." The first three and one-half years are only the beginning of sorrows for the Jews.

Verse 9 is when Antichrist turns against the Jews in the middle of the tribulation, and they suffer much affliction and death at the hands of Antichrist. Antichrist will be responsible for many more Jewish deaths than Hitler.

Verses 10, 11, and 12 record the Jewish reaction to the unprecedented persecution of the Jews by Antichrist. Verse 13 speaks of the remnant of the Jews who will endure to the end and be saved. One-third of the Jews will pass through the Great Tribulation and be physically saved on the Day of Atonement when Jesus Christ returns in power and glory and the nation of Israel is saved in one day.

Verse 14 speaks of the gospel of the kingdom being preached throughout the world as a witness to all nations before the end of the age arrives. This verse is probably the most misinterpreted verse in all of Scripture. The gospel of the kingdom is not currently being preached. The gospel of grace is currently being preached, but the gospel of the kingdom will be preached by the 144,000 Jews during the last half of the seven year tribulation. The two witnesses— probably Elijah and Moses—will also preach the gospel of the kingdom during this period. The gospel of the kingdom will be for the Gentiles, and numerous Gentiles will enter into the earthly portion of the kingdom of God the Son. This will take place at the sheep and goat judgment that will be explained in the Gentile section of the Olivet Discourse.

Verse 15 jumps back to the middle of the tribulation to fill in more details of the last three and one-half years known as the "time of Jacob's trouble." The abomination of desolation is the Antichrist who sets himself up in the Jewish temple and claims to be god. This act is the beginning of the "time of Jacob's trouble."

Verse 16 gives instructions to the Jews living in Judea at the time that Antichrist sets himself up in the temple. The Jews will flee to the wilderness Southeast of the Dead Sea and hold up in the ancient city of Petra in modern day Jordan.

Verses 17 and 18 depict the rapidity that must be adhered to in order to escape the vengeance of Antichrist. Verse 19 describes the danger for pregnant women and women with young babies since they will be fleeing for their lives on foot. Verse 20 commands that they pray that their flight will not be in winter, and that it will not be on the Sabbath day since they will have to travel further than the Talmud allows for a Sabbath journey.

Verse 21 describes the last three and one-half years as the worst tribulation that the world has ever known. The tribulation will be so great that verse 22 says that no one would have survived if the days had not been shortened. This verse has been misinterpreted by numerous theologians. The tribulation will still be three and one-half years long but the days will literally be shortened by one-third for a part of the tribulation. This will be accomplished by speeding up the rotation of the earth on its axis so that the days will only be sixteen hours long (Rev 8:12).

Verses 23-26 warn the Jews against believing that the Christ (i.e., the Messiah) will come by ordinary means. Verse 27 depicts the coming of Jesus as being a supernatural event as visible as the lightning out of the East after a major storm has passed. Verse 28 alludes to the carnage that will take place at his return. This is the time that Jesus will tread the winepress of the wrath of God and the blood will flow up to the horses' bridles (Rev 14:20).

Verse 29 describes the unusual displays in the heavens just prior to the coming of Jesus in power and great glory. The sun shall become dark and the moon will not shine. This could be from the dust and debris ascending into the atmosphere from the nuclear devastation, but the description is more like that of a nova of the sun. This is also in accord with the fourth and fifth vial in Revelation 16:8-11 since there is first intense heat and then darkness and cold. In a nova the sun burns very intensely for a time and then decreases below normal output for a time. It then returns to its normal intensity. Stars much larger than our sun tend to supernova or virtually blow up. A nova would cause the sun to become dark, and this would result in a failure of the moon to shine since the moon merely reflects light from the sun. Some scientists in the past have estimated that the conditions of the sun make it ripe for a nova. Whatever the cause, the world will experience the exact condition described in the prophecy.

Verse 29 also states that the stars shall fall from heaven and the powers of the heavens will be shaken. The stars falling will almost certainly be apparent from the perspective of those on the earth. The earth tilting on its axis will most likely be the cause of this according to the following Scripture:

> Isa 24:20 (KJV) The earth shall reel to and fro like a drunkard, and shall be removed like a cottage; and the transgression thereof shall be heavy upon it; and it shall fall, and not rise again.

The falling stars and powers of the heavens being shaken will probably also have another figurative fulfillment with the fallen angels (i.e., principalities and powers) losing their positions of sovereignty over the earth.

Verse 30 describes the appearance of the Son of man in power and great glory at the end of the tribulation period. The Scriptures do not say what the sign of the Son of man will be, but it will be clear to all when it happens since all the tribes of the earth will mourn. Verse 31 describes the gathering of the elect of Israel from all over the earth. The description of this gathering likely includes a resurrection of the elect of Israel in addition to the gathering of the elect upon the earth who are still alive.

This concludes the section of the Olivet Discourse addressed to the Jews. At this point the desolation of the house of Israel has ended, and Jesus Christ has returned to establish his kingdom upon the earth. The disciples' questions have been answered as regards the nation of Israel. It is at this point that the restoration of Israel takes place with Jesus as their Messiah.

Church Section (Mat. 24:32-25:30)

This section of the Olivet Discourse is addressed to the Church. It describes the return of Jesus Christ as it regards the Church so the frame of reference is not the seventieth week of Daniel but the entire Church Age. It is very important for the reader to understand that everyone involved in the parables in this section are Christians, whether faithful or unfaithful. The lessons in the parables are for the exhortation and edification of Christians, and all warnings are for Christians. The entire discourse in this section pertains to rewards and punishments that will be meted out at the Judgment Seat of Christ, and salvation in the evangelical sense is not an issue anywhere in this section. It bears repeating that parables are peculiar to the Church and the Church Age.

> Mat, 24:32-35 (KJV) Now learn a parable of the fig tree; When his branch is yet tender, and putteth forth leaves, ye know that summer is nigh: 33 So likewise ye, when ye shall see all these things, know that it is near, even at the doors.

34 Verily I say unto you, This generation shall not pass, till all these things be fulfilled. 35 Heaven and earth shall pass away, but my words shall not pass away.

These verses describe one of the two signs given to the Church that signals the return of Jesus Christ. The parable of the fig tree is addressed to Christians and points to Israel as a sign to the Church since Israel is symbolized in the Bible by a fig tree. An understanding of this parable requires an understanding of the following verses:

Mat. 21:19-21 (KJV) And when he (i.e., Jesus) saw a fig tree in the way, he came to it, and found nothing thereon, but leaves only, and said unto it, Let no fruit grow on thee henceforward for ever (i.e., for the age). And presently the fig tree withered away. 20 And when the disciples saw it, they marveled, saying, How soon is the fig tree withered away! 21 Jesus answered and said unto them, Verily I say unto you, If ye have faith, and doubt not, ye shall not only do this which is done to the fig tree, but also if ye shall say unto this mountain, Be thou removed, and be thou cast into the sea; it shall be done.

A fig tree normally produces fruit before it produces leaves. When Jesus saw no fruit on the fig tree, he knew it was barren so he placed a curse on it for the age—not forever. Since the fig tree symbolizes Israel, it was Israel that was found barren (i.e., no fruit), so Israel was the recipient of the curse for the age. Jesus is saying that when Israel puts forth its leaves (i.e., shows signs of life), the generation that sees this will not pass away until all the prophecies about Jesus' second coming will be fulfilled.

Matthew 24:32-34 above simply says that the generation that sees Israel reestablished as a nation will still be in existence when all the prophecies about the return of Jesus have been fulfilled. Since Israel was established May 14, 1948 and man's years upon the earth are three score and ten (i.e., 70), then the beginning of the seven year tribulation must be very close. Verse 35 as follows is a special emphasis on the certainty of these prophecies coming to pass.

Mat 24:35 (KJV) Heaven and earth shall pass away, but my words shall not pass away.

Verses 36-51 refer to the second advent of Christ for the Church. This section is specifically referring to the Firstfruits Rapture of Christians who have been faithful to the Lord. In verse 36 Jesus states that no man knows the day and hour of the parousia (i.e., second coming) of the Lord. Since this verse says that only the Father knows, many have taken it to mean that even Jesus Christ did not know the day and hour of his return, but this is highly doubtful since He is God Incarnate. Jesus had the fullness of the Spirit, and this means He was fully God. He knew all things and all men, and nothing was hidden from him. Jesus Christ was God the Father manifest in the flesh. He remained deferent to the Father, but He was equal in knowledge. The meaning in the original language is that Jesus would not have known if he were not also the Father. This is also true for the passage in Mark 13:32. The main point is that the deity of Jesus cannot be separated from his humanity throughout his earthly life from his incarnation until his ascension. As the God-Man He was as much fully God as He was fully man

Verse 37 is the second major sign for the Church to know that the *parousia* (i.e., second coming) of Jesus Christ was very close. This verse simply says that it will be as the days of Noah when the Lord returns. A description of the days before the flood is recorded in chapters 4, 5 and 6 of Genesis so a study of these chapters of the Bible will help the reader see that the days we live in now exactly parallel the days before the flood.

Chapter 4 of Genesis describes the economic picture at the time of Noah. Eight specific conditions are mentioned in chapter four, and they are religious apostasy, travel, city building, polygamy and sexuality, great agricultural advances, music, metallurgy, and violence and crime. All eight are the outstanding characteristics of today's world. Space prohibits an in-depth discussion of these characteristics, but the reader should be able to make the connections. Religious apostasy is probably the most significant since large numbers of Christians have fallen away from the faith because of a lack of understanding of the two aspects of our salvation (see pp. 46-48), and the great majority of Christians are Biblically illiterate.

There is a tremendous upsurge in interest in religion but very little interest in walking with God and studying his Word. We are at the end of the Church Age of Laodicea, and apostasy and lukewarmness are the prevailing characteristics for the largest segment of Christianity. It is ironic that one of the primary characteristics of Laodicea is self-deception in believing that it is spiritually rich when it is actually wretched, miserable, poor, blind, and naked.

Chapter 5 of Genesis gives God's dispensational picture during the days before the flood. Enoch was the seventh from Adam and the number seven speaks of divine perfection. There were six generations of men who died, and then Enoch was raptured before he saw death. Enoch was a type of the rapture of the Firstfruits of the Church. He walked with God and was raptured or translated to heaven because of his faithfulness according to the following Scripture:

> Heb 11:5 (KJV) By faith Enoch was translated that he should not see death; and was not found, because God had translated him: for before his translation he had this testimony, that he pleased God.

Enoch preached of the second coming of Christ, and he preached of coming judgment. This is the same message Paul gives to the carnal Christians in Corinth in 1 Corinthians 3. Enoch knew that his son would be the last generation to exist before the flood since he named his son Methuselah. The name *Methuselah* means, "when he is gone, then it will happen." The meaning of the name proved to be accurate beyond measure since the flood began the same year and day that Methuselah departed this earth. Thus, Methuselah is a type of the main harvest of the Church which remains on the earth right up to the very day that God's judgments are poured out upon the earth. This is also seen in carnal Lot who was taken out of Sodom the very same day that God rained down judgment in the form of fire and brimstone.

In conclusion of typology in this text of Scripture, Noah is left as a type of God's people who are sealed and pass through the judgments of God miraculously protected by Christ himself. The three arks in the Bible all symbolize Jesus Christ who makes atonement for the sins of his people. Thus, the sealing of Noah in the ark by God symbolizes the 144,000 Jews who are sealed in their foreheads because of their faithfulness.

Noah is also a type of the nation of Israel and the Gentiles who will be preserved throughout the last half of Daniel's seventieth week and enter into the millennial kingdom as God's earthly people. The 144,000 Jews are the Firstfruits of the nation of Israel who are saved in a day in the prophetic fulfillment of the feast of Atonement.

Matthew 24:38-39 depicts the second coming as a time when individuals will be going about their normal activities without realizing the closeness of coming judgment. This is exactly the way it is for the world and much of the Church right now. Most Christians are totally oblivious to the present signs signaling the soon return of our Lord and Savior Jesus Christ.

Verses 40 and 41 are routinely taken to mean a saved and an unsaved person standing next to each other and only the saved person will be taken. When these verses are read carefully within their context, the picture is that of two saved individuals together and only one of them will be taken. It is important to repeat that the promise of Christ's return and the judgment is only for believers. In the context, Jesus is talking to his disciples and these two verses are a warning to them that they must be ready when the Lord comes or they will be left behind to endure the persecution of Antichrist.

Verse 42, "Watch therefore: for ye know not what hour your Lord doth come," is clearly a warning to the disciples that they must be prepared for the return of Jesus or they will be left behind. The following verse also addresses this warning:

> Luke 21:36 (KJV) Watch ye therefore, and pray always, that ye may be accounted worthy to escape all these things that shall come to pass, and to stand before the Son of man.

The criterion for being the one taken is clearly preparation for the Lord's return by being alert and prepared. The admonition is not "believe on the Lord Jesus Christ," since the above verse is addressed to believers who have already been saved.

An Old Testament type of this New Testament truth is the example of Elijah and Elisha who were walking along two by two. They were separated by a fiery chariot and only Elijah was taken up into heaven by a whirlwind. Elijah is a type of the Firstfruits who are raptured at the beginning of the tribulation, and Elisha is a type of the tribulation

Christian who will be raptured from the tribulation.

When Elisha saw Elijah ascend into heaven, he immediately rent his clothes, a picture of repentance. This is exactly what much of the Church will do when they realize that certain ones have been taken, and they have been left behind. Elisha then took the mantle of Elijah, parted the Jordan River, and crossed over. Crossing over Jordan is a picture of entering the spirit filled life, and this is exactly what numerous Christians will do after the Firstfruits rapture has taken place. Elisha then purified a spring of water, a picture of leading others into the spirit filled life. This is also a prophecy of the Church in the coming tribulation.

Elisha was then mocked for his bald head and teased by a group of young men because he was not raptured like Elijah. They taunted him by saying, "Go up, thou bald head; go up, thou bald head" (2 Kings 2:23). Baldness in Scripture is a symbol of defilement, and those carnal Christians who are defiled by the world and not cleansed by the Lord Jesus Christ will be left behind at the Firstfruits rapture. Thus, Elisha is a primary type of that part of the Church left to go through the tribulation, and Elijah is a primary type of that part of the Church that is raptured as Firstfruits.

It is also very important to understand that Elisha received a double portion of Elijah's spirit. This is a picture of Christians who will go through the first half of the seven year tribulation. The tribulation will be a return to the Old Testament method of empowerment by the Holy Spirit. The Holy Spirit would come on people to empower them for special assignments. Thus, Christians during the first half of the tribulation will be both indwelled by the Holy Spirit and empowered by the Holy Spirit coming upon them for acts of service. This will be the prophetic fulfillment of Elisha having a double portion of spirit. Christians during the tribulation will need this double portion of spirit to endure until the main harvest of the Church in the middle of the tribulation.

Matthew 24:45-51 is a description of two courses available to a servant of the Lord. It is important to note that the servant is the same individual in both courses of action. This is done to illustrate that a servant of the Lord (i.e., a saved or spiritually reborn person) has the choice of being a faithful or unfaithful (i.e., evil) servant, and he will be justly recompensed for his actions either way. The faithful servant will be blessed, and he will be made a ruler in the coming millennial kingdom.

The unfaithful or evil servant is described as one who disregards the second coming of our Lord Jesus Christ. Many Christians who attend church services weekly are guilty of delaying or minimizing the importance of the return of Jesus Christ. This simply means that they are not looking for the return of Jesus, and they push it off into the distant future in their own minds. This is the same Christian who mocks those Christians who are actively looking for the return of Jesus. This is what is meant by the unfaithful servant smiting his fellow servants. Many Christians have ceased talking about the return of Jesus because they have been smitten so much by these unfaithful servants. These unfaithful servants will also "eat and drink with the drunken." This simply means that these Christians will be caught up in the affairs of the world. Like the people of Noah's time they will be busy enjoying their life with little time for spiritual things.

Verse 50 makes it clear that these servants will not be looking for the return of Jesus, and they will not even be aware in the hour when Jesus does come. They will be the ones who are left at the Firstfruits rapture. They will be "cut asunder" (i.e., separated) and assigned their portions with the hypocrites. This verse refers to carnal Christians suffering in the world during the first half of the tribulation. This is a message the carnal Laodicean church members of today do not want to hear, and unfortunately, few pastors are as bold as Paul was in 1 Corinthians 3.

The Ten Virgins (Mat. 25:1-13)

This parable points to the same time in which the story of the faithful and unwise servant took place. It occurs during the time of the Lord's absence from the earth. The parable of the ten virgins gives additional insights into that which has preceded, and it is specifically addressing the Church.

Ten is one of the four perfect numbers in Scripture, and it speaks of ordinal completion or perfection. Thus, the ten virgins represent the entire Church during the present dispensation. Five of the virgins were wise, but five were foolish. The five wise virgins represent the same segment of the Church as the faithful servant in the Lord's house. The five foolish servants represent the same segment of the Church as the unfaithful servant in the Lord's house.

It should be noted that all ten are called *virgins* by Jesus, and it is completely untenable that Jesus would refer to unsaved reprobates, tares, children of the devil, etc., as *virgins*. Also, all ten virgins had lamps filled with oil, and the lamps were burning, a picture of the indwelling of the Holy Spirit. In addition, all ten "took their lamps and went forth to meet the bridegroom." If the five foolish virgins are unsaved reprobates, then words in Scripture have no stable meaning and cannot be trusted to enlighten us regarding spiritual truths.

The reason that the parable of the ten virgins has been misinterpreted so often is the fact that it contains some hard truths that the majority of the Church is unwilling to accept. It makes Christians accountable for their lives, and it shows consequences for being a foolish Christian. It is more palatable to assign the foolish virgins to the ranks of the lost than to face the realities of what this parable teaches. This is an uncomfortable message for casual and lukewarm Christians.

The oil in the lamps and the burning lamps are a picture of Christians who are indwelled by the Holy Spirit and who are provided with light for the journey. The burning lamps also typify their outward profession of faith. The correct translation of verses 7-8 is given in the Montgomery New Testament as follows:

> Then all those maidens arose, and trimmed their lamps. And the foolish said to the wise, "Give us some of your oil, for our lamps are *going out*."

It may seem trivial to some as to whether the lamps had gone out or were going out, but the doctrine of the eternal security of the believer is not a trivial matter. The lamps of the foolish and unfaithful Christian may dim and even flicker, but they will never be totally extinguished. The Greek word for going out (G#4570) is the same word for quench when referring to Christians quenching the spirit (1 Thess. 5:19). To say that the lamps had "gone out" is to say that the Holy Spirit has departed from the believer.

The only difference between the wise and the foolish virgins is the extra measure of oil that the wise virgins carried with them. This is a picture of an abundance of oil and speaks of the filling of the spirit rather than the indwelling of the spirit. It is also very important to note that the extra measure of oil had to be bought, and this speaks of works. The indwelling spirit is a free gift from God at the point of salvation, and it cannot be bought. Being filled (i.e., controlled) by the Holy Spirit requires effort on the part of the Christian, and there is even a crown for the Christian who successfully crucifies the flesh nature and submits to the control of the Holy Spirit through daily confession of sin (1 John 1:9).

It should be clear that the five wise virgins were prepared for the return of Jesus Christ because they had prepared themselves by being spirit-filled Christians. Since they were prepared at the return of Jesus, they were taken in the Firstfruits rapture as faithful Christians. They received the open door.

The foolish virgins knock on the door where the wedding is taking place. Could this be a picture of the "one left in the field" who sees the "open door" and cries out to God? Like the foolish virgins they call Jesus "Lord, Lord," but He professes that He does not *know them*. Those left behind after the open door rapture are like the foolish virgins in that they are rejected for the prize of the high calling of God, which is to qualify as the bride of Jesus Christ. This does not mean that they are unsaved but that they never established an intimate relationship with Jesus Christ.

One further point about the parable of the ten virgins concerns the "midnight cry" described in verse 6. The cry was a warning to the Church that the Bridegroom was coming, and the Church was to prepare to meet him. This cry is apparently from the five wise virgins who are awake, and could be initiated by a social or economic upheaval a day or perhaps a week before the open door rapture. This is the warning that the bridegroom is at the door.

It is important to understand that verse five states, "While the Bridegroom tarried, they all beckoned or slept." The five wise virgins are awake beckoning for Jesus to return, but the five foolish are sound asleep. At the midnight cry, the five foolish virgins "arose and trimmed their lamps," and this indicates that the main body of the Church awakens to the reality of the return of Jesus at the time of the midnight cry. Trimming the lamps is a picture of repentance, which is confession and turning away from sin. The five wise virgins would have already trimmed their lamps, and their lamps are burning brightly. They also have the extra measure of oil, which is the filling of the Holy Spirit.

In this passage the midnight cry and the open door are not simultaneous since the foolish virgins trim their lamps and have time for conversation with the wise virgins. There is not enough time for the foolish virgins to buy more oil. Immature Christians will not have time to mature and grow to qualify for the open door rapture.

Millions of Christians in the Church today have been taught that they are prepared to meet Jesus at His return because of the fact of simple evangelical salvation. These Christians are still babes in Christ and will not be prepared. Growing is not something that can take place over night. It takes time to become a mature Christian. If a Christian is not prepared when he hears the "midnight cry," it will be too late. He will likely be aware of the rapture, but he will be left behind just like Elisha. When this happened to Elisha, he rent his clothes in anguish. Many Christians will do likewise. This will be the beginning of their three and one-half years of spiritual growth during the tribulation period.

The great majority of the Church today is spiritually ignorant of the truths concerning the appearance of the Bridegroom and his coming kingdom. Those Christians who study, give thought to, and understand these truths represent only a small minority in the Church today. These are the Philadelphia Christians who will be taken out through the open door of Revelation 3:8. They are the Firstfruits (i.e., hasty fruit) who have believed the Word and matured early before the hot summer sun. These are the Christians described in the following Scripture:

> 2 Cor 6:17-18 (KJV) Wherefore come out from among them, and be ye separate, saith the Lord, and touch not the unclean thing; and I will receive you, 18 And will be a Father unto you, and ye shall be my sons and daughters, saith the Lord Almighty.

> 2 Cor 7:1 (KJV) Having therefore these promises, dearly beloved, *let us cleanse ourselves from all filthiness of the flesh and spirit, perfecting holiness in the fear of God.*

Parable of the Talents (Mat. 25:14-30)

The parable of the talents also pertains to the Church, but it focuses on three servants who are left behind at the Firstfruits rapture. The three servants in this parable typify the evil servant described earlier, and the five foolish virgins in the previous parable. Verse 14 states "For as a man traveling into a far country called his own servants, and delivered unto them his goods." The man traveling into a far country is Jesus Christ at the Firstfruits rapture, and He delivers unto these servants all of his goods for the purpose their working during the time of their testing during the tribulation period.

The three servants received five talents, two talents and one talent respectively, and each was to use the talents working in the Lord's business. The various denominations received indicates that there are varying abilities in the servants to perform in the Lord's work.

The return of the "lord" after a long time is a picture of the return of Jesus at the Main Harvest rapture of the Church, and His "reckoning" with His servants is a picture of the Judgment Seat of Christ.

It is also important to note that the servant who received the five talents exactly doubled his capital, and the servant who received two talents also doubled his capital. Therefore, both servants were equally faithful so both received important positions in the coming millennial kingdom of Jesus Christ.

It is also very important to note that the best servant only doubled his master's capital, and this is in stark contrast to the hundred-fold reaping in the parable of the sower in Matthew 13:8. It is also important to note that these two faithful servants are only "good and faithful" as compared to the "faithful and wise" servant described earlier in Matthew 24:45-47:

> Matt 24:45 (KJV) 45 Who then is a *faithful and wise servant*, whom his lord hath made ruler over his household, to give them meat in due season? 46 Blessed is that servant, whom his lord when he cometh shall find so doing. 47 Verily I say unto you, That he shall make him *ruler over all his goods*.

Also, the good and faithful servants are only made ruler over many things, but the faithful and wise servant is made ruler over all things.

The faithful and wise servant was raptured at the Firstfruits rapture, but the three servants in this parable are raptured in the Main Harvest rapture.

The servant who had received one talent was afraid so he hid his talent in the ground. He also accused the master, the Lord Jesus Christ, for being a hard or stern master. He was afraid because he was in the tribulation period, and he felt the master was hard because he had been left behind.

The unfaithful servant, a believer, was called wicked and slothful, and his talent was taken away from him. In addition, he received no sovereign authority in the coming kingdom. He was called an unprofitable servant, and he was cast into "outer darkness" where there will be weeping and gnashing of teeth. "Outer darkness" is a position outside the sovereign dominion of Jesus Christ in the upcoming millennial kingdom. Outer darkness is not hell. The phrase comes from an ancient oriental idiom that means "to receive the displeasure of the master." There will be much weeping and gnashing of teeth by Christians when they are not allowed to enter into the kingdom of Jesus Christ. This does not mean exclusion from heaven but exclusion from being a sovereign or ruler in the one thousand year kingdom of Jesus Christ. God the Father promises to wipe away all the tears at the end of the Millennium (Rev. 21:4).

Gentile Section (Mat. 25:31-46)

This section is commonly called the sheep and goat judgment. The time of this judgment is immediately after the return of Jesus at the end of the tribulation period. Verse 31 states that it is: "When the Son of man comes in his glory." Therefore, it is not a judgment of Jews, nor of Christians, but a judgment of Gentiles who have performed good works in their treatment of the brethren of Jesus (i.e., the Jews). The fact that they perform good works during the last half of the tribulation demonstrates that they had been saved by faith in the Lord Jesus Christ at some point in the early part of the tribulation. Therefore, these Gentiles are those who respond to the Gospel of the Kingdom, which is preached by the 144,000 Jews during the last half of the seven-year tribulation. None of these Gentiles will be members of the Church since they will be saved after the Church Age has ended.

The 144,000 Jews who preach the Gospel of the Kingdom during the last half of the tribulation will be saved by the preaching of those in the Church who have been left behind to participate in the main harvest rapture. These Gentiles who respond to the preaching of the Gospel of the Kingdom during the last half of the tribulation will be those Gentiles who respond to the preaching of Christians during the first half of the tribulation. In other words, many Christians who are unfaithful in their witnessing now will be faithful witnesses during the three and one-half years in which they are persecuted by Antichrist. These are the Christians who will have "washed their robes" (Rev. 7:14).

It is important to understand that the Gospel of the Kingdom is always a message for believers, whether they are Jews, Christians, or Gentiles. This was true when Jesus, the Twelve, and the Seventy preached the Gospel of the Kingdom at the first advent of Jesus, and it will be true at His second advent. The Gospel of Grace is the message for the lost to "believe and be saved." The Word of the Kingdom is the message to believers to "repent," "obey," and "seek the kingdom."

Summary

It is necessary for the reader to understand the dispensational aspects of the Bible in order to grasp the prophetic truths taught throughout Scripture. Admittedly, it is no easy task to understand these truths, but the effort devoted to understanding them will be greatly rewarded.

The three different sections of the Olivet Discourse must be understood in relation to the people being addressed. For example, the Christian would not be looking for the signs in the section addressed to the Jews, nor would he be looking for the sheep and goat judgment applicable to the Gentiles who will be saved during the tribulation period. Instead, the Christian should be looking forward to the Rapture of the Firstfruits, and he should be praying that he will be accounted worthy to receive the "open door."

Watch ye therefore, and pray always, that ye may be accounted worthy to escape all these things that shall come to pass, and to stand before the Son of man (Luke 21:36).

**VIEW OF THE TEMPLE MOUNT
FROM THE MOUNT OF OLIVES**

Chapter 7

THE SEVEN PARABLES OF THE KINGDOM

The Good Seed are the Children of the Kingdom

Many twenty-first century Christian pastors and theologians are essentially proclaiming the same thing as the first century Jewish religious leaders: "We are guaranteed inclusion in the millennial kingdom on Earth." But John and Jesus aren't talking about the *earthly* kingdom of Messiah. They are preaching about how to qualify to be part of the *heavenly* kingdom. Inclusion in the heavenly ruling realm is only for those saints who qualify through obedience and faithfulness...There are many disciples in the multitude that are listening to Jesus in Matthew 13, but mixed into the crowd are also many who think they are guaranteed inheritors of the kingdom. They don't see a need to change, and assume they qualify automatically. They are not open to the truth; they are unteachable; they are hard-hearted. This is what prompts Jesus to begin teaching using parables.
James S. Hollandsworth – *Keys For Inheriting the Kingdom*

Salvation is by grace, and rewards are according to works! This simple and true statement seems almost profound when it is compared to the teaching and preaching in most local churches today. Failure to rightly divide the Bible in regard to salvation and rewards causes many teachers to incorrectly interpret the parables.

There are two popular movements that confuse grace and works in Christian circles today. They are Lordship Salvation on one side and Ultra Grace on the other extreme.

Lordship Salvation states that a person must first make Jesus Lord before he can make him Savior. They often use verses addressed to believers exhorting faithfulness and obedience, and they preach it to the lost as a salvation message. They avoid calling it works salvation by simply saying that those who do not do these works are not really saved. These preachers and teachers use terms like truly saved or real believers even though these terms are not from the Bible.

Ultra Grace is on the other extreme. These Christians lump together salvation and rewards on the grace side. They teach that salvation and rewards are by grace at the point of salvation. They teach that all Christians will be the bride of Christ and will be equally rewarded in Heaven. Thus, the emphasis on teaching is related to getting saved and getting others saved.

Both groups tend to make rewards automatic for believers.

The parables are a problem for both of these groups since the parables typically illustrate the differences in rewards for both the carnal and faithful Christian. The easy solution to this problem for both Lordship Salvation and Ultra Grace teachers is to make the parables pertain to the saved and lost since this assigns all the good things to believers and all the bad things to the lost.

The parables will not become clear until one understands the Biblical teaching that *salvation is by grace, and rewards are according to works!*

The 13th chapter of Matthew is a connected discourse given by Jesus Christ concerning the mysteries of the kingdom of heaven. It consists of seven parables about the present dispensation which has been called the mystery aspect of the kingdom. The Church was unknown in the Old Testament even though it can now be seen in various types such as Ruth and Orpah. This is why the Church is called a mystery by Paul (Eph. 1:9). Each analogy will be consistent throughout all of the parables, and we must begin with the interpretations that Jesus gave in order to understand the parables. This interpretation is key to understanding the parables.

> Mat 13:37-39 (KJV) He answered and said unto them, He that soweth the good seed is the Son of man; 38 The field is the world; *the good seed are the children of the kingdom*; but the tares are the children of the wicked one; 39 The enemy that sowed them is the devil; the harvest is the end of the world; and the reapers are the angels.

Please note that the "good seed" are not the lost or the gospel message. The "good seed" are born again, regenerated, "children of the kingdom."

The Parable of the Sower

Mat 13:3-9 (KJV)   And he spake many things unto them in parables, saying, Behold, a sower went forth to sow; 4 And when he sowed, some seeds fell by the way side, and the fowls came and devoured them up: 5 Some fell upon stony places, where they had not much earth: and forthwith they sprung up, because they had no deepness of earth: 6 And when the sun was up, they were scorched; and because they had no root, they withered away. 7 And some fell among thorns; and the thorns sprung up, and choked them: 8 But other fell into good ground, and brought forth fruit, some an hundredfold, some sixtyfold, some thirtyfold. 9 Who hath ears to hear, let him hear.

The parable about the sower is not a parable of salvation but of fruit-bearing by Christians in the present dispensation. All the seed sown are good seed and represent believers. The parable relates the reactions to the Word of the Kingdom of four different types of Christians in the present age in which we are living. All are saved but their reactions to the Word of the Kingdom vary greatly. Remember that the Word of the Kingdom pertains to qualifying for positions in the coming kingdom of our Lord and Savior Jesus Christ. This is the message Jesus taught his disciples in Matthew 16:24-27. One must lose his life now so he will gain it in the coming kingdom.

A person can be saved without comprehending the coming kingdom of our Lord. Indeed, most Christians in the world today do not understand the truths about the coming kingdom of our Lord. Salvation depends solely upon faith in the Lord Jesus Christ (Acts 16:30,31). It is an *easy believism*.

The first group of Christians in the parable of the sower hears the Word of the Kingdom, but they do not understand it, and Satan devours (i.e., seizes upon and destroys) these Christians before they have a chance to mature and produce fruit. Most faithful Christians who attend church and witness know of Christians who trust in Jesus Christ and then immediately become entangled in sin and desires of the world. Many in the Church today would say that these people were never really saved, but the Bible says differently. These people are good seed but they just never take root and produce fruit.

The second group of Christians hears and understands the Word of the Kingdom and receives it with joy. Unfortunately, teaching and speaking about the return of Jesus is not a popular subject in the Church today, and the believer who does so can expect sarcasm, indifference, ostracism, and outright mockery from his/her fellow Christians. Many Christians can not bear this persecution, and they fall away from speaking and teaching about the coming kingdom of our Lord and Savior Jesus Christ. These Christians have "no roots" and the heat of the sun causes them to be "withered away."

The third group of Christians hears and understands the Word of the Kingdom, but "the care of this world and the deceitfulness of riches, choke the Word, and he becometh unfruitful." This passage of Scripture refers specifically to those who do not have enough of this world's goods and to those who have an abundance of this world's goods (i.e., the poor and the rich). Numerous Christians in both groups love the things of this world, and they have very little interest, if any, in the coming kingdom of Jesus Christ. Neither group is content with what they have of this world's goods. Christians who covet money destroy themselves, and it is ironic that the very poor and the very rich are the ones who are most susceptible to this temptation (1 Tim. 6:7-11). These Christians bear no lasting fruit for the kingdom.

The first three groups represent three types of children of the kingdom and their response to the Word of the Kingdom. They do not bear any fruit and will not have any rewards in the coming kingdom. Their salvation is not affected since salvation is by grace and not of works.

The fourth group represents those Christians who hear, understand and obey the Word of God. They produce fruit in varying degrees and their rewards will be commensurate with the proportions of fruit yielded in accordance with their abilities.

This parable marks the inception of the Christian era since our Lord began sowing the children of the kingdom while he was on earth, and the sowing continues even until today. Also, the seven parables of Matthew 13 are parallel teachings with the seven churches of Revelation 2 and 3. The church of Ephesus represents the first century church and the initial sowing by the Lord Jesus Christ.

A cursory reading of the parable of the sower seems to be discrepant with the interpretation that Jesus gave in verses 37-39. The reason for this discrepancy is a mistranslation of portions of verses 19, 20, 22 and 23. The translation in verse 19, "This is he which received seed by the wayside," should have been translated, "This is he which was sown by the wayside." Verse 20 should read, "But he that was sown in the stony places..." Verse 22 should read, "He that was sown among the thorns..." Verse 23 should read, "But he that was sown in the good ground..."

It bears repeating that the parable of the sower is not a parable of salvation but of fruit-bearing for the kingdom. This is confirmed by verse 23 which is the last verse in the parable. The seed sown in the good ground "beareth fruit, and bringeth forth, some an hundredfold, some sixty, some thirty." The decreasing yields picture the decline in fruit-bearing as the Christian era approaches its end. This is also confirmed in the history of the church revealed in the seven churches of Revelation 2 and 3.

The correct translation of verses 19, 20, 22 and 23 can be found in *The New Testament, An Expanded Translation* by Kenneth S. Wuest, Teacher Emeritus of New Testament Greek at the Moody Bible Institute. *Wuest's Word Studies From the Greek New Testament* is a standard in the field of New Testament studies. *The American Standard Bible of 1901* and a few other unpopular translations currently out of print also have the correct translation of these verses. *The Montgomery New Testament* and *The Interlinear Bible* translated these verses correctly, and they are still in print. The transliterated Greek word for seed is *sperma* and it is the common Greek word for offspring or descendants throughout the New Testament. Of course, the simple statement of Jesus in verse 38 should be sufficient for the correct understanding of who the seed are in this parable, but tradition dies hard.

Numerous Scriptures have been traditionally interpreted as pertaining to salvation or spiritual rebirth when they actually pertain to fruit-bearing or faithfulness in serving the Lord and the "just recompense of reward" (Hebrews 2:2) that will be meted out by Jesus at the Judgment Seat of Christ. The Greek word apistia means unbelief or unfaithfulness, and it most often refers to the unfaithfulness of Christians. This is confirmed by Mark 16:14 where it is applied to the eleven disciples after the resurrection of Jesus. Its use in Hebrews 3:12 also applies to Christians.

Parables of the Tares

This parable in Matthew 13:24-30 is generally interpreted correctly by exegetes (i.e., Bible interpreters who utilize set principles called hermeneutics). The reason for this is the interpretation by Jesus in verses 37-43. The parable of the sower and this parable are linked chronologically and personally. After the children of the kingdom have been placed in the field (i.e., the world), Satan comes along and sows tares (i.e., children of the devil) among the wheat which represents Christians.

A tare is someone who has heard the true gospel and rejected it. He has seen and heard and rejected the testimony of Christians. Tares look like Christians, act like Christians, and talk like Christians. Many tares are people who can not accept salvation by faith only. They insist on working for it.

It is only at harvest time that they can be distinguished from true Christians. Jesus said to leave them alone, but many Christians do not take this advice. Jesus also said that in the time of harvest the reapers (i.e., angels) would gather the tares together into bundles so they could be burned. We are in the time of the harvest and the tares are being gathered together into bundles. If these bundles were labeled they would be called Mormons, Jehovah's Witnesses, Christian Science, Christadelphians, the Way International, Worldwide Church of God, etc. All of these cults have burgeoned in the twentieth century and most of their members have come out of orthodox Christianity. They all call themselves Christians and numerous true Christians believe that they are Christian. They all deny the deity of Jesus Christ so this means that they have heard the true gospel and rejected it. The very recent surge in the growth of cults should not cause undue concern for true believers. It is simply the work of the angels gathering the tares into bundles so they can be burned at the appropriate time after the wheat has been harvested.

The concern of true Christians should be obedience. Our goal should be reaching maturity before the harvest of the Firstfruits. Otherwise, Christians will have to mature in the hot summer sun (i.e., the fires of the tribulation). Upon maturity wheat dies from the roots up so the Christian who still has strong, deep roots in the earth (i.e., he loves the things of the world) is not ripe for harvest.

It is important to note that the orthodox Christian churches still have tares in them, and it is impossible for believers to tell which ones are the tares. We are admonished to judge not (Rom. 14;10). It is not productive for Christians to try to determine who the tares are since true believers could be rooted up in the process. Frequently, tares are more self-disciplined, hard-working, and prosperous than true believers. You will not find tares coming to the altar weeping over and confessing to fleshly sins and weaknesses. They are frequently the leaders in the church, and are sometimes found in the pulpit and other high positions of authority. They often have a cherubic countenance, and they know all the phrases and clichés indigenous to Christianity. They are the fine upstanding citizens in the community and few people doubt their sincerity. As stated above, they look, act and talk just like Christians, and true Christians are not able to tell the difference. This is why Jesus said to leave them alone.

Parable of the Mustard Seed

> Mat 13:31-32 (KJV) Another parable put he forth unto them, saying, The kingdom of heaven is like to a grain of mustard seed, which a man took, and sowed in his field: 32 Which indeed is the least of all seeds: but when it is grown, it is the greatest among herbs, and becometh a tree, so that the birds of the air come and lodge in the branches thereof.

The parable of the mustard seed is the third parable in this discourse and it runs parallel with the message to the church of Pergamum in Revelation 2:12-17. Its true message is overlooked by the majority of exegetes. The message of this parable describes the growth of Christianity from insignificant beginnings, but this growth is not represented as something good according the correct interpretation of the parable. The smallness of the mustard seed represents the growth of Christianity from a minute beginning, but most commentators overlook the statement that the mustard bush, the greatest of herbs, *became a tree* which is abnormal and unnatural.

Also, after it became a tree, the birds came and lodged in its branches. In Scripture the tree symbolizes a world power. Trees represent nations in Judges 9:8-15, and a tree represents a world power in Daniel 4. The nation of Israel is symbolized by a fig tree and an olive tree. From these symbols this parable teaches that Christianity started from a small and insignificant beginning and grew into a bush which is normal. Then something abnormal took place.

The bush became a tree or a world power. This unnatural phenomenon was the result of Constantine the Great who decreed on October 28, 312 A.D. that Christianity would be the world religion. Constantine's fiat did great damage to the spiritual condition of the Church because of the political and ecclesiastical intrigue involved in the Church being a world power. The Church became worldly and corrupt, and the birds which symbolize Satan and his emissaries found lodging in its organization.

The current age is the time the world rejects Christ, and a faithful church would share in this rejection. Instead, the Church became a political power and she is misguided by Satan into programs of world betterment and reform instead of evangelism and discipleship of believers. Even the formal Sardis churches that are evangelistic neglect the very important function of discipling its members and teaching the deeper truths of Scripture. This is why so many Christians with shallow roots will fall away and become unfaithful as soon as persecution appears, financial disaster hits, or material prosperity happens. Numerous Christians attend church, witness, and perform works for a period of months, years, etc. and then become disinterested and fall away from the faith as soon as they slack off in their church attendance.

The faithful Christian who studies the Word of God and lives according to its precepts is like the marathon runner who finishes the race with respect to the faith. The racetrack of the narrow way is strewn with Christians who have sprinted for a time and then dropped out before the course is finished. Rewards will be awarded to only those Christians who finish the race (1 Cor. 9:24-27).

The Church was robbed of its spiritual power the day it became a world power. It was a sad day for the cause of our Lord when the mustard bush became a tree. The tree sends its roots down deeply into the earth, and this is exactly what the Church has done. Many in the Church are distracted with political events for advancing the power of Christianity. They are not focused on the fulfillment of prophecies which signal the soon return of our Lord Jesus Christ. The world system belongs to Satan, and Christians who strive for position and status in the current system are striving in the wrong kingdom. Unfortunately, this is the scenario for the majority of Christians in the world today.

Power, popularity and prestige in the community and society are not the lot of the faithful Christian in the world system. Persecution, rejection and suffering are in store for the Christian who sincerely strives to walk in obedience to the Lord Jesus Christ.

Parable of the Leaven

Mat 13:33 (KJV) Another parable spake he unto them; The kingdom of heaven is like unto leaven, which a woman took, and hid in three measures of meal, till the whole was leavened.

The parable of the leaven runs parallel with the message to the church of Thyatira in Revelation 2:18-29. Leaven in the Scriptures is always used symbolically to represent evil, sin and false doctrine. Leaven is never used for anything good in the Bible, and it definitely does not represent the gospel spreading throughout the world until the whole world has been evangelized.

Jesus told his disciples in Matthew 6:6-12 to beware of the leaven of the Pharisees and the Sadducees. The leaven of the Pharisees was the substitution of ritualism and formalism for true worship. They were substituting the letter of the law for the spirit of the law. They were concerned about cleaning up the outside of the person with no attention given to the inside. The leaven has permeated the Church. The faithful Christian would describe this as substituting religion for a relationship with Christ. It has also been called legalism.

The leaven of the Sadducees was the emphasis on rationalism and denial of the supernatural. The Sadducees were the rich and sophisticated Jews in the time of Jesus. They were in control of the Sanhedrin which was the supreme judicial council of Judaism. The Sadducees did not believe in angels or in the resurrection. This leaven has also permeated the Church, and it is spread by Christians when they offer rational and logical explanations for miracles in the Bible. An example is the futile attempt by Christians to prove that a man can really be swallowed by a whale and survive three days. A careful reading of Jonah reveals that Jonah died and spent three days in Sheol while his body was in the great fish. God raised him from the dead on the third day and Jonah thanked and praised God for raising him up and bringing him out of Sheol. The fish then promptly vomited Jonah up on dry land. The book of Jonah is filled with the supernatural (i.e., miracles), and it is dishonoring to God to try to explain Jonah rationally. This is only one example of many.

In Mark 8:15 Jesus enjoined his disciples to beware of the leaven of Herod. The leaven of Herod is the belief that politics and reform movements are the panacea for all the world's problems. If Christians spent as much time studying the Bible and warning fellow believers of the coming Judgment Seat of Christ as they do in campaigning for politicians or political reform, there would be many more crowns and a lot less chastisement at the Judgment Seat of Christ. The Christian's involvement in politics is striving in the wrong kingdom.

Abraham was a key type in the Old Testament for the spiritual believer and he was totally divorced from politics and the world system. Lot was a primary type in the Old Testament for the carnal believer and he was mayor of Sodom. The statement in Genesis 19:1, "And Lot sat in the gate of Sodom," means that Lot was an elected official of Sodom and this most likely means that he was the top official in Sodom. It does not require much reflection to see how much impact Lot had on the immorality and degradation of Sodom.

The reader should take the advice of Jesus and beware the leaven of Herod which has also permeated the Church. Christians should stop politicking and start warning believers and unbelievers of the coming judgment. When John the baptist was beheaded by Herod, Jesus went off to himself then returned to heal the sick (Mat 14:10-13). When Paul and Silas were unjustly imprisoned they prayed and witnessed to the prison guard and he was saved (Acts 16:16-34) Christians are to be in this world but not of this world.

The interpretation of the parable of the leaven is as follows: Christendom is the mystery aspect of the kingdom of heaven, and the woman in the parable is the false church which is the papal worship system. This woman takes false doctrine and hides it in the three measures of meal. The three measures of meal symbolize the truth and teaching of the Godhead (i.e., the Trinity) with special emphasis on Jesus the Christ. The Greek word for meal is "aleuron" and literally means "what is ground" so it can refer to corn meal or flour. The meal offering in the Old Testament was offered with oil and frankincense which symbolize the Holy Spirit and prayer. Thus, the meal offering symbolizes the fruit (i.e., flour comes from wheat) of believers which is acceptable when combined with the Holy Spirit and with prayer.

Leaven is a corrupting or putrefying agent which produces deterioration in the flour in which it is placed. Jesus was speaking of the degeneration of the fruit produced by Christians because of the false doctrine interjected into the truth of the gospel. It does not mean fewer Christians but less fruitful Christians. The work of the leaven has been so subtle and pervasive that virtually all churches have been affected in some way. A knowledgeable student of the Bible does not have to look far to find leaven in any church.

Only one thing destroys the work of leaven and that is fire or heat which kills the germ or bacteria in the flour. Unfortunately, only a relatively few Christians are purging out the leaven (i.e., evil) in their lives. Those who do not purge out the leaven through confession of sin will be purged in the fires of the tribulation. Jesus rejects the Laodicean church (Rev. 3:16) and cautions it to buy from Him gold refined in the fire (Rev. 3:18). These Christians are rejected at the harvest of the Firstfruits and will have to wait for the main harvest which will take place in the middle of the tribulation. Unfaithful Christians will be turned over to Antichrist for three and one half years (Dan. 7:25) and will have another opportunity to bear fruit.

Parable of the Hidden Treasure

Mat 13:44 (KJV) Again, the kingdom of heaven is like unto treasure hid in a field; the which when a man hath found, he hideth, and for joy thereof goeth and selleth all that he hath, and buyeth that field.

Contrary to popular opinion this parable has nothing to do with the gospel of grace or the salvation of individuals. It refers specifically to the nation of Israel. The following Scriptures reveal to us that Israel is God's treasure:

Exo 19:5-6 (KJV) Now therefore, if ye will obey my voice

indeed, and keep my covenant, then ye shall be a peculiar treasure unto me above all people: for all the earth is mine: 6) And ye shall be unto me a kingdom of priests, and an holy nation. These are the words which thou shalt speak unto the children of Israel.

Psa 135:4 (KJV)   For the LORD hath chosen Jacob unto himself, and Israel for his peculiar treasure.

Because of Israel's disobedience God destroyed her cities and dispersed her among the nations. Israel was first separated into two nations consisting of the Northern kingdom and the Southern kingdom, and then she was carried off into captivity. The Northern kingdom was called Israel and it consisted of ten of the tribes of Israel. The Southern kingdom was called Judah, and it was made up of the tribes of Judah, Benjamin and Levi.

Those in the world today who are known as Jews are primarily made up of those three tribes. The ten tribes of the Northern kingdom were carried off into captivity by Assyria in 722 B.C. Some of the ten tribes filtered back to the Southern kingdom, but the majority of these tribes disappeared from the pages of history. They are currently hidden in the world today and they are not known as Jews. Their true identity is even unknown to them.

There is evidence that the American Indian may be from the tribe of Ephraim. This is speculation, but there is much evidence that the traditions and heritage of the American Indians are amazingly close to that of Israel. Also, they meet all of the descriptions that God gave of Israel about keeping them few in number, keeping them separate and distinct, causing them to be a persecuted people, and being a people who tend toward much alcohol and violence, and not having a place that they can call home and reside in peace. The Indians also have physical traits that are Jewish such as the straight black hair, prominent nose, and the dark brown skin. The American Indian is also an enigma in regard to their origin.

A stone tablet found in a Cherokee Indian mound 103 years ago contains inscriptions which archaeologists had assumed represented an early Indian alphabet. Recently, a discovery was made identifying them instead as old Hebrew inscriptions. This recent discovery has baffled scientists, but could be explained if a lost tribe of Israel were the origin of the early Cherokee nation.

There is another group of people that could possibly belong to the ten lost tribes of Israel. This identification took place during the war with Iraq when a mysterious group of people started making the headlines in the newspapers. They also became the topic of television newscasts and national news magazines. These people are the Kurds and their origin is also a mystery to the world and themselves. They are not Turks, Persians, or Arabs and they were not called Kurds until the 7th century.

The Kurds have lived in the area known as Kurdistan since long before Josephus, the Jewish historian, wrote his chronicles. The Bible states that the ten tribes were taken into Assyria, and prophecy says they will be brought out of Assyria (Isa. 11:11, 16). It is not coincidental that Kurdistan is in the area of ancient Assyria. Josephus said that they were there in 70 A.D., and Jerome wrote in his notes on Hosea in the 5th century that the people of Kurdistan were the ten lost tribes. The Kurds have the same physical traits as the Jews, and the centuries of oppression qualify them as likely candidates. Their traditions, culture, and dreams of one day having a conquering king and a nation they could call their own also identify them as the ten lost tribes of Israel. They also have many modified observances of the Mosaic Ritual such as Peace Offerings, Vows, Firstfruits, and Tithes.

Unlike God's hidden Jews, the Bible calls Christians "the light of the world" (Mat. 5:14). It should now be clear that the treasure hidden in the field (i.e., the world) is not Christians but the nation of Israel. The nation of Israel has been hidden in the world, and it is represented by the treasure. The treasure is definitely not the gospel, and the man is not a lost soul trying to find salvation. It is not man seeking after God but God seeking after man which brings about salvation. Ezekiel 37:15-25 clearly teaches that God will bring the nations of Judah and Israel back together again before Jesus returns in power and glory at the end of the seven year tribulation. When Jesus returns He will reclaim Israel from the world, restore her to her land, and she will be recommissioned as Jehovah's witnesses in the world just like Jonah was commissioned a second time to preach to the Gentiles of Nineveh.

Parable of the Pearl of Great Price

Mat 13:45-46 (KJV) Again, the kingdom of heaven is like unto a merchant man, seeking goodly pearls: 46 Who, when he had found one pearl of great price, went and sold all that he had, and bought it.

It should first be stated that the merchant man is not a lost man seeking to be saved with the pearl representing salvation. In harmony with the other parables in this discourse, the leading character in this parable is the Lord Jesus Christ. The last three parables of the seven parables address three separate groups of people who are to be in the kingdom of the heavens. The first group in verse 44 represents Israel converted and restored. In verses 45 and 46 we have a second group symbolized by the pearl of great price. This second group of people is the Church, and the pearl is an appropriate stone to symbolize the Church.

The pearl is not an Old Testament stone and the word is not even found in the Old Testament. The occurrence of the word in Job 28:18 is a mistranslation since the Hebrew word actually means crystal. The pearl comes from the oyster which is considered unclean to the orthodox Jew. The oyster which bears the pearl comes from the sea which symbolizes the Gentile nations from which the Church is gathered. The pearl is born out of injury to the oyster as a foreign particle enters the side of the oyster the same as the spear entered the side of Jesus.

The pearl is gradually built up from living tissue as the oyster coats the particle to protect itself. The Church is also gradually built up as a living organism. The pearl is the only precious stone which cannot be divided and made into two or more stones. It is also the only stone which may be called a living stone since it grows while in the oyster. It should be clear by now why the Lord chose the pearl of great price to symbolize the Church. Jesus gave everything He had to buy the pearl of great price. By his incarnation He made himself of no reputation and gave His life on Calvary to purchase the Church. Christ died for us so that we might live for Him.

Parable of the Dragnet

Mat 13:47-50 (KJV) Again, the kingdom of heaven is like unto a net, that was cast into the sea, and gathered of every kind: 48 Which, when it was full, they drew to shore, and sat down, and gathered the good into vessels, but cast the bad away. 49 So shall it be at the end of the world: the angels shall come forth, and sever the wicked from among the just, 50 And shall cast them into the furnace of fire: there shall be wailing and gnashing of teeth.

This parable concerns the third group of saved people that will populate the kingdom. This action takes place at the full end of the age just before the kingdom is established upon the earth. The cast net is thrown from the land into the sea. The land symbolizes Israel, and the sea symbolizes the Gentiles. This is a clear description of the 144,000 Jewish evangelists who are the Firstfruits of the Jews preaching the gospel of the kingdom during the 42 months of the tribulation period. Numerous Gentiles will be saved during this proclamation of the gospel of the kingdom.

These saved are not part of the Church and will not be raptured since they were saved after the Church Age ended. They will enter into the millennium in their bodies of flesh and blood, but the unsaved will be supernaturally placed in the winepress of the wrath of God outside of Jerusalem. Jesus will tread the winepress alone and his robe will be stained with the blood of his enemies. The following Scriptures describe the sequence of this literal event:

Mat 24:14 (KJV) And this gospel of the kingdom shall be preached in all the world for a witness unto all nations; and then shall the end come.

Mat 25:31-34 (KJV) When the Son of man shall come in his glory, and all the holy angels with him, then shall he sit upon the throne of his glory: 32 And before him shall be gathered all nations: and he shall separate them one from another, as a shepherd divideth his sheep from the goats: 33 And he shall set the sheep on his right hand, but the goats on the left. 34 Then shall the King say unto them on his right hand, Come, ye blessed of my Father, inherit the kingdom prepared for you from the foundation of the world:

Mat 25:41 (KJV) Then shall he say also unto them on the left hand, Depart from me, ye cursed, into everlasting fire, prepared for the devil and his angels:

Mat 25:46 (KJV) And these shall go away into everlasting punishment: but the righteous into life eternal.

It bears repeating that the parable of the dragnet (i.e., cast net) does not refer to Christians or Jews, but it refers to Gentiles saved during the preaching of the 144,000 Jews. The type in the Old Testament is Jonah being commissioned a second time to preach to the city of Nineveh with the whole city repenting as a result of Jonah's preaching.

In summary, the parables of the kingdom in Matthew 13 run parallel with the history of the Church in Revelation 2 and 3. Both teach the degeneration and deterioration of the Church as the age approaches its end. Fruitfulness (i.e., faithfulness) will occur in only one out of four groups of Christians in the parable of the sower and in only one church (i.e., Philadelphia) out of the four churches in existence (i.e., Thyatira, Sardis, Philadelphia, and Laodicea) at the time that Jesus Christ returns to set up his kingdom on the earth.

The Church age will end in the judgment of Christians at the Judgment Seat of Christ, the judgment of the Jews during the time of Jacob's trouble, and the judgment of the Gentiles at the sheep and goat judgment at the end of the tribulation.

Chapter 8

THE SEVEN CHURCHES

The Faithful and the Carnal

The assertion that all believers are overcomers is so plainly contrary to fact and to Scripture that one wonders it ever has been made. It involves the false position that no believer can be a backslider. It avoids and nullifies the solemn warnings and urgent pleadings of the Spirit addressed to believers, and, by depriving Christians of these, leaves him dangerously exposed to the perils they reveal.
> G.H. Lang – *The Revelation of Jesus Christ*

It has been pointed out that the Lord names overcomers in every one of His seven letters to the Churches (Panton). What a remarkable encouragement and revelation is this fact, especially for those of us who have been overcome, and have failed Him so often in the past! If we repent, and honestly and genuinely seek His help and strength to obey His word, we also can be overcomers. Let's not allow ourselves to be side-tracked by those 'who consider reward to be beneath the notice of a CHRISTIAN.' Let's be like Paul and "press on toward the goal to win the prize…"(Phil. 3:14)
> Robert Govett – *Seek First His Kingdom and His Righteousness*

Chapter 1 of Revelation is a picture of the Person of Christ as Judge at the Judgment Seat of Christ. Chapters 2 and 3 of Revelation are an amazingly accurate and detailed prediction of the history of the Church. Before explaining this prophetic history of the Church, it must first be understood that Scripture has three interpretations, and all three are important. The three interpretations are the literal, the figurative, and the prophetic.

The first interpretation is the *literal* interpretation, and it is the primary, basic meaning. The seven churches were literal churches in existence at the time John received his revelation from Jesus Christ while on the island of Patmos. These churches had the characteristics that Jesus expounded to John. This interpretation is correct.

The second interpretation is the *figurative*. This interpretation is used for personal application and as an example for Christian living. Each local church as a whole in existence today could fit into the description of one of these seven churches. Also, each born-again Christian could be characterized by one of the seven churches. Thus, each local church today is a combination of these seven "types" of Christians as members.

If a local church has the character of Laodicea, then it is most likely that the majority of Christians in that church have the character of Laodicea, or at least the pastor and church leaders have the character of Laodicea. There are numerous combinations that are possible. For example, a Philadelphia Christian could be a member of a Sardis church. It is highly probable that he would not be very popular in the church, and he would not be satisfied with the church character. Many practical applications can be made from the seven churches of Revelation and these applications are correct Biblical interpretation.

The third interpretation is the *prophetic*. All three interpretations must be considered in order to have a balanced approach to God's Word. This is true for the book of Revelation and all Scripture. Unfortunately, the majority of Christians today avoid the prophetic interpretation of Scripture.

The prophetic revelation of the seven churches is a progressive picture of the history of the Church from the first coming of Christ to his second coming. In unmistakable detail and clarity, each of the seven churches describes a certain period of Church history. Even the names of the seven churches are prophetic and revelatory.

Even though the character of the seven churches is descriptive of the Church during seven periods of history, we must not forget that the condition of the seven local churches as Jesus described was their exact condition in John's day.

It is also important to note that the first three church periods were consecutive, but the last four church periods overlap and extend up until the rapture. We are currently living at the end of the Laodicean Church age and the dominant character of the Church is Laodicean.

However, the characters of Thyatira, Sardis, and Philadelphia are still in existence, but they are secondary to Laodicea.

For example, most Southern Baptist churches have the character of Sardis or Laodicea, but a few have the character of Philadelphia. Most Presbyterian churches are Sardis in character. Most of the television ministries and many of the charismatic churches of today have the character of Laodicea. The following chart summarizes the seven church periods.

Overview of Seven Church Periods			
Church	Period	Meaning of Name	Character
1 Ephesus	1st Century	To let Go, Relax	Apostolic, Loveless
2. Smyrna	100 - 312 A.D	Myrrh	Persecuted
3. Pergamum	312 - 606 A.D.	Married	Compromising, State Church
4. Thyatira	606 A.D. - End	Continual Sacrifice	Papal, Corrupt, Ritual
5. Sardis	1517 A.D - End	Remnant	Protestant, Dead, Formal
6. Philadelphia	1750 A.D. - End	Brotherly Love	Great Awakening, Faithful
7. Laodicea	1900 A.D. - End	People's Rights	Apostate, Lukewarm

Briefly summarized, Ephesus was the Apostolic church of the first century that maintained correct doctrine but gradually lost its love for the Person of Christ toward the end of the century. Smyrna was the persecuted church of the second and third centuries. Pergamum was the compromising or State church that began under Constantine in 312 A.D. and continued until 606 A.D. when Boniface III was crowned "Universal Bishop" of the Roman Church. These periods of church history have ended. The next four periods of church history overlap and run concurrently until Jesus returns.

Thyatira represents the Roman Catholic Church from 606 A.D. that continued through the Dark Ages and will continue until the return of the Lord. Sardis is the church of the Renaissance and the Reformation that began in 1517 A.D. and will continue until the return of the Lord.

Philadelphia is the church of the Revival that began about 1750 A.D. and will continue until the return of the Lord. Laodicea is the end time church of apostasy and lukewarmness that began about 1900 A.D. and will continue until the return of the Lord.

It is important to understand that periodization of history is an artificial mechanism to organize history into manageable segments. The beginning and ending dates are not always as clear-cut as the chart would indicate. For example, some scholars would end the Pergamum age of Church history with the fall of the last Roman emperor, Romulus Augustulus, in 476 A.D. The year 590 A.D. might be chosen as the beginning of Thyatira since Gregory I, often called Gregory the Great, was consecrated as the first medieval pope, and he ushered in a new era of Church power in the West. The precise beginning and ending dates are not as important as the sequence and overall characterization of each period. A general, basic knowledge of Church history should be sufficient to see the prophetic significance of the seven churches of Revelation.

It is very important to understand that the people addressed by Jesus in these seven churches are true believers who are part of the body of Christ, though many of them are carnal like those in chapter three of 1 Corinthians. Jesus was not addressing "professing believers" or "the visible church" calling them to salvation. The letters to the seven churches in Revelation are to true believers calling them to a maturity in the faith.

John's use of the word us in Revelation 1:5-6, and the word brother in Revelation 1:9 confirms that the message of the book of Revelation is to believers. The only admonition to the lost in the Bible is "believe on the Lord Jesus Christ."

A study of the seven churches and their good and bad works, along with the admonitions and promises to the overcomers, gives much insight to Christians today.

Ephesus

Jesus commended the Church of Ephesus for its works in Revelation 2:2 but He complained that the Church had left its first love which was Jesus Christ. The character of the Ephesian Church is seen in its very name for Ephesus means "to let go" or "to relax." Ephesus had become a backslidden church having lost its "First Love" so the Lord was about to chastise it for the express purpose of causing it to return to him. Thus, the Ephesian period of Church history ended and the Smyrna period of Church history was about to begin.

Smyrna

Smyrna means "Myrrh" and has for its root meaning "bitterness". It is associated with death and persecution, and it is a prophecy of the persecution and death of Church members under the Roman Emperors beginning with Nero in 64 A.D. and ending with Diocletian in 310 A.D. Constantine ended the persecution of the Church upon his accession in 312 A.D. Thus, the Smyrna period of Church history ended in 312 A.D.

Pergamum

Pergamum means "Married" and it is an accurate description of the period of Church history from the accession of Constantine in 312 A.D. up until the crowning of Boniface III as "Universal Bishop" of the Roman church. It was a period when the church entered into a union with the State. Jesus called Pergamum "Satan's Seat" (Rev. 2:13). Under the Attalid dynasty Satan shifted his capital from Babylon to Pergamum when Pergamum became the capital of a powerful prosperous Hellenistic kingdom also known as Pergamum. At first, Satan persecuted the followers of Christ, and Antipas was one of the martyrs (Rev. 2:13). According to tradition, Antipas was roasted in a brazen bowl at Domitian's request.

The Smyrna Church grew rapidly in number and faithfulness so Satan changed his tactics and began to exalt the Church via Constantine's unification of Church and State. Constantine's motive was more political than religious since his purpose was to meld his Christian and Pagan subjects into a unified Empire.

However, the union of Church and State resulted in two false and pernicious doctrines being introduced into the Church. The first was the Doctrine of Balaam, and the second was the Doctrine of the Nicolaitanes. The Nicolaitanes were not a sect but a party in the Church seeking to establish a "Priestly Order" similar to the Old

Testament order of Priests, Levites, and common people. This comes from the word "Niko", to conquer, to overthrow, and "Laos" the people or laity. The object was to establish a "Holy Order of Men" to control the laity and call them Clergy, a thing God "hates" (Rev. 2:6). The Doctrine of the Nicolaitanes secured a strong and permanent foothold in the Church at the First Great Council of the Church held at Nicaea in 325 A.D.

The Doctrine of Balaam is found in Numbers in Chapters 22 to 25. It is essentially the doctrine of worldly compromise, laxness and loss of the separated position of the believer. This is a doctrine that teaches worldly success over personal holiness and that God's rewards are based on grace rather than works. This doctrine is rampant in the Church today.

The Balaam method employed by Constantine was to provide imposing buildings and superb vestments for the clergy. A sensuous form of worship was provided and the character of preaching changed. Paganism was mingled with Christianity, and it has continued in the Church until this day. It was at this time that Postmillennialism originated. The Church had become rich and powerful through the union of Church and State, and it became tenable that the Millennium could be ushered in without Christ.

There has been a resurgence of Postmillennialism in recent years. It was claimed that the Jews had been cast off forever, and the prophecies of Israel's future glory were intended for the Church. The marriage ended when Boniface III was crowned Universal Bishop of the Roman Church in 606 A.D. As government was breaking down, religious order was increasing and the Roman Catholic Church became a unifying force in Western Europe.

Thyatira

It is also important to note that Thyatira represents the true believers of the Catholic Church and its offshoots, while ecclesiastical Babylon represents the false Papal Worship System headed up by John Paul II. This system is called the Great Harlot in Revelation 17 and it will be finally destroyed by the Antichrist of Revelation 13. Ecclesiastical Babylon is not the same as political Babylon, that Great City Babylon, which is destroyed according to Revelation 18. Chapter three describes political Babylon and the Scriptures delineating its destruction.

The message of Jesus to the Church of Thyatira is an accurate characterization of the Roman Catholic Church from 606 A.D. up until the present time. This Church period will continue up until the Lord comes since this is the first message where Jesus mentions his return, "But that which ye have already hold fast till I come" (Rev 2:25).

Jesus commended this Church for its works but complained about it allowing a woman named Jezebel to remain in the Church and teach her pernicious doctrines. It is unsure whether her real name was Jezebel, but she was so much like her prototype in the Old Testament that Jesus called her by that name. There is no doubt that Jezebel typified the Papal Worship System that introduced images and pictures into its churches and which devolved into idolatry.

A careful study of the Papal Worship System from 606 A.D. to the Reformation in 1517 A.D. reveals the characteristics of Jezebelism in the sacrifice of the mass and other pagan rites. It is also seen in the Jezebelistic persecution as seen in the wars of the Crusades and the rise of the Inquisition. A comparison of the message to the Church of Thyatira with the Parable of the Leaven reveals that the Jezebel of the Church of Thyatira is the woman who inserted the leaven of false doctrine into the meat of the gospel.

The word "Thyatira" literally means "a continual sacrifice", and it refers to the false doctrine of transubstantiation. It denies the finished work of Christ and requires that Jesus be sacrificed over and over again in the Eucharist. Thus, the celebration of the mass is a constant repetition of Calvary and adds works, ceremonies, rituals and sacrifices as necessary for salvation. This is a synthesis of faith and works, and it is very much akin to Lordship Salvation which is now even taught in Southern Baptist churches. The leaven of false doctrine has worked its way through the entire Church and most Christians are not even aware of its presence.

The Church of Thyatira will be rejected for its unfaithfulness at the return of the Lord, and it will be cast into the tribulation under the reign of Antichrist (Rev. 2:22). There are some in this Church who are faithful overcomers, and they will be taken out at the beginning of Daniel's seventieth week. This is what is meant by "I will give him the morning star" (Rev. 2:28). The morning star appears just before the darkest part of the night, and this is typified by Ruth, the Bride, who sleeps safely at the feet of Boaz during the dark night of threshing and winnowing.

Threshing and winnowing is not the separation of the saved from the unsaved, but the separation of the chaff from the wheat which symbolizes the purification or refining of the Church which is made up of true believers. Most Bible readers forget that Orpah became a member of the family of God before she apostatized by going back to Moab, a picture of the world. Ruth is a type of the Bride who remained faithful while Orpah is a type of the unfaithful Church who must remain on earth for the threshing and winnowing. An interesting side note is that the beating tool used to thresh the grain is called a *tribulum* from which we get our word tribulation.

Sardis

The message of Jesus to the Church of Sardis is an accurate characterization of the Church of the Reformation period which has continued in the mainline Protestant denominations and will continue up until the return of Jesus. The Church at Sardis was called a Dead Church even though it had a reputation for being alive. Worship in the Sardis Church was formalistic and ritualistic. It had a form of Godliness but no power. The word "Sardis" means the "escaping one", "remnant", or those who "come out" so it is an excellent picture of the Protestant Church which came out of the Reformation.

The Reformation was that period in Church history when Martin Luther, John Calvin, and other reformers protested the false teaching and claims of the Papal Church. This period in Church history began October 31, 1517 A.D. when Martin Luther nailed his 95 Theses to the Church door at Wittenberg, Germany. The circulation of the Holy Scriptures was initiated and the doctrine of Justification by Faith without works was revived.

The cry of the Reformation was "Sola Fide" (i.e., Faith Alone), and it is amazing how many evangelists and pastors still tack on the work of repentance as a prerequisite for spiritual rebirth. The gospel of John was written as a testimony so that people would believe and be saved (John 20:31). The word "repent" cannot be found in this Gospel. Repentance is a condition for entrance into the Kingdom of God and this is not the same as spiritual rebirth. The teachings of Lordship Salvation has accelerated the leavening process by making works (i.e., repentance and obedience) a condition for spiritual rebirth.

The Church of the Reformation reverted to simpler modes of worship, but the increase in the number of sects led to bitter contentions and interfered greatly with the spiritual state of the Church until it could be truthfully said, "That she had a name to live and was dead" (Rev. 3:1).

The reformers did sweep away much ritualistic and doctrinal error, but they did not recover the promise of the second advent. They returned to God from idols but not to watch for the return of Jesus. This truth would be regained by the Church of Philadelphia, but it would remain a derisive doctrine in the Sardis Church. This is why Sardis Christians have a distaste for teachings and sermons on the return of Jesus. Those in the Church of Sardis who repent and watch for the return of Jesus will be taken out before the beginning of the seventieth week of Daniel. Those who are not watchful will be surprised and will not even know the hour that Jesus takes out the faithful, undefiled overcomers (Rev. 3:3).

Philadelphia

The word "Philadelphia" means "brotherly love" and characterizes the Church age which began with the Great Awakenings under George Whitefield in 1739 and was followed by John Wesley, Charles G. Finney and D. L. Moody. The evangelistic and missionary labors of this period were carried out in the power of the Holy Spirit, and the doctrine of the second coming was revived. It was during this period that the midnight cry went out and the five foolish virgins (i.e., the Main body of the Church) awoke to the truths of the second coming of Jesus. The Philadelphia Church remains faithful to the Lord and will be taken out through the "open door" before the seventieth week of Daniel (Rev. 3:10). Those in the Philadelphia Church will not pass through the tribulation like most of those in the Church of Thyatira and Sardis, and all of those in the Church of Laodicea.

Laodicea

The word Laodicea means the "peoples rights" and refers to the Church age which began about 1900 A.D. and will continue until the return of Jesus. This Church age is characterized by apostasy and lukewarmness. This Church is a self-satisfied, proud and self-righteous group. It has become wealthy with material possessions, and the primary emphasis is on financial matters and organization. There is a zeal and fervor for organization and works that are to be seen by men but very little communion with God and in-depth Bible study for the express purpose of knowing God through His Word. Most of the activities in these churches today are largely mechanical and of a social character. Committees and clubs are numerous but there is an absence of spiritual fervor.

Many Laodicean churches have Cathedral-like buildings, stained glass windows, eloquent preachers, paid singers and large congregations. Some have large land interests and are well endowed. Many of the members are worldly, prosperous business men. The poor and the saintly are not in such churches because their presence is a rebuke. These churches are self-deceived and do not see that they are wretched, miserable, poor, blind, and naked. It must be remembered that these wretched, miserable, poor, blind, and naked people are true Christians saved by the blood of Jesus. However, they are carnal like the Christians in Corinthians chapter three. They are immature Christians, caught up in the affairs of this world, and they represent the largest segment of Christianity today.

A primary characteristic of the Laodicean Church is a lack of interest in the doctrine of the second coming. This Church is not interested in Bible prophecy, and Scriptural knowledge is very superficial and grounded upon tradition and the powers of the intellect rather than a sound exegesis of the Scriptures in the power of the Holy Spirit. The emphasis of teaching is on victorious living through self-help, psychology, and finding joy and peace in the world. They are not looking for the coming Kingdom or watching for Jesus to come back.

The character of the Church today is Laodicean, and the Laodicean period will continue until the faithful, Philadelphia Christians are removed before the Antichrist is revealed. This is when the remainder of the Christians who were in Thyatira, Sardis, and Laodicea will wake up to their true spiritual poverty and seek the spirituality that only comes through intimate communion with the Lord Jesus Christ.

The Rapture of these Christians will take place after the 42-month reign of Antichrist. Many of these Christians will be purified and mature in the faith as a result of the persecution during the 42-month reign of Antichrist. This is part of the threshing and winnowing process that John the Baptist described (Luke 3:17). Most Christians relate the fire that burns up the chaff to unbelievers, but the chaff is part of the wheat and represents the "wood, hay and stubble" produced by Christians (1 Cor. 3:12). Part of the reason for the great power and wealth of the Laodicean church is that she is based in America, the most powerful end-time nation in the world.

THE SEVEN CHURCHES OF REVELATION

	Angel at Ephesus	Angel at Smyrna	Angel at Pergamos	Angel at Thyatira	Angel at Sardis	Angel at Philadelphia	Angel at Laodicea
Addressed to							
Attributes of Christ	Holds 7 Stars	First & Last Dead > Alive	Sharp Two Edged Sword	Eyes - Flame Feet - Bronze	7 Spirits & 7 Stars	Holds Key of David	Faithful Witness
Commendation	Have Zeal Works	Know Your Tribulation	Did Not Deny My Name	Know Your Endurance	Few Worthy	Kept Word Not Denied	
State of Church	Lack 1st Love for Christ	Willing to Die for Christ	Stumbling Block	Tolerate False Teaching	Reputation Alive-But Dead	Willing to Live for Christ	Lukewarm Christ Outside
Warning	Repent Do 1st Works	Faithful Unto Death: Crown	Repent Sword	Repent	Wake Up Watch!	Hold Fast	Buy Gold & Garments
Exhortation	Hear What Spirit Says	Hear What Spirit Says	Hear What Spirit Says	Hold Fast	Do Not Soil Your Garments	Don't Loose Crown	Knocking on Door
Promise to Overcomers	Grant to Eat Tree of Life	Will Not Be Hurt 2nd Death	Give Hidden Manna	Authority Over Nations	Clothed In White Raiment	Pillar - Temple New Name	Sit on Throne

Chapter 9

BABYLON THE GREAT

The Last Great Nation

My goal [in this book] is to seek to unlock the threefold imagery of the depiction of Mystery Babylon as "a woman sitting on a beast which has ten horns" (Rev 17). The premise I am setting before you is that this threefold imagery is America as the beast, Catholicism as the religious harlot woman riding the beast, and the EU as the ten horns of the beast. This scenario could be dismissed as mere speculation apart from the existence of a unifying common denominator linking all three together. Let us consider that common bond. America, Catholicism and the EU have a historical and cultural thread that links them together: all three are Roman in origin. Mystery Babylon is Roman to the core. Scriptures teach that the last great world empire that will be on the face of the earth just prior to the second coming of Jesus Christ is a kingdom that has its roots in the Roman Empire. It is this common denominator that links them together as one identity namely, Mystery Babylon.
      Pastor Randy Shupe – *Babylon The Great*

Scripture records three Babylons. The first Babylon was Ancient Babylon ruled over by Nebuchadnezzar and conquered by the Medes and Persians in 539 B.C. Ancient Babylon was never destroyed like the Biblical description of the destruction of the New Babylon described in Revelation 18 and Jeremiah 50 and 51. Thus, Ancient Babylon and New Babylon are two distinct places with different geographical locations and distinctive characteristics.
     The second Babylon recorded in Scripture is Ecclesiastical or Religious Babylon. This Babylon is the harlot church described in Revelation 17 and headed up by the False Prophet of Revelation 13. The identity of Religious Babylon has been known for hundreds of

years and a sincere reading of the Scriptures reveals that the Papal Worship System is the Great Harlot of Revelation 17. It is no longer any secret among prophetic scholars that John Paul II is also the False Prophet of Revelation 13.

There are several books that thoroughly document the identity of the Great Whore of Babylon as the Papal Worship System incorporated into the Roman Catholic Church like the working of leaven in dough. Peter Lalonde's book, *One World Under Antichrist* is an excellent example. Also, Dave Hunt's book, *Global Peace* identifies John Paul II as the False Prophet, and Pastor Randy Shupe's volume *Babylon the Great* gives an excellent, in-depth analysis of the three components of this end time mystery.

John Paul II came up out of Poland, and the name Poland literally means "the people of the earth". The miter the Pope wears has two points on it that strongly resemble horns. Thus, John Paul II came up out of the earth and he has two horns like a lamb (Rev 13:11). He also came to the papacy with full knowledge and appreciation of the geopolitical power of his position.

It was revealed in "Newsweek" magazine in late 1990 that President Bush and Soviet Premier Mikhail Gorbachev consulted with the Pope on a weekly basis. Soviet Foreign Minister Gromyko described the Pope as a man with a weltanschauung (i.e., world view). Also, President Clinton flew to Denver, Colorado expressly to visit with the Pope. Karol Wojtyla, the Pope's given name, speaks numerous languages and almost a billion people come under his direct authority as the head of the Catholic Church. He has also been working feverishly to bring the other world religions under his influence. He has been very successful at this for even Billy Graham extols his virtues.

It seems certain that the False Prophet described in Revelation 13, will arise from the papacy. He is the "beast coming up out of the earth" who will identify the Antichrist as the Messiah and "causeth the earth and them who dwell in it to worship the first beast, whose deadly would was healed" (Rev. 13:12).

The third Babylon in Scripture has been called Political Babylon, the New Babylon, New Testament Babylon and the Great City Babylon. Scripture gives a detailed and unmistakable description of the Great City Babylon. The Biblical description of the New Babylon is that of a great end-time nation that will be totally destroyed in one hour.

There is no doubt that the United States of America is the great end-time nation so aptly described in Scripture as a nation immensely blessed by God but which turns its back on God just before the return of the Lord Jesus Christ. It is extremely easy to allow one's emotions and biases to cause spiritual blindness when the truth is so painfully close to that which we dearly love. Christians who dearly love America should also remember that their true home is that "...city which hath foundations, whose builder and maker is God" (Heb 11:10).

> Rev 18:4 (KJV)   And I heard another voice from heaven, saying, Come out of her, my people, that ye be not partakers of her sins, and that ye receive not of her plagues.

God's people are in the Great City Babylon and this includes Jews, Christians and some of the Gentiles who will be saved during the tribulation.

God's judgment on New Babylon is described in detail in Jeremiah 50 and 51, and the description of New Babylon is an amazingly detailed and accurate description of America. The time of judgment is when Israel and Judah return to their land (Jer. 50:4-5). This is near the end of the tribulation after all Christians have been raptured. God is urging the Jews to flee Babylon because He is going to stir up a nation from the North. This refers to Russia which is due north of Israel since directions in the Bible are always given in relation to Israel.

Babylon will be destroyed by "arrows" (i.e., Missiles) which will come out of the North (Jer. 51:48). Each one of these "arrows" will hit its mark as if it were shot by a mighty expert (Jer. 50:9). This is a perfect prophetic description of Russia's Intercontinental Ballistic Missiles (ICBM) which have guidance systems and are aimed at America's cities over the North Pole.

A fire will be kindled in the cities of Babylon which will consume everyone around the cities (Jer. 50:32). This accurately describes the aftermath of the detonation of nuclear missiles over American cities. Russia's ICBMs have maintained full fallout lethality to guarantee that people in the cities and around the cities would be killed by the nuclear radiation. Babylon will be totally desolated and the people left in other countries will be astonished and horrified at her plagues. Babylon will not be inhabitable after its destruction (Jer. 50:13). This is clearly because of the nuclear radiation.

The Lord has opened his arsenal and brought out the weapons of his wrath to destroy Babylon completely without even a remnant left (Jer. 50:25-26). God's arsenal contains weapons powered by the atom which is held together by his might. His weapons utilize nuclear energy which is the same energy that powers the sun and all the stars.

The New Babylon is called "O daughter of Babylon" in Jeremiah 50:42. Ancient Babylon did not have a mother since it was founded by Nimrod. Not only does New Babylon have a mother, but she is in existence at the time the New Babylon is destroyed. Also, New Babylon will be a young nation in contrast to the rest of the nations of the world (Jer. 50:12). This is a perfect description of America which is a young nation relative to all other nations, and her mother, Great Britain, is still in existence.

Babylon has been "a golden cup in the Lord's hand" (Jer. 51:7). This means that God has blessed this nation with unprecedented wealth, and it is a nation used by God to accomplish His purpose. However, this nation has turned against God in pride and arrogance. This one verse identifies America as the nation being judged. No other nation has been blessed so abundantly as America, and no other nation has changed so dramatically from being God-centered to being man-centered. America has been dramatically used by God in the area of missions, and this was especially true during the Philadelphia Church Age. But the Church has become lukewarm and indifferent in the current Laodicean Church Age.

God "would have healed Babylon" if she would have repented, but she would not be healed (Jer. 51:9). The judgment that befalls Babylon "reaches unto heaven." This is a graphic description of the mushroom clouds that ascend into the heavens after the detonation of the nuclear missiles which destroy Babylon.

Babylon "mounts up to heaven" to fortify her defenses (Jer 51:53). This is a classic description of America's use of satellites in our defense systems. Satellites are useless against the ICBMs though, and verse 53 clearly delineates the futility of these defenses. The knowledge that the missiles are coming does not stop them. America's

Patriot Missiles are not fast enough to catch the Russian ICBMs which travel at 20,000 MPH.

The New Babylon is situated "upon many waters" (Jer. 51:13), and this one verse alone proves that Political Babylon is not Ancient Babylon rebuilt. Of course, the overall description of New Babylon also clearly excludes Ancient Babylon as the nation under judgment at the close of this age.

Chapter 17 of Revelation describes "the great whore that sitteth upon many waters." This harlot is representative of both Ecclesiastical and Political Babylon. Ecclesiastical Babylon, the papal worship system, will be destroyed by the Ten-Horned Beast and its leader, the Antichrist. Chapter 18 of Revelation describes in detail Political Babylon, America, and its sudden catastrophic destruction through the providential act of God. Russia is the instrument used by God to rain down his judgment upon America. The destruction of chapter 17 is a separate event from the destruction of chapter 18 of Revelation.

New Babylon has "become the habitation of devils, and the hold of every foul spirit, and a cage of every unclean and hateful bird" (Rev. 18:2). This clearly enunciates how patently evil America has become. Birds in Scripture represent evil and the growth of evil. In America, adultery, fornication, drunkenness, drug-use, abortion, arrogance, murder, homosexuality, gluttony, gossip, covetousness, materialism and numerous other demonstrations of outright wickedness have become so commonplace that even Christians have become desensitized to them. America has gone past the point of no return in its wickedness and is now being ripened for God's judgment. Of course, Antichrist will first be given his authority for 42 months, and God's people will be removed before the judgments of God will be rained down.

"For all the nations have drunk the wine of the wrath of her fornication" (Rev. 18:3). America is the only nation that has fulfilled this prophecy completely. It is common knowledge that American popular culture is overrunning the world. The phenomenon is called "the Americanization of the world," and even secular figures from the world of scholarship, entertainment and communications do not believe it is good.

The export of America's music, movies and television is spreading the dark, self-indulgent side of American civilization throughout the world. Pop culture is not only trashing America's values but that of the entire world. This spread of American pop culture has been credited with the fall of communism, but it teaches a hedonistic and destructive lifestyle that debases the audiences that receive it. God's assessment is accurate.

"The merchants of the earth are waxed rich through the abundance of her delicacies" (Rev. 18:3). This is a concise and amazingly accurate description of America's infatuation with the god of materialism. America has become a nation drunk with the desire for more and more possessions and wealth. Americans are no longer content to have reliable means of transportation. That transportation must now be a Mercedes, Lexus, BMW, Ferrari or some other vehicle whose primary function is to impress friends and neighbors. Even Christians are drunk with these desires and will have to account for their use of the wealth that they have received. This accountability will take place at the Judgment Seat of Christ.

America will receive as much torture and grief as the glory and luxury she gave herself (Rev. 18:7). She boasts as a "Queen" who "shall see no sorrow." America sees herself as being invincible, and this arrogant attitude is a sure sign of a coming fall.

> Rev 18:2 (KJV) And he cried mightily with a strong voice, saying, Babylon the great is fallen, is fallen...

The diadem worn by the Statue of Liberty is identical with the one worn by Ishtar, the ancient Babylonian goddess of love and war. It is also highly significant that New York City, the city that represents America to the world, is called "Babylon on the Hudson." The idea that political Babylon will be a rebuilt city in Iraq is a futile attempt at escaping reality and a determined attempt to delay the coming of the Lord Jesus Christ. The Biblical description of the New Babylon is such a perfect and comprehensive description of America that it is difficult to understand why all Christians cannot see this. It has become clear that this blindness is motivated by self-deception rather than a lack of Biblical evidence.

The clincher for the identification of America as the New Babylon is in Revelation 18:16. This Scripture describes Babylon the Great as being clothed in red, white and blue. The word for "blue" is translated as "purple", but no Greek word is translated "blue" in the New Testament, and the corresponding Hebrew word in the Old Testament is translated "blue".

All cargoes imported and exported by Babylon the Great are listed in Revelation 18:11-13, and all of these cargoes are imports or exports of America. They have caused the world's ship owners to become wealthy (Rev. 18:19). Of key importance is the trafficking in "bodies and souls of men" (Rev. 18:13). This is a reference to America's purchase of African slaves prior to the Civil War.

Babylon the Great will be totally destroyed in one day when she will be consumed by fire as the Lord God judges her (Rev. 18:8). Three times the Scriptures state that her doom will come in "one hour" (Rev. 18:10,17,19). It is not coincidence that one hour is the time estimated for Russia's missiles to be fired and detonate over our cities. They are aimed at us over the North Pole and they take about 20 minutes to reach their destination.

One final prophecy about Babylon is that she will be caught in "a snare" (Jer 50:24). She "wast not aware," and she will be totally annihilated. Babylon lowered her guard. This is exactly what is happening right now in America. We are unilaterally disarming by dismantling nuclear weapons and decreasing defense spending. America has been tricked into complacency by Russia's collapse and overtures for peace. Russia has not dismantled one nuclear missile and has no intention of doing so.

The above prophecies about Babylon the Great are only a smattering of the prophecies in Scripture that give a detailed description of her. They are representative and should provide the reader with a clear picture of America's part in the prophetic puzzle. This means doomsday for America and those who have never placed their faith and trust in Jesus Christ. It is not a doomsday scenario for believers since God's people will be removed before His wrath is released upon the earth.

God judged the earth with a flood, and He judged Sodom and Gomorrah with fire and brimstone. America will surely be judged for its sins.

Before the destruction of America, the "man of sin" must be revealed. He is the Antichrist, "the beast that was, and is not, and yet is" (Rev. 17:8).

The book of Revelation describes a great harlot seen riding on Daniel's beast with seven heads and ten horns (Revelation 17:1-3). The Apostle John describes this great harlot as the "beast out of the earth" (Revelation 13), also known as the false prophet.

The above pictures are provided courtesy of Pastor Randy Shupe, whose books may be found in the Bibliography on page 203.

Chapter 10

ANTICHRIST

The Idol Shepherd

An often overlooked aspect of Daniel's description of the Antichrist (little horn) is his persecution of the saints:"He shall speak words against the Most High, and **shall *wear out the saints of the Most High,....and they shall be given into his hand*** *for a time, times, and half a time[3½ years]"* (Dan 7:25 – ESV). Those believers who subscribe to the strictly dispensational view of the rapture are perplexed by this verse since they have been taught that all believers are taken away before the tribulation begins. One of the main purposes of this author's ministry has been to alert the church to this critical truth: the Lord will deliver His firstfruits (overcomers) before the trials begin; however, those who are not ready and looking for their Lord to return will face this 3½-year period of trial at the hands of the Antichrist. Daniel 7:21 and 7:25 warn believers that the Antichrist will make war with them, and the Apostle John confirms it in Rev 12:17 and 13:7. The believers who remain will be given this great test of their faith, requiring them to stand up to the beast. They will be able to triumph over him because Jesus overcame death for them (see Rev 12:11). They will then learn to be overcomers and proclaim the final victory and get to witness the destruction of the Antichrist (Dan 7:26).

James T. Harman – ***Daniel's Prophecies Unsealed***

The identity of the Antichrist has been one of the most intriguing questions since the time of Christ. Many have been identified as the Antichrist based on their evil natures and heinous acts committed against God and their fellowmen. Such characters as Nero, Hitler, Mussolini, Napoleon, Juan Carlos, Judas Iscariot, Saddam Hussein, Henry Kissenger and Gorbechev have at one time or another been tagged as the Antichrist. The fact that none of these men fulfill the

Biblical prophecies about Antichrist does not seem to deter men from tagging these individuals based on some perceived evil trait that these men personify.

The one and only method of identifying the Antichrist is to search the Scriptures for the detailed description of him, which has been given by God the Holy Spirit. Knowledge of what the Scriptures say about Antichrist can provide an unmistakable picture of him.

A big mistake that most people make is looking for someone whom the world hates or despises. In Revelation Antichrist is often called the "beast". God calls him a beast because he is evil and worldly, but to the world he is a wonderful charismatic figure who is admired and loved.

> Rev 17:17 (KJV) For God hath put in their hearts to fulfil his will, and to agree, and give their kingdom unto the beast, until the words of God shall be fulfilled.

The Biblical description of Antichrist pictures someone whom the world loves and reveres. The leaders of the world will turn to him in a time of crisis. He must be a great world leader that is highly admired. For this to happen, Antichrist has to be a figure known and loved throughout the world. He must have a charismatic and a magnetic personality. He has to be an individual who has captured the fame of the world. He will be the subject of books, movies, television programs, magazines and newspaper articles.

> Rev 13:3 (KJV) And I saw one of his heads as it were wounded to death...

The Scriptures are clear that the world will witness the death of the Antichrist. The whole world will witness his death, and there will be great mourning over this popular world leader. Common sense reveals that Antichrist will have to be someone who has been around a while in order to establish his power base and credibility.

He must also be perceived as a peace lover who exudes the ideals of a democratic society, since the new world order will begin this way before it degenerates into an autocratic government led by a dictator. He will be the type of individual who will have buildings, parks, schools, libraries, and airports named after him. In brief, the searcher for Antichrist should look for a man greatly admired, respected and well thought of by the majority of the world, but the world must believe that he is dead. Also, the Scriptures depict someone who has apparently died as a result of a mortal head wound.

> Psa 68:21 (KJV)   But God shall wound the head of his enemies, and the hairy scalp of such an one as goeth on still in his trespasses.

The Antichrist's head wound was prophesied in Gen 3:15 where the mortal head wound is first mentioned. The phrase "goeth on still" indicates that he continues in his sin even though the world thinks he is dead. The whole world must be convinced that he is dead, since the world will be astonished that Antichrist has recovered from his mortal head wound. It will have to be a very famous person for the world to pay attention to his death.

The wound will have to be highly visible to the entire world. The only way this could happen is if the head wound had been recorded in some way for the world to witness over and over again. This is a wound that the whole world will witness repeatedly. It will be a famous "assassination."

The Scriptures say he will be a world leader. His death will only increase the reverence for him, and his legend will increase irrationally in the minds of the people of the world. He will become the superhero in death that would be impossible in real life.

The "hairy scalp" in Psalm 68:21 indicates he will be a man with a full head of hair and the scalp will be part of the wound.

> Rev 13:3 (KJV) And I saw one of his heads as it were wounded to death; and his deadly wound was healed: and all the world wondered after the beast.

The whole world will be amazed when the beast is healed and he returns from the dead. This "resurrection" healing will make him seem like a god, and the world will turn to him to be their supernatural leader in a time of crisis (see Appendix A for more on this marvel).

Hab 3:13 (KJV) Thou wentest forth for the salvation of thy people, even for salvation with thine anointed; thou woundedst the head out of the house of the wicked, by discovering the foundation unto the neck. Selah.

Habakkuk 3:13 reveals another clue to the identity of Antichrist. In addition to the scalp wound, it appears that Antichrist will have some damage at the base of his neck. A wound at this very critical place may explain another prediction in the Bible that he will have a withered arm.

Zec 11:17 (KJV) Woe to the idol shepherd that leaveth the flock! the sword shall be upon his arm, and upon his right eye: his arm shall be clean dried up, and his right eye shall be utterly darkened.

Perhaps the wound to the head and scalp caused the blind right eye and this indicates that the wound is on the right side of the head. Also the nerves to the arms come out of the spine at the base of the neck. A wound here could cause a paralyzed arm.

Dan 7:20 (KJV) And of the ten horns that were in his head, and of the other which came up, and before whom three fell; even of that horn that had eyes, and a mouth that spake very great things, whose look was more stout than his fellows.

Antichrist will be a great orator and the wounds will not affect this. He will still be able to speak and hold a crowd spellbound. His speeches will be part of his fame.

His physical appearance is one of strength and health as compared to his contemporaries. He looks good on television since this is how most of the world will see him. He will probably be youthful and athletic looking for his age. He is clearly a desirable and charismatic personality.

Rev 13:12 (KJV) And he exerciseth all the power of the first beast before him, and causeth the earth and them which dwell therein to worship the first beast, whose deadly wound was healed.

The Antichrist will work closely with the false prophet, the Pope. The Pope will cause the world to worship the Antichrist. This presents another clue to his identity. The Antichrist will be closely aligned with the Catholic Church. Even though he is privately evil and ungodly, outwardly he will support the Catholic Church and worship as a Catholic.

> Rev 17:11 (KJV) And the beast that was, and is not, even he is the eighth, and is of the seven, and goeth into perdition.

This is perhaps the most revealing verse for identifying the Antichrist. This verse tells us that Antichrist will be the leader of the eighth world power, the revived Roman Empire. The ten toes of iron and clay mentioned in Daniel 2:42-43 represent this empire. This means that he will be the leader of the European Common Market. This is also the Ten-Horned Beast mentioned in Revelation 13:1.

The most intriguing part of this verse is that the Antichrist is also of the seventh power. The seventh power is Babylon the Great, which is the United States of America. This means that Antichrist will have been a President of the United States of America

Antichrist is a real individual who will fulfill every Biblical prophecy concerning him. Many of these prophecies have already been fulfilled, and when the Antichrist emerges on the world's scene he will fulfill the remaining prophecies about himself.

While the whole world witnessed his death, the Bible says that he "goes on in his sin" influencing world events and leaders. God is waiting for the right moment for his reappearance as the "resurrected" messiah to save the world in a time of crisis.

Antichrist will graciously accept the world's bidding to take over the reigns of government to extract the world and its economy from wars and depression. He will bring peace to the world

> Dan 8:25 (KJV) And through his policy also he shall cause craft to prosper in his hand; and he shall *magnify himself in his heart*, and *by peace shall destroy many*: he shall also stand up against the Prince of princes; but he shall be broken without hand.

The Antichrist is filled with pride. He has seen the world worship his memory, and he has magnified himself. Through words and peace he will take power and destroy sovereign nations and their leaders. He will have a power so great that only the return of Christ will be able to stop him.

The Bible also tells us what the leaders of Babylon will be like just before the "vile person" comes.

> Dan 11:15 (KJV) So the king of the north shall come, and cast up a mount, and take the most fenced cities: and the arms of the south shall not withstand, *neither his chosen people*, neither shall there be any strength to withstand.
>
> Dan 11:16 (KJV) But *he that cometh* against him shall do according to his own will, and *none shall stand before him*: and he shall stand in the *glorious land*, which by his hand shall be consumed.

A king comes against God's "chosen people" and threatens them. But a defender comes who none can stand against. This one comes literally to the glorious land of Israel. In modern terms this is like sending Patriot missiles to defend Israel.

> Dan 11:17 (KJV) He shall also set his face to enter with the *strength of his whole kingdom*, and *upright ones with him*; thus shall he do: and he shall give him the *daughter of women*, corrupting her: but she shall not stand on his side, neither be for him.

This one "that cometh" comes with the "strength of his whole kingdom." He has the power and support of his people. He comes with "upright ones." Christians and churches are behind him. God's people are praying for this war. When he leaves he gives them the "daughter of women." These are not soldiers, but ones who are without power. This would be a good description of the UN peacekeepers who are neither for nor against each side.

> Dan 11:18-19 (KJV) After this shall he turn his face *unto the isles*, and shall take many: but a prince for his own behalf shall cause the reproach offered by him to cease; without his own

reproach he shall cause it to turn upon him. 19 Then he shall turn his face toward the fort of his own land: but he *shall stumble and fall, and not be found.*

Nations are always referred to in the Bible based on their geographical relationship to Israel. Therefore, the "isles" refers to the land across the seas from Israel (i.e., America). In victory, the President returns but surprisingly he "stumbles" and is "not found." He loses his power.

Dan 11:20 (KJV) Then shall stand up in his estate a raiser of taxes in the glory of the kingdom: but within few days he shall be *destroyed, neither in anger, nor in battle.*

Following this President will be a new one who is a *"raiser of taxes."* And like his predecessor, he is gone before his time "neither in anger, nor in battle." And it happens in a "few days" which means a short span of time in the Bible.

Dan 11:21 (KJV) And in his estate shall stand up a *vile person,* to whom they shall not give the honour of the kingdom: but he shall *come in peaceably, and obtain the kingdom by flatteries.*

Now we see the Antichrist appear and he is not given the "honour of the kingdom." He is not made President again, but he "obtains the kingdom by flatteries." Here again we see a reference to the Antichrist's great speaking skills and promises of "peace". With just words and his very presence he is given the power of the kingdom. The nations of the world will follow and obey.

Like the story of Camelot, the king who once was, and will be again, has returned. The world will want to believe that the fairytale has come true. It will be hard to believe even when they see him with their own eyes, but they will have living proof.

Can it really be true? Will JFK be brought back by God? And if so, then we must be at the end of the age, the rapture is near, and our lives are about to be judged.

As you have seen from the Bible, the evidence is overwhelming. Our nation is awash in selfish lusts. There is a pervasive nostalgia for free sex of the sixties. The music, clothes and haircuts of Kennedy's era are returning. It is because of television, books and movies that a whole new generation has fallen in love with JFK's legend. JFK fulfills all the Scriptures identifying the Antichrist, and the time for him to be revealed is rapidly approaching.

Every detail of Scripture concerning the Antichrist must be fulfilled, and prophecies already fulfilled identify him as John F. Kennedy. Genesis 3:15 gives us the first detailed information on Antichrist. In this Scripture the Seed of the Woman is Christ, and both Judas Iscariot and Antichrist are the Seed of the Serpent. The Serpent is Satan. Judas Iscariot and Antichrist are the only two people mentioned in Scripture who have been or will be indwelled by Satan.

Genesis 3:15 simply states that the Seed of the Serpent (i.e., Judas Iscariot) will cause the heel of the Seed of the Woman to be bruised. This was literally fulfilled at the crucifixion when the feet of Jesus were overlapped and nailed to the Cross with a long spike. The process would have severely bruised the heel of Jesus since it was violently smashed against the upright of the wooden cross with the hammer.

There is also a current theory that Hitler is the Antichrist. Since the Antichrist will have to be someone who is loved and revered by the world, Hitler would definitely not be a candidate for this position. This theory also speculates that Hitler will use a pseudonym, but the Scriptures are clear that Antichrist will come using his real name (John 5:43). It is admitted that Hitler was one of the many antichrists who were to come (1 John 2:18), but he is not The Antichrist.

Antichrist is also the Seed of the Serpent, and he had his head "bruised" November 22, 1963 when an assassin's bullet ripped through his head giving him a "mortal" or "fatal" wound. The Hebrew word for "bruise" in the injuries of both Jesus and Antichrist means "to injure or wound greatly; to break or smite in pieces." Both fulfillments were accurate in detail.

Revelation 13:3 describes the head wound, "One of the heads of the beast seemed to have had a fatal wound...." Unknown to the world at the time, this "fatal wound" would be healed without the world's knowledge, and when the world discovers that the wound was healed, it will be astonished. Revelation 13:3 also states this very succinctly, "...but the fatal wound had been healed. The whole world was astonished and followed the beast." Revelation 13:12 reiterates the fact that the fatal wound of Antichrist "had been healed."

The world has seen the infliction of the fatal head wound literally hundreds of times in living color on television and in books and magazines. Numerous books and magazines have published the sequence of the fatal wound frame by frame with the head wound occurring in frame 313 of the infamous Zapruder film. There has recently been a tremendous surge of interest in JFK and the assassination since the release of the movie "JFK". There have been so many programs on television focusing on JFK that it is difficult for a person to watch all of them. This intense interest in JFK will not subside, and he will one day soon reveal himself and fulfill the remaining prophecies about Antichrist.

Zechariah 11:17 gives us more amazing details about the wounds experienced by the "idol shepherd" (i.e., the Antichrist). This verse states:

> Zec 11:17 (KJV) Woe to the idol shepherd that leaveth the flock! the sword shall be upon his arm, and upon his right eye: his arm shall be clean dried up, and his right eye shall be utterly darkened.

The Scriptures do not reveal to us which arm will be paralyzed, but the actual fulfillment of this prophecy confirms that it will be his right arm. The first bullet that struck John F. Kennedy pierced his trapezius muscle on the right side of his spinal column and struck the nerve root coming from the first thoracic vertebra. This nerve root enters the brachial plexus, a group of nerves which controls the muscles of the right arm among other things.

The fact that the bullet struck this nerve root is confirmed by JFK's arm reflex immediately after the first shot. This nerve damage is responsible for JFK's "withered" (i.e., paralyzed) right arm. Some pictures taken of JFK on the Island of Scorpios in 1971 by George Duncastle, a British civil service employee, also confirm the withered right arm. The pictures are legitimate, and they have surfaced several times since 1971. They were even shown on television at one point in time.

The second bullet entered the back of JFK's head tangentially and blew a fist-sized portion of his skull out on the right rear of his head.

The right parietal and temporal lobes of his brain were almost completely blown away. One fragment of the bullet went all the way through the brain and lodged to the upper part of his right eye. The path of the bullet would have severed or severely damaged the optic nerve to his right eye. This caused his right eye to be totally blind.

Thus, the two bullet wounds suffered by JFK fulfilled the prophecies about Antichrist in Genesis 3:15, Zechariah 11:17, and Revelation 13:3,12. The fulfillment of these three prophecies alone defies the probability of mere coincidence.

2 Thessalonians 2:1-17 confirms that the biggest single factor in the rise of Antichrist is deceit. This deceit is on a grand scale since the whole world will be fooled. The fake autopsy and funeral of JFK have been the world's grandest deception. Literally millions of people in the U.S.A., Europe and the world watched the greatest assembly of world leaders in history who came to attend the funeral of a man who still lay in a hospital room on the seventeenth floor of the National Naval Hospital in Bethesda, Maryland.

The body in the casket was that of a cadaver brought over from the medical school at Bethesda. Dr. Humes was the medical doctor who performed the autopsy, and he refuses to be interviewed by anyone in regard to the autopsy. He admitted to the Assassination Committee that the report he wrote was given to JFK's doctor, Admiral Burkley, who rewrote the autopsy report. This is an incredible admission since Admiral Burkley did not perform the autopsy. No rationale has been offered as to why the autopsy report was completed this way.

The rationale is very simple when it is understood that Dr. Humes performed an autopsy on a cadaver with a head wound significantly different from JFK's head wound. The report had to be edited to agree with JFK's head wound, and that is exactly why Admiral Burkley rewrote the report.

This is also the reason why no conical section was performed on Kennedy's brain. A conical section is where the brain is removed and literally sliced into numerous thin slices so the path of the bullet can be traced. Students in the medical school had already worked on the cadaver that was used for the autopsy, and the brain was missing when the autopsy was begun. The bullet wound would not have matched Kennedy's wounds anyway. This is the reason why Kennedy's brain was missing from the National Archives when a forensic pathologist was finally allowed to view the autopsy material 15 years later.

Jacqueline Kennedy had supposedly taken the brain to the National Archives, but it has never been located and no one has attempted to explain how it became missing. No one in the family ever became concerned about the location of Kennedy's brain, since its precise location is well known to them.

Although missing the right parietal and temporal lobes, JFK's brain is very much intact inside his somewhat scarred cranium. The parietal and temporal lobes of the brain control motor areas of the body. Since JFK is right-handed, his left parietal and temporal lobes are the dominant control centers for his body so they have taken over the control of his body.

JFK's thought processes and verbal abilities have not been affected by his wounds. He is simply blind in his right eye, and his right arm is "withered" (i.e., atrophied and drawn) because of the nerve damage to his brachial plexus, a network of nerves that control the chest, shoulder and arm. The blind right eye was caused by the damaged optic nerve. For those who are unfamiliar with symbolism in Scripture, a blind right eye and a crippled right arm signify a foe who has already been defeated. This defeat took place at Calvary almost two thousand years ago.

Revelation 17:9-11 is one of the most mysterious passages in Scripture. It refers specifically to the Antichrist. The "seven heads" are the leaders of the seven world empires: (1) Egypt, (2) Assyria, (3) Babylon, (4) Medo-Persia, (5) Greece, (6) Rome, and (7) New Babylon (United States of America).

At the time John wrote Revelation, five of the empires had fallen and the sixth empire, Rome, was in power. The leader of the seventh empire had not yet come to power. When he does come to power he will remain for a little while. This prophecy has been fulfilled since JFK has come to power and he was leader of the seventh empire for approximately one thousand days.

He now "is not" but he will also be the eighth king who will reign over the eighth empire, which is the ten-horned beast or the revived Roman Empire. "Of the seven" means that the origin of Antichrist was the seventh empire. Even though "seven" in verse eleven is a cardinal number in the Greek, it is specifically referring to the seventh empire. The grammatical construction is almost identical to Matthew 22:26

where the cardinal number "seven" in the Greek is even translated "seventh" in most translations.

Thus, JFK is "Rex quondam Rexque futurus" (i.e., the King who once was and will be again). This quotation from Sir Thomas Malory was the impetus for a book by Terence H. White called *The Once and Future King*. Sir Thomas Malory wrote *Le Morte D'Arthur*, which is one of the classic works on the Arthurian legend—the most famous of medieval legends. Space prohibits a detailed comparison between the legends of King Arthur and John F. Kennedy, but the numerous analogies are not coincidental.

President Kennedy loved the play "Camelot," and his administration is still nostalgically remembered as the era of Camelot. Time Incorporated published a book in 1988 called *Life in Camelot: The Kennedy Years*.

For those unfamiliar with Arthurian legend, King Arthur was a British king who ruled over a utopian kingdom called Camelot. He suffered a mortal head wound by the sword, and he was carried off to a Celtic paradise called the Isle of Avalon where he was to be healed. At some point in the future he is to return from the Isle of Avalon and again rule over Great Britain.

John F. Kennedy also suffered a mortal head wound. He was secretly carried off to the island of Skorpios where he was healed. In God's perfect time He will return and reign over Great Britain as leader of the Ten-Horned Beast or the revived Roman Empire.

It is highly significant that the Island of Skorpios means the Island of the Scorpion, and in the Mazzaroth (i.e., the Zodiac) the Scorpion is symbolic of the Seed of the Serpent (i.e., the Antichrist). It is also not coincidental that in the Mazzaroth the scorpion's head is crushed by Ophiuchus, the symbol of Jesus Christ or the Seed of the Woman. The Mazzaroth has been called the gospel in the stars, and much can be learned from a study of it. This is not the same as Astrology, which is a Satanic perversion of the Mazzaroth. The original Mazzaroth is a heavenly portrayal of the struggle between the Seed of the Serpent and the Seed of the Woman. Two excellent books on the subject are *The Gospel in the Stars* by Joseph A. Seiss and *The Witness of the Stars* by E. W. Bullinger.

The Mazzaroth exalts Jesus Christ and points to his final victory over Satan and the Antichrist. Satan has perverted the Mazzaroth into the system called Astrology, which is so widespread in the world today. It is because of this perversion that the great majority of Christians who have a little knowledge believe that anything pertaining to the Mazzaroth is satanic. God created the stars and gave man the gospel of Jesus Christ in them long before He gave man his written Word in the form of the Bible. It is tragic that only a relatively few Christians are able to appreciate the true significance of the Mazzaroth.

Will Antichrist be an Israelite? Scriptures strongly imply that Antichrist will be an Israelite, and that he will specifically be a member of the tribe of Dan (Gen. 49:16-17; Dan. 11:37). The Scriptures also indicate that he will rise to power "out of the sea" (Rev. 13:1) which implies that he will be a Gentile. The grand mystery is how both can be true. In actuality, he did rise up out of the Gentile nations, but he is a real Israelite from the tribe of Dan.

The rising "up out of the sea" has been fulfilled both literally and figuratively. In August 1943 during World War II, JFK's PT boat was cut in two and sunk from underneath him by a Japanese destroyer named "Amagiri". John F. Kennedy literally came up "out of the sea" and survived the destruction of the PT 109, which he commanded. The incident made him a hero since he was personally responsible for saving most of his crew. A book and a movie were made about the incident, and it was the impetus for JFK's rise to power. John F. Kennedy is also well known for his love of the sea and his vacations to Martha's Vineyard on the seacoast of Massachusetts. The Sea in Scripture is symbolic of the Gentile nations, so this is the figurative fulfillment of this same prophecy.

The tribes of Dan and Ephraim are part of the ten lost tribes of Israel, and they are conspicuously absent from the 144,000 Jewish evangelists who will preach the Gospel of the Kingdom during the last half of Daniel's seventieth week. They will, however, receive their inheritance when Jesus returns in power and glory at the end of the tribulation (Ezekiel 48:1,5). In other words, the world will not know that Antichrist is an Israelite until the end of the tribulation and when Jesus identifies the people of Antichrist as being of the tribe of Dan. The following Scripture describes this event:

> Isa 56:8 (KJV) The Lord GOD which gathereth the outcasts of Israel saith, Yet will I gather others to him, beside those that are gathered unto him.

It may be that Ephraim is another group of people in the world not recognized as Israelites. The parable of the hidden treasure (Matthew 13:36-44) refers specifically to the nation of Israel being hidden in the world until the Lord returns. The identification of the people who make up the rest of the 10 lost tribes is explained in Chapter 7, The Seven Parables of the Kingdom.

It should be clear by now that if Antichrist is of the tribe of Dan, then the Irish people are Israelites, since JFK is of Irish descent. This may sound absurd on the surface, but thorough research into the traditions and heritage of the Irish people, including their physical and familial traits, will reveal that they are remarkable in their similarities with the Israelites

The Irish people perfectly match God's description of the nation of Israel. Throughout the Old Testament, God describes Israel as being a persecuted people. The history of the Irish confirms this description even down to the persecution in America when they migrated here around the turn of the century. They have also been kept "few in number" (Lev. 26:22), and they remain Irish where ever they settle in the world just like the Jews remain Jews regardless of the country in which they settle.

There are numerous traits and traditions that link the Irish people to the lost tribe of Dan. The tribe of Dan was stonecutters, and Ireland is known for its stone buildings, walls and fortresses that have stood for well over a thousand years without benefit of mortar. The national instrument of Ireland is the harp (clarsech), which is very much like the harp played by David. The tribe of Dan tended toward violence and "much wine" which is a stereotype of the Irish people.

The Irish are gifted intellectually and they are highly religious. Both of these traits are Jewish. The Irish are the only group of people in the world who equal the Jews in the number of Nobel prizes based on a "per capita" basis.

The Irish people can only be traced back to about 400 B.C., which is 200 years after the tribe of Dan disappeared from history. The Irish were able to defend Ireland because of iron weapons and the use of chariots with iron wheels, which they introduced into Ireland. The tribe of Dan was familiar with iron and iron chariots long before they were introduced into Ireland. They had learned about iron from the Philistines and Canaanites, and they were very much aware of the advantage of using iron rather than bronze in the forging of weapons.

The ancient traditions and heroes of Ireland are fascinating, and their origins are as mysterious as they are fascinating. The mystery slowly begins to dissipate with the understanding that the ancient history of the Irish people can be studied in the Old Testament by studying about Israel and especially the tribe of Dan. The Irish have an ancient hero simply known as the Giant Killer. This fact standing along is trivia until we realize that this Giant Killer was David and the giant he killed was Goliath.

Another ancient tradition of the Irish was that the land of Ireland was a land that was given them by God. It is a mystery where the Irish got this tradition, but the mystery clears up when we realize that they received it from their forefathers, Abraham, Isaac and Jacob who were promised a land as an inheritance from God. Ireland is not the land of promise, but the tradition of being given some land by God is of legitimate origin.

The changing seasons of the year were highly significant for the ancient Irish, and festivals were held marking the passage of the year. This ancient custom can be clearly linked to the seven festivals that God ordained for Israel to mark the passage of the year and especially the various stages of the harvest (Lev. 23).

The Irish have numerous other legends and myths that can be linked to the history of Israel as revealed in the Bible. One is that the Irish people will someday be married to God, but they are currently married to the wrong spouse. Another is that they will one day have a King who was chosen by God to be King and who was born to be King. No explanation should be necessary linking this to Israel who is called God's unfaithful wife. She will one day be restored (See the book of Hosea).

Also, Jesus is their King and He will reign over them during the millennium. Another interesting legend related to this one is that the King must be without physical blemish. The origin of this has to be the sinless nature that the Messiah was to have at his appearance.

Of course, these Irish myths and legends have changed over time and many adulterations to the original truths have been added. The basic ideas of the legends have not changed, and they can be clearly linked to the historical facts pertaining to the nation of Israel, and even to the tribe of Dan in some cases.

Historical Analysis

One of the most difficult tasks in persuading Christians that John F. Kennedy is the Antichrist is in convincing them that he is did not die at the time of his assassination. People have a tendency to believe what they read in the newspapers, and the more times they read and hear about something, the stronger that belief becomes.

One of the world's biggest mysteries is the events that took place on November 22, 1963 and related events subsequent to that date. It is as if the events of that day have been frozen in time and everyone old enough to recall that day remembers in detail where he was and what he was doing. The infliction of that fatal head wound has been indelibly impressed on our minds after having witnessed it countless times on television in slow motion.

The mysteries of the events of that day are still researched extensively, and numerous articles, books and videotapes have been created attempting to explain those mysteries. None have been successful in answering the mysteries of that day. The following is a brief summary of the events of that day and related events subsequent to that day with an explanation of the mysteries surrounding these events.

After the fatal head wound, JFK was rushed to Parkland Memorial Hospital where he received emergency treatment. The doctors and emergency personnel quickly set about infusing the President with large quantities of blood and Ringer's solution in order to re-establish peripheral circulation and prevent hemorrhagic shock (i.e., blood loss). Parkland was a research hospital for hemorrhagic shock, and it is not coincidence that it was probably one of the best trauma hospitals in the nation. Dr. Carrico had forced an endotracheal tube down JFK's throat, but Dr. Perry performed a tracheotomy when it became clear that the endotracheal tube had failed to increase the air volume in JFK's lungs.

Doctors Charles J. Carrico and Malcolm O. Perry have to be credited with saving the life of JFK even though they probably do not know it even now. Several other doctors were involved in the emergency treatment, but it was Dr. Clark who pronounced him dead in the absence of neurological, muscular or heart response. This was not the first time that someone had been pronounced dead when he was in fact very much alive.

A nurse was called in to clean JFK up for removal of the body. This nurse made a comment that should have triggered another medical check of JFK but has gone virtually unnoticed. Her comment, "His body was still supple," shows that she was surprised that rigor mortis had not set in, but more importantly, it was evidence that he was not dead.

An expensive $10,000 bronze casket was requisitioned from a local funeral home, and JFK was placed in the casket in the nude after a sheet had been spread out in the casket. This casket mysteriously disappeared later at the National Naval Hospital in Bethesda, Maryland under the close scrutiny of the CIA, FBI and family members of JFK. The mystery of the lost casket has never been resolved. The truth is that the casket contained evidence that JFK was still alive so it had to be disposed of to maintain the cover-up.

After being placed in the casket, JFK was illegally spirited away to Love Field where the casket was loaded inside the airplane after quickly removing some seats. The departure was illegal since a homicide was involved and Texas law required an autopsy in Texas to keep from breaking the chain of evidence. The cover-up of JFK's survival would never have been possible if Texas law had prevailed.

Arrangements were made with a funeral home in Washington, D.C. to embalm and dress the body after an autopsy was to be performed at the Bethesda Naval hospital. The arrangements were later mysteriously canceled when it was decided that the embalming could be done at the hospital even though it was against regulations. The explanation for this mystery is very simple since JFK was alive and the cadaver brought over from the medical school at Bethesda did not require embalming.

After loading the bronze casket aboard Air Force One, Lyndon B. Johnson was sworn in as President, and Air Force One lifted off from Love Field in Dallas. At this point the world had been informed that JFK was dead, and everyone aboard the airplane thought he was dead. It was at some point in the flight back to Washington, D.C. that it was discovered that JFK was still alive. This is where the numerous discrepancies and mysteries begin and the obvious cover-up by the CIA, the FBI, the family of JFK, the administrators of Bethesda hospital, and the doctors who performed the fake autopsy.

According to Oliver Stone who produced the movie "JFK," all of this cover-up was to conceal whether the bullets came from the front or the rear, and this was done to cover-up the fact of a conspiracy rather than a lone gunman acting along. This theory says that JFK was removed from the casket aboard the airplane, and the wounds were altered to make them look like they came from the rear rather than the front. The ludicrousness of this theory should be obvious to anyone reflecting on the logistics and planning that would be required for such an operation. A mission of this scope would make the old "Mission Impossible" series look like child's play.

The simple truth is that JFK was discovered alive and removed from the casket. Kennedy's doctor, Admiral Burkley, enlarged the tracheotomy to help JFK breathe. This is why the picture of the tracheotomy was described by Dr. Charles a Crenshaw as different and much larger than when JFK left Parkland Hospital. The decision had to be made whether to reveal to the world that JFK was still alive or to let it continue in the belief that he was dead. It appeared obvious that JFK would not survive the gunshot wounds to the neck and head, or that if he did survive he would remain a vegetable for the remainder of his life due to the severe brain damage.

At the time this decision was made, there was no constitutional provision for the vice-president to take over the Presidency if the President were merely incapacitated. In other words, there was a constitutional crisis with no immediate solution if the world was told that JFK was alive. The correct decision was obvious so the cover-up began which involved the Kennedy family and the upper echelons of government.

Another major factor in the decision to cover-up that JFK was still alive was the obvious fact that the attempted assassination was the handiwork of organized crime. The Kennedy family and aides knew that a contract put out on someone's life by the Mafia was never rescinded. This is the primary reason JFK has been living in obscurity.

It is highly significant that organized crime under the leadership of the Mafia is now considered dead with the conviction and incarceration for life of John Gotti, the last of the Godfathers. All of the traditional leaders of the Mafia are now dead or incarcerated for life, and this presents an opportune time for JFK to reveal himself without fear of retaliation by the Mafia.

It is now common knowledge that the Mafia was responsible for the assassination of JFK and RFK, and both were conspiracies. Unfortunately, Oliver Stone's movie "JFK" was not able to distinguish between the conspiracy of the Mafia to kill JFK and the conspiracy of the government and family of JFK to conceal the fact that he was still alive. What the government and JFK's family did not foresee was the extent of JFK's recovery.

Air Force One landed at Andrews Air Force Base and the numerous mysteries about the assassination began. The empty bronze casket was unloaded from the starboard side of the aircraft. The honor guard that had been requested to unload the casket were not allowed by General McHugh and others aboard the aircraft to carry the casket. This mystery is easily resolved since they knew that the honor guard would easily detect that the casket was empty. It has now been conclusively established that the bronze casket was empty when it was unloaded.

News videos later showed that a helicopter was approaching Air Force One from the port side of the aircraft at the time the bronze casket was being unloaded. The attention of the news media was focused on the bronze casket. While the hearse carrying the bronze casket was on its way to Bethesda with the news media following, JFK was carried aboard the helicopter to Bethesda where he received emergency surgery. It is established fact that a helicopter landed at Bethesda before the bronze casket arrived, but it is still unknown who the injured person was who received so much attention when the helicopter arrived.

Another hearse arrived at the hospital back door before the bronze casket arrived at the front door. It supposedly contained the body of JFK, but the discrepancies were numerous. The body was in a Viet Nam type body bag, and it was in a cheap metal shipping casket. Also, the head had a towel wrapped around it covering the face. The head wound was massive, and it was totally different from the head wound described by the doctors at Parkland hospital. Aides who helped unload the body were astounded because surgery had already been performed on the body and the entire brain was missing.

This body was actually a cadaver brought over from the medical school at Bethesda. This body received the so-called autopsy, and it was the body buried at Arlington National Cemetery. This is the reason why none of the Kennedy family ever visit the grave site except on ceremonial occasions. This is also why JFK's children said in a recent interview that they never think about JFK's death but only think about his life. Jacqueline's friends are also very curious as to why she still refers to "Jack" in the present tense after almost 30 years. They reason that she has never really been able to accept his death.

One of the mysteries that has never been resolved is why LBJ set up his presidential office in a building across the street from the White House and remained there for several weeks. It was common knowledge that RFK, the Attorney General, would not allow LBJ to set up his office in the oval office. It was several weeks later that RFK changed his mind and allowed LBJ into the oval office

This mystery is easily resolved when it is understood that LBJ was not legally the President until Congress passed an amendment to the constitution allowing the vice-president to become President if the President became incompetent. LBJ would not have submitted to this intimidation if he had legally been the President. He hated the Kennedys, and he was a ruthless and egotistical individual.

One significant fact that has never been addressed by the Kennedy family or the administrators of Bethesda is Jacqueline Kennedy's frequent visits to the hospital for several years after the assassination. The answer to this mystery ties in with another mystery that has never been explained. The seventeenth floor of Bethesda hospital is the VIP suite, and it was completely closed off to hospital personnel and visitors for several years. It certainly is not coincidence that the seventeenth floor was reopened for use after Jacqueline Kennedy married Aristotle Onassis in 1968 and she moved to the Island of Skorpios.

Most people are not aware that JFK and Onassis were good friends before the assassination. The Island of Skorpios was a perfect place for the care and rehabilitation of JFK, and Jacqueline and the children could be isolated from the news media. Therefore, a marriage between Aristotle and Jackie was arranged with Cardinal Cushing's blessings.

Cardinal Cushing was the Kennedy's spiritual counselor, and he was criticized for blessing the marriage since Aristotle was divorced. He responded by saying that the world would approve of the marriage if they knew the circumstances. The marriage was a complete sham with a contract for them to have separate bedrooms. This is why Cardinal Cushing could grant his blessings to the marriage without violating his conscience. The reader should take note that Jackie has not been romantically linked with anyone since the death of Aristotle Onassis.

Several people have seen John F. Kennedy on the Island of Skorpios. Ardash Tookoian, a Greek tour guide, has stated that he often saw JFK in his wheelchair on the island. A Greek nurse named Koula Markopolis was hired by Aristotle Onassis to care for JFK. George Duncastle, a British civil service employee even took some pictures of JFK with a telephoto lens in 1971. The pictures show JFK being assisted out of his wheelchair by Jackie and two secret service men. JFK's hair is "white like wool" and his "withered" right arm is clearly visible.

God gave us a detailed portrait of Antichrist in the Scriptures, and the idea that Christians will be unable to identify him has no Scriptural basis. Antichrist has to be someone, and the fact that JFK perfectly fulfills numerous prophecies about the Antichrist should cause Christians to wake up to the prophetic truths about the return of the Lord Jesus Christ. In addition to having already fulfilled numerous prophecies about Antichrist, JFK will be in a position to fulfill the remainder of the prophecies about this individual.

Since Antichrist will be the world leader, it is common sense that he will have to be someone well-known throughout the world. He will also have to be someone admired and respected throughout the world and especially in Europe since he will be leader of the European Common Market. JFK was the most respected world leader in history. He was especially loved throughout Europe, and numerous Europeans have pictures of him in their homes.

He lived and traveled in Europe when his father, Joseph Kennedy, was ambassador to Great Britain. He also took frequent vacations to Europe. JFK actually knew more about Europe than he knew about America at the time he became President.

Six months before the assassination JFK visited six of the then nine members of the European Common Market. He and Jackie received a resounding welcome in all six countries. Europe openly demonstrated its love for John F. Kennedy, and this was just a preview of Europe's attraction for JFK when he returns as the Roman Prince.

Since the Jews will reveal the Antichrist as their messiah, it seems only fitting that he be highly regarded by the Jews. John F. Kennedy was loved and highly respected by the Jews in the world. When he was elected President 82% of Jews voted for him, and this was the highest percentage of any ethnic group in America.

The Jews throughout the world also mourned his death, and a large memorial building looking like the sun with rays extending out from it was constructed outside of Jerusalem. The building sits on top of a mountain, and a forest of trees surrounds it. JFK was loved and admired by the Jews of the world, and he will be readily accepted by the Jews as their messiah when he is revealed in God's timing.

A primary accomplishment of Antichrist will be his successfully negotiated treaty (i.e., covenant) with Israel and the Arabs. JFK has already proven himself with Israel when he guaranteed their security for the first time in 1961. He followed up a year later with this promise by selling Israel a major defense system, the Hawk anti-aircraft missile. It is also significant that JFK's daughter, Caroline, married a Jew. To the Jewish mind this is highly symbolic of a covenant relationship which is verified by the Old Testament. Caroline recently had her first son who is named John Kennedy Schlossberg. This will only enhance the endearment that the Jews have for John F. Kennedy.

One major difficulty in convincing anyone that JFK is the Antichrist is convincing them that he could have possibly survived the massive head wound that he received. The primary argument for this is the Scriptural description of this exact situation. The whole world will be astonished when the Antichrist is brought on the world scene. A simple belief in what the Scriptures say should be sufficient, but the Church is filled with doubting Thomases. Therefore, the following case history should provide additional evidence that a person can survive a massive head wound with his mental faculties unimpaired:

The writer personally knows of a man in a nursing home approximately two miles from his home who attempted suicide 20 years ago by shooting a bullet into his temple. He almost completely destroyed the parietal and temporal lobes on both sides of his brain. The doctors informed the wife at the time that it was impossible for the man to survive more than a few hours because of the extensive brain damage. Not only did he survive but the doctors are still amazed that the man's mental faculties and verbal abilities are totally unaffected.

He is totally paralyzed except for his ability to move his right arm. It must be remembered that JFK only lost the parietal and temporal lobes on the right side of his brain. Since he is right-handed, the left lobes are dominant and have taken over the control of the motor functions of his body. The brain has an amazing ability to compensate for portions that have been destroyed. Medical history is replete with examples of this nature, but ignorance still predominates in the arena of physiological understanding.

Another area of unbelief that plagues Christians when they hear that JFK is the Antichrist is the doubt that anyone could actually worship him. The first argument for this inevitable state of affairs is a simple quotation from the Encyclopedia of American Religions, 3rd Edition.

"*1582"
KENNEDY WORSHIPPERS
No central headquarters.
Shortly after the death of the charismatic President John F. Kennedy, people began to claim contact with his spirit. They began ascribing healings of many serious diseases, some congenital and/or terminal, to that spirit. By 1970 more than 100 such reports were on file. Coincidental with these accounts of miracles was the emergence of a loosely organized movement in which John F. Kennedy was an object of worship. The first manifestations were home shrines centered upon pictures of Kennedy. In 1972 Farley McGivern organized a John F. Kennedy Memorial Temple in Los Angeles to provide headquarters for the movement. To believers, Kennedy is thought of as a god. McGivern believed that Kennedy gave his life for his people to warn them of the evil around them.
The existence of this movement has been known only through the occasional encounters by reporters with people who claim to be a part of it. To Most people involved in it, their belief is a very private matter which is rarely shared with others, even close friends. Hence, little information about it exists.
Membership: In the 1970s, 2,000 adherents around the United States were reported."

A second argument for the reality of JFK being an object of worship is some quotations from the book **Smiling through the Apocalypse, Esquire's History of the Sixties**. The following quotations are from the chapter "The Holy Family" by Gore Vidal, which expounds on the dynastic tendencies of the Kennedy family:

> "From the beginning the godhead shone for those who had eyes to see."
>
> "From the triumph to triumph the hero proceeds to the convention at Los Angeles where the god is recognized. The only shadow upon that perfect day is cast, significantly, by Lyndon B. Johnson. Like Lucifer he challenged the god at the convention; and was struck down only to be raised again as son of morning."
>
> "From this point on the thousand days unfold in familiar sequence and, though details differ from gospel to gospel, the story already possesses the quality of a passion play; disaster at Cuba One, triumph at Cuba Two; the eloquent speeches; the fine pageantry and always the crowds and glory, ending at Dallas.
>
> With Lucifer now rampant upon the heights, the surviving Kennedys are again at work to regain the lost paradise, which means that books must be written not only about the new incarnation of the Kennedy godhead but the old. For it is the dead hero's magic that makes legitimate the family's pretensions. As the Osiris-Adonis-Christ figure, J.F.K. is already the subject of a cult that may persist, through the machinery of publicity, long after all memory of his administration has been absorbed by the golden myth now being created in a thousand books to the single end of maintaining in power our extraordinary holy family."

The above quotations clearly depict the religious overtones connected with JFK and his "sacrificial death" to warn his people of the evil around them. It is not coincidental that this is the same theme in new age teaching, which centers on Lucifer and attributes to him a sacrifice to teach mankind about evil. According to new age teaching, Lucifer will one day be reconciled to God and reign over the earth.

An incarnation must take place before this reign can begin, and that incarnation will take place in the "Man of Sin" who is better known as the Antichrist. Genesis 3:15 refers to him as the Seed of the Serpent.

On July 18, 1969, at 11:15 p.m. Ted Kennedy drove a car off a bridge at Chappaquiddick Island in Martha's Vineyard, Massachusetts and killed a young lady named Mary Jo Kopechne. The true facts of what happened that night are still a mystery, but there is one mystery that stands out from the others.

About 2:30 a.m. on the morning of July 19, 1969 after having just killed someone, Ted Kennedy made a telephone call to the home of Jacqueline Kennedy Onassis. Jackie was in Europe at the time, but Ted talked to someone at her house for 20 minutes. Ted refused in court to divulge the name of the person with whom he had talked.

Telephone company records confirmed the telephone call and its length, but the person with whom Ted talked is still a mystery. The identity of the mystery person should be clear to the reader, but a few edifying statements are in order for those unfamiliar with the legendary Kennedys. Ted Kennedy reverenced his older brother Jack since Ted was a child. Big Brother Jack would be the first person Ted would call in just such an emergency as Chappaquiddick. It is logical that JFK would be at Jackie's house at 2:30 in the morning even with Jackie in Europe

Also, JFK would be the one person that Ted would not be able to identify as the other party on the line. In addition, it was not until 1971 that JFK was photographed on the Island of Skorpios. Thus, the timing would also be appropriate for JFK to have left Bethesda hospital but not yet have gone to Skorpios.

One recent mystery involves one of the Kennedy Estates in Virginia which is located just outside Washington D.C. World leaders including the Queen of England have been observed visiting this estate under mysterious circumstances. The primary mystery is the identity of the host receiving the world leaders. It is inconceivable that these world leaders would be coming to visit with Ted Kennedy whose popularity in Europe is virtually nil.

The implication has even been made that maybe JFK really is still alive as rumors have maintained since the date of the assassination. Stories about JFK being alive have circulated throughout the world long before the tabloids became popular and turned the story into an object of ridicule. No credible journalist interested in a career would dare write anything even hinting that JFK could be alive after 30 years

Truman Capote did write an article shortly after the assassination saying JFK had survived, but he retracted the article and said he was wrong. Anyone voicing this opinion now needs to have tough skin and a stout heart in order to handle the fiery darts of the devil since this world scam is his creation. Satan is the father of lies and deceit and this is his masterpiece. The purpose of this chapter is to enlighten the children of God in regard to this plan and help them prepare to meet the Lord when He returns in the near future.

Jesus Christ came to earth and lived in obscurity for 30 years and was then proclaimed as the messiah by John the Baptist. He ministered for 3.5 years and then went into Jerusalem and claimed to be God. When the Antichrist comes out, the false prophet will proclaim him as the messiah. He will be given authority for 3.5 years and then he will enter Jerusalem and claim to be God.

Antichrist will mimic Jesus Christ, and God has His perfect timing for his reappearance. The Bridegroom is coming soon, and Christians need to prepare to meet Him.

Books Quoted or Referenced

Flowers, Peggy J. – *Will The Real Rapture Feast Stand Up?*, Spring Hill, Centerville, TX

Govett, Robert – *Seek First His Kingdom and His Righteousness* Tract (for the entire tract, please see the Supplemental Articles for the book *Salvation of the Soul*, which can be found at: (www.ProphecyCountdown.com)

Harman, James T. – *Daniel's Prophecies Unsealed – Understanding the Time of the End*, Prophecy Countdown Publications, LLC © 2018, (www.ProphecyCountdown.com)

Hollandsworth, James S. – *Keys for Inheriting the Kingdom: Unlocking the Parables of Jesus*, Hollypublishing © 2017, (www.TruthOverTraditions.com)

Lang, G. H. – *The Revelation of Jesus Christ*, Schoettle Publishing Co., Inc. © 2006 (www.schoettlepublishing.com)

Panton, D. M. – *The Judgment Seat of Christ*, Schoettle Publishing Co., Inc. © 1984 (www.schoettlepublishing.com)

Seiss, Joseph A. – *The Apocalypse: Lectures on the Book of Revelation*, Cosimo Classics © 2007

Shupe, Pastor Randy – *Babylon the Great*, Apostolic Missions, Inc. © 2007 (www.PastorRandyShupe.com)

Shupe, Pastor Randy – *Is America Mystery Babylon the Great?*, Apostolic Missions, Inc. © 2015 (www.PastorRandyShupe.com)

Simpson, Albert B. – *The Christ In The Bible Commentary: Volume Six*, Christian Publications © 1994

Even So Come

by Kristian Stanfill

All of creation

All of the earth

Make straight a highway

A path for the Lord

Jesus is coming soon

Call back the sinner

Wake up the saint

Let every nation

Shout of Your fame

Jesus is coming soon

Like a bride

Waiting for her groom

We'll be a church

Ready for You

Every heart longing for our King

We sing

Even so come

Lord Jesus come

To view a recent YouTube video of this beautiful song, please see our article entitled *Even So Come* on the **Recent Posts** section on our website (www.ProphecyCountdown.com).

Appendix A – More On the Antichrist

In the original edition of this book, Lyn Mize presented the startling belief that JFK survived the assassination attempt in Dallas, Texas on November 22, 1963. On hearing this for the first time most people immediately scoff and surmise that such a scenario is too preposterous to be true.

When I read Lyn's synopsis for the first time back in 1992, my spirit said, "I believe Lyn could be correct." I remember specifically asking the Lord that if he is correct, then his number must add up to 666:

> Here is wisdom. Let him who has understanding calculate the number of the beast, for it is the number of man: his number is 666 (Revelation 13:18).

Being a CPA having dealt with numbers throughout my career, within the next day or so, the Lord showed me the number of the Antichrist's name does, in fact, add up to 666! When I saw this I became excited because in my mind, the Lord was confirming his identity.

While I believe JFK is the Antichrist and I feel Lyn's analysis on his survival is correct, I also believe that JFK must have passed away by now. On May 29, of this year he would be 105, which makes it highly improbable that he is still alive, even though his mother lived to the age of 104.

A more likely scenario is that God's timing for the Antichrist's appearance has not arrived or has been postponed according to His perfect timing.

In Pastor Randy Shupe's excellent book: *Is America Mystery Babylon the Great?* he makes a good case that JFK is the most likely candidate and that God will cause him to arrive on the world scene according to His designed time:

> "If the antichrist is to come from the American presidency, then we cannot rule out the possibility of a previous president fulfilling

"AND I SAW ONE OF HIS HEADS AS IF IT HAD BEEN MORTALLY WOUNDED, AND HIS DEADLY WOUND WAS HEALED. AND ALL THE WORLD MARVELED AND FOLLOWED THE BEAST. SO THEY WORSHIPED THE DRAGON WHO GAVE AUTHORITY TO THE BEAST; AND THEY WORSHIPED THE BEAST..." Rev. 13:3-4

"AND THOSE WHO DWELL ON THE EARTH WILL MARVEL, WHOSE NAMES ARE NOT WRITTEN IN THE BOOK OF LIFE... WHEN THEY SEE THE BEAST THAT WAS, AND IS NOT, AND YET IS." Rev. 17:8

that role...Because of the fact that the false prophet will come from the Roman Catholic papacy, I am suggesting the antichrist may be JFK!

Notice the Scripture describes this man as "WAS, and IS NOT, and YET IS" (Rev 17:8). Being a prophetic passage that is to be fulfilled at the appearance of the Antichrist, the whole world will remember him as an American president who WAS but then WAS NOT because he was killed and now YET IS once again alive many years after his death. Would you not marvel if you witnessed such a sight? Multitudes who saw him die may be on the earth to see him brought back to life!

Perhaps the thought bothers you that Satan does not have the power to resurrect JFK (or anyone else) from the dead. It is true; he does not have ANY power other than what God Almighty grants to him. We are taught this clearly in the story of Job. Satan had no power of his own making against Job. He received God-regulated power to inflict Job. Satan could not go beyond what God said he could and could not do (see Chapters 1 and 2 of Job). The point I am after is that it will be God who enables Satan to bring forth the Antichrist:

"The coming of the lawless one is according to the working of Satan, with all power, signs and lying wonders, and with all unrighteous deception among those who perish, because they did not receive the love of the truth, that they might be saved, and for this reason God will send them a strong delusion, that they should believe the lie..."
(2 Thessalonians 2:9-11)

Notice it is God who sends forth this strong delusion (the coming of the lawless one – the antichrist), a lying wonder brought forth by the working of Satan! Because the people have rejected the truth in the person of Jesus Christ, God will permit Satan to perform a lying wonder, in which he will bring forth the lie personified, the antichrist. However, the appearance of antichrist is, in reality, God's strong delusion, the beginning of His wrath upon a Christ rejecting world!

Scripture abounds with God raising people from the dead for His glory, both in the Old Testament and in the New. If God can raise someone for His Glory, He can also raise someone form the dead as an act of His righteous judgment upon a Christ-rejecting world! It becomes a lying wonder because Satan will take credit for it and be worshipped by all who are deceived by it:

> "And I saw one of his heads as if it had been mortally wounded, and his deadly wound was healed. And all the world marveled and followed the beast. So they worshiped the dragon who gave authority to the beast; and they worshiped the beast…" (Rev. 13:3-4)

> "And those who dwell on the earth will marvel, whose names are not written in the book of life…when they see the beast that was, and is not and yet is…" (Rev. 17:8)

Moses died, yet God will send him back to earth during the tribulation as one of His two witnesses to glorify His name. He will be killed a second time (Rev. 11:3-11). Why then should we reject the idea that God could resurrect an evil and corrupt person like JFK and bring him back as an act of His judgment, a strong delusion sent from God to glorify Satan in his hour allotted to deceive the world?"

Pastor Randy Shupe's fine analysis paints a dramatic picture of how God plans to bring a conclusion to the remarkable time just ahead. His perceptive analysis provides us with a probable explanation of how the Antichrist will be revealed in the very near future.

Partial or Phased Rapture

It is important to point out that our Lord alludes to the doctrine of a "partial" or "phased" Rapture of believers in both the earlier and later portions of His ministry. First, in the Sermon on the Mount, Jesus teaches His disciples to pray for deliverance from the Tribulation period (Matthew 6:13). Towards the very end of His ministry when He gives His famous discourse on the Mount of Olives He also instructs His followers to always pray for escape from the same Tribulation period (Luke 21:34-36).

Jesus chose to teach His disciples this principle of a "partial" or "phased" Rapture on two different occasions. Both times were on a "Mount," both times He taught this privately to His disciples, and both times He included this important instruction in a prayer for His disciples to follow. The overcomer has the ears to hear and the heart to understand this teaching while the rest of the Church prefers to follow the Traditions of man (Colossians 2:8).

The overcomer heeds the Lord's advice and prays for deliverance from the coming Tribulation period on a continual basis.

---

*34) And take heed to yourselves, lest at anytime your hearts be overcharged with surfeiting, an drunkenness, and cares of this life, and so that day come upon you unawares. 35) For as a snare shall it come on all them that dwell on the face of the whole earth. 36) **Watch ye therefore, and pray always, that ye may be accounted worthy to escape all these things that shall come to pass, and to stand before the Son of Man***
(Luke 21:34-36 – KJV)

Appendix B – Signs of Christ's Coming

Many modern Bible teachers and students believe that the rebirth of the nation of Israel represents the budding of the *fig tree* that Jesus described to His disciples as he sat on the Mount of Olives, and we are living in the generation that won't pass away before He returns.

Verily I say unto you, this generation shall not pass,
till all these things be fulfilled. (Matthew 24:34 – KJV)

With Israel becoming a nation in 1948, we have been alerted that the Lord's return is fast approaching. Jesus also told his disciples a second sign to look for in the parable of Noah:

As it was in the days of Noah,
so it will be at the coming of the Son of Man.
(Matthew 24:37 – NIV)

Here the Lord is telling the Church that just prior to His return, things will be the same as they were back in Noah's day. This pictures life going on right up until the day that the rapture occurs, and the judgments of God are suddenly released upon the earth. A careful study of Genesis 6 will alert the reader to the fact that living in these end times is almost parallel to the time before the flood. The world has become a great cesspool of corruption, violence, sex, drugs, idolatry, witchcraft and other perversions. Reading the account in Genesis is like reading today's newspaper or listening to the daily news.

In the Lord's parable concerning Noah, Jesus was also giving us a second important sign that His return is drawing very near. Several years ago a famous comet passed though our solar system and it was hailed at the most watched comet of all times.

Sign of Christ's Coming

April 8, 1997

Comet Hale-Bopp Over New York City
Credit and Copyright: J. Sivo
http://antwrp.gsfc.nasa.gov/apod/ap970408.html
"What's that point of light above the World Trade Center? It's Comet Hale-Bopp! Both faster than a speeding bullet and able to "leap" tall buildings in its single orbit, Comet Hale-Bopp is also bright enough to be seen even over the glowing lights of one of the world's premier cities. In the foreground lies the East River, while much of New York City's Lower Manhattan can be seen between the river and the comet."

As it was in the days of Noah,
so it will be at the coming of the Son of Man.
(Matthew 24:37 – NIV)

These words from our wonderful Lord have several applications about the Tribulation period that is about to ensnare this world.

Seas Lifted Up
Throughout the Old Testament, the time of the coming Tribulation period is described as the time when the "seas have lifted up," and also as coming in as a "flood" (please see Jeremiah 51:42, Hosea 5:10, Daniel 11:40 and Psalm 93:3-4 for just a few examples).

This is a direct parallel to the time of Noah when the Great Flood of water came to wipe out every living creature except for righteous Noah and his family, and the pairs of animals God spared. While God said He would never flood the earth again with water, the coming Judgement will be by fire (II Peter 3:10). The book of Revelation shows that approximately three billion people will perish in the terrible time that lies ahead (see Revelation 6:8 and 9:15).

2 Witnesses
A guiding principle of God is to establish a matter based upon the witness of two or more:

> ...*a matter must be established by the testimony of two or three witnesses* (Deuteronomy 19:15 – NIV)

In 1994, God was able to get the attention of mankind when Comet Shoemaker-Levy crashed into Jupiter on the 9th of Av (on the Jewish calendar). Interestingly, this Comet was named after the "two" witnesses who first discovered it.

In 1995, "two" more astronomers also discovered another comet. It was called Comet Hale-Bopp, and it reached its closest approach to planet Earth on March 23, 1997. It has been labeled as the most widely viewed comet in the history of mankind.

Scientists have determined that Comet Hale-Bopp's orbit brought it to our solar system 4,465 years ago (see Notes 1 and 2 below). In other words, the comet made its appearance near Earth in 1997 and also in 2468 BC. Remarkably, this comet preceded the Great Flood by 120 years! God warned Noah of this in Genesis 6:3:

> *My Spirit shall not strive with man forever, for he is indeed flesh; yet his days shall be one hundred and twenty years.*

Days of Noah

What does all of this have to do with the Lord's return? Noah was born around 2948 BC, and Genesis 7:11, tells us that the Flood took place when Noah was 600, or in 2348 BC.

Remember, our Lord told us: ***"As it was in the days of Noah, so it will be at the coming of the Son of Man.***
(Matthew 24:37 – NIV)

In the original Greek, it is saying: ***"exactly like"*** it was, so it will be when He comes (see Strong's #5618).

During the days of Noah, Comet Hale-Bopp arrived on the scene as a harbinger of the Great Flood. Just as this same comet appeared before the Flood, could its arrival again in 1997 be a sign that God's final Judgement, also known as the time of Jacob's Trouble, is about to begin?

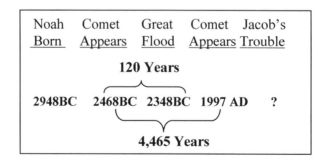

Comet Hale-Bopp's arrived 120 years before the Flood as a warning to mankind. Only righteous Noah heeded God's warning and built the ark, as God instructed. By faith, Noah was obedient to God and, as a result, saved himself and his family from destruction.

Remember, Jesus told us His return would be preceded by great heavenly signs: *"And there shall be signs in the sun, and in the moon, and in the stars; and upon the earth distress of nations, with perplexity; the sea and the waves roaring..."* (Luke 21:25)

Just as this large comet appeared as a 120-year warning to Noah, its arrival in 1997 tells us that Jesus is getting ready to return again. Is this the **"Sign"** Jesus referred to?

> Jesus was asked 3 questions by the disciples:
> *"Tell us, (1) when shall these things be"* (the destruction of the city of Jerusalem), *" and (2) what shall be the **sign** of thy coming, and (3) of the end of the world?"* (Matthew 24:3)

Sign of Christ's Coming

The **first** question had to do with events that were fulfilled in 70 AD. The **third** question has to do with the future time at the very end of the age.

The **second** question, however, has to do with the time of Christ's second coming. Jesus answered this second question in His description of the days of Noah found in Matthew 24:33-39:

> *(33) So likewise ye, when ye shall see all these things, know that it is near, even at the doors. (34) Verily I say unto you, This generation shall not pass, till all these things be fulfilled. (35) Heaven and earth shall pass away, but my words shall not pass away. (36) But of that day and hour knoweth no man, no, not the angels of heaven, but my Father only. (37) **But as the days of Noe were, so shall also the coming of the Son***

of man be. *[(38)]For as in the days that were before the flood they were eating and drinking, marrying and giving in marriage, until the day that Noe entered into the ark, [(39)] And knew not until the flood came, and took them all away; so shall also the coming of the Son of man be.*

Jesus is telling us that the **sign** of His coming will be as it was during the days of Noah. As Comet Hale-Bopp was a sign to the people in Noah's day, its arrival in 1997 is a sign that Jesus is coming back again soon. Comet Hale-Bopp could be the very sign Jesus was referring to, which would announce His return for His faithful.

Remember, Jesus said, *"exactly as it was in the days of Noah, so will it be when He returns."* The appearance of Comet Hale-Bopp in 1997 is a strong indication that the Tribulation period is about to begin, but before then, Jesus is coming for His bride!

Keep looking up! Jesus is coming again very soon!
As Noah prepared for the destruction God warned him about 120 years before the Flood, Jesus has given mankind a final warning that the Tribulation period is about to begin. The horrible destruction on 9/11 is only a precursor of what is about to take place on planet Earth. We need to be wise like Noah and prepare. Always remember our Lord's instructions:

Watch and Pray

*(34)And take heed to yourselves, lest at any time your hearts be overcharged with surfeiting, and drunkenness, and cares of this life, and so that day come upon you unawares. (35) For as a snare shall it come on all them that dwell on the face of the whole earth.(36)**Watch ye therefore, and pray always, that ye may be accounted worthy to escape all these things that shall come to pass, and to stand before the Son of man** (Luke 21:34-36).*

Footnotes to Appendix B

(1) The original orbit of Comet Hale-Bopp was calculated to be approximately 265 years by engineer George Sanctuary in his article, *Three Craters In Israel*, published on 3/31/01 found in the Supplemental Articles at www.ProphecyCountdown.com

Comet Hale-Bopp's orbit around the time of the Flood changed from 265 years to about 4,200 years. Because the plane of the comet's orbit is perpendicular to the earth's orbital plane (ecliptic), Mr. Sanctuary noted: "A negative time increment was used for this simulation...to back the comet away from the earth.... past Jupiter... and then out of the solar system. The simulation suggests that the past-past orbit had a very eccentric orbit with a period of only 265 years. When the comet passed Jupiter (*around 2203BC)* its orbit was deflected upward, coming down near the earth 15 months later with the comet's period changed from 265 years to about *(4,200)* years." (*added text for clarity*)

(2) Don Yeomans, with NASA's Jet Propulsion Laboratory, made the following observations regarding the comet's orbit: "By integrating the above orbit forward and backward in time until the comet leaves the planetary system and then referring the osculating orbital elements...the following orbital periods result: Original orbital period before entering planetary system = 4200 years. Future orbital period after exiting the planetary system = 2380 years."

This analysis can be found at:
http://www2.jpl.nasa.gov/comet/ephemjpl6.html

Based upon the above two calculations we have the following:

265 [a] + 4,200 [b] = 4,465 Years

1997 AD – 4,465 Years = 2468 BC = Hale Bopp arrived

(a) Orbit period calculated by George Sanctuary before deflection around 2203 BC.

(b) Orbit period calculated by Don Yeomans after 1997 visit.

Tract Included In Appendix B

This tract was written in 1997 when Comet Hale-Bopp entered our solar system. In 2027 it will be the 30th Anniversary of its last appearance. Bullinger wrote, "30, being 3x10 denotes in a higher degree the perfection of Divine order, as marking the **right moment**. Christ was thirty years of age at the commencement of His ministry. David was also 30 when he began to reign." (Bullinger, p. 265). Was Comet Hale-Bopp giving us a sign that the bride of Christ is about to begin her reign very soon? NOT setting a date, just sounding the alarm (please see Ezekiel 33:2-6).

How Long is a Generation?

Now learn a parable of the fig tree; When his branch is yet tender, and putteth forth leaves, ye know that summer is nigh: So likewise ye, when ye shall see all these things, know that it is near, even at the doors. Verily I say unto you, **This generation shall not pass, till all these things be fulfilled**. (Matthew 24:32-34 – KJV)

What was the average life expectancy at the time of Jesus?

Those living in the days of **Jesus** (as mentioned in the New Testament) had an **average life span** that was similar to human life spans before the arrival of modern medicine and technology. At the time Jesus spoke the above words, the **average life expectancy** was around 30 to 35 years, similar to the **life span** of those in classical Rome.

32 AD + 35 = 67 AD around the time that the Romans' siege of Jerusalem began (3½ years of judgment), ending in 70 AD.

In 1948 the average life expectancy was approximately 70 years (or 80 because of strength, as in Psalm 90).

1948 +70 = 2018 +?

The days of our life are **seventy years**— *Or even, if because of strength,* **eighty years**; *Yet their pride [in additional years] is only labor and sorrow, For it is soon gone and we fly away.* (Psalm 90:10 – AMP)

Special Invitation

This book was primarily written to those who have been born again. If you have never been born again, would you like to be? The Bible shows that it's simple to be saved...

- **Realize you are a sinner.**
  "As it is written, There is none righteous, no, not one:"
  (Romans 3:10)
  "... for there is no difference. For all have sinned, and come short of the glory of God;" (Romans 3:22-23)

- **Realize you CAN NOT save yourself.**
  "But we are all as an unclean thing, and all our righteousness are as filthy rags; ..." (Isaiah 64:6)
  "Not by works of righteousness which we have done, but according to his mercy he saved us, ..." (Titus 3:5)

- **Realize that Jesus Christ died on the cross to pay for your sins.**
  "Who his own self bare our sins in his own body on the tree, ..." (I Peter 2:24)
  "... Unto him that loved us, and washed us from our sins in his own blood," (Revelation 1:5)

- **Simply by faith receive Jesus Christ as your personal Savior.**
  "But as many as received him, to them gave he power to become the sons of God, even to them that believe on his name:" (John 1:12)
  " ...Sirs, what must I do to be saved? And they said, Believe on the Lord Jesus Christ, and thou shalt be saved, and thy house." (Acts 16:30-31)

WOULD YOU LIKE TO BE SAVED?

If you would like to be saved, believe on the Lord Jesus Christ right now by making this acknowledgment in your heart:

> Lord Jesus, I know that I am a sinner, and unless You save me, I am lost forever. I thank You for dying for me at Calvary. By faith I come to You now, Lord, the best way I know how, and ask You to save me. I believe that God raised You from the dead and acknowledge You as my personal Saviour.

If you believed on the Lord, this is the most important decision of your life. You are now saved by the precious blood of Jesus Christ, which was shed for you and your sins. Now that you have received Jesus as your personal Saviour, you will want to find a Church where you can be baptized as your first act of obedience, and where the Word of God is taught so you can continue to grow in your faith. Ask the Holy Spirit to help you as you read the Bible to learn all that God has for your life.

Also, please see the Bibliography, as well as the pages that follow for information on several books that will help you on your wonderful journey and help you prepare for the days ahead.

Endtimes

The Bible indicates that we are living in the final days and Jesus Christ is getting ready to return very soon. This book was written to help Christians prepare for what lies ahead. The Word of God indicates that the Tribulation Period is rapidly approaching and that the Antichrist is getting ready to emerge on the world scene.

Jesus promised His disciples that there is a way to escape the horrible time of testing and persecution that will soon devastate this planet. The main purpose of this book is to help you get prepared so you will rule and reign with Jesus when He returns.

About The Author

Lyn Mize was a gifted disciple of Christ who founded *Meat In Due Season Ministries* to help advance the important gospel of the Kingdom. Lyn was a prolific writer and teacher of the prophetic Word. His writings included a verse by verse exegesis of the following books of the Bible:

Colossians	Habakkuk	Jude	Revelation
Daniel	James	1 Peter	Romans
Esther	1 John	2 Peter	Ruth
Galatians	2 John	Philippians	

Lyn's detailed analysis of the above books of the Bible may be found at: www.ffwthb.org On his website you will also discover over 50 in-depth articles covering the following important topics: Salvation, Parables, Prophecy and Warnings.

Jim Harman was fortunate to have been a close personal friend of Lyn Mize who understood and taught the deeper truths of the Bible. It is Jim's strong desire to carry on the legacy of his good friend through the republication of this book so that many will come to realize the importance of seeking the Kingdom and seeking Christ's righteousness as we approach the soon return of our Lord and Saviour Jesus Christ.

The burden of both Lyn and Jim's hearts is to see many believers come to know the joy of Christ's triumph in their life as they become true overcomers; qualified and ready to rule and reign with Christ in the coming Kingdom.

To contact Jim for questions or to arrange for speaking engagements:

Jim Harman
P.O. Box 941612
Maitland, FL 32794
JimHarmanCPA@aol.com

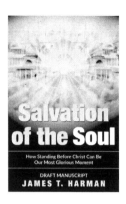

HOW STANDING BEFORE CHRIST
CAN BE OUR MOST GLORIOUS MOMENT

The topic of the Judgment Seat of Christ is often neglected by today's modern church.

"For we must all appear before the judgment seat of Christ, that each one may receive the things done in the body, according to what he has done, whether good or bad" (2 Corinthians 5:10).

When Jesus returns, He will review all of our lives to determine whether we have been faithful and obedient doers of His Word. The purpose of this book is to prepare believers so they will be able to hear Him say:

"Well done, good and faithful servant....
Enter into the joy of your lord" (Matthew 25:21).

MUST-READ FOR ALL BELIEVERS

NEW DISCOVERY – LEARN ABOUT
- Difference between the salvation of spirit and soul.
- What Jesus meant by *"take up your cross."*
- How the Word of God can save our souls.
- When the salvation of our soul takes place.
- Sign of Christ's Coming

Download your FREE copy: www.ProphecyCountdown.com

Or from Amazon.com–Available in Paperback and/or Kindle Edition

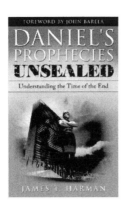

"Go your way Daniel, because the words are closed up and sealed until the time of the end...none of the wicked will understand, but those who are wise will understand."
(Daniel 12:9-10)

The Archangel Michael told Daniel that the prophecies would be sealed until the time of the end. Discover how the prophecies in the book of Daniel are being unsealed in the events taking place today.

Since Daniel was told that the wise will understand the message and lead many to righteousness, while the wicked will not grasp its meaning and will continue in their wickedness, it is imperative for everyone living in these end times to diligently examine and attempt to comprehend the vital message Daniel has recorded for us. The wise will diligently search the word of the Lord and ask for wisdom in order to understand God's plan.

When Jesus came the first time, the wise men of the day were aware of His soon arrival and they were actively looking for Him. Today, those who are wise will be passionately sharing this message and helping others prepare. Those doing so will *"shine like the stars forever and ever."*

May the Lord grant us a heart of wisdom to understand the time we are living in so we can prepare for what lies ahead!

Download your FREE copy: www.ProphecyCountdown.com

Or from Amazon.com–Available in Paperback and/or Kindle Edition

An Interpretation of the Song of Solomon
Foreword by John Zajac
James T. Harman

God placed the Song of Solomon in the heart of the Bible for a special reason. *Come Away My Beloved* helps reveal that reason in a most enchanting way. In this refreshing commentary you will realize why this ancient love story has perplexed Bible students and commentators down through the ages.

Find out the prophetic importance veiled within the Song's poetic imagery and experience a renewed love for the Lord as you explore one of the most passionate love stories of all time.

Witness the wonderful joys of romance and devotion shared by two young lovers. Discover enduring lessons of virtue and faithfulness, and learn amazing truths that have been hidden within the greatest love Song ever written.

Written almost 3,000 years ago this brilliant Song of love reflects God's desire for every man and woman; not only in their present lives but also in their relationship with Him.

This book will revive your heart with a fervent love for your Saviour. It will also help you prepare for your glorious wedding day when Jesus returns for His devoted bride.

Allow this beautiful story of love and passion to ignite a flame in your heart and let this inspirational Song arouse your heart to join in the impassioned cry with the rest of the bride:

"Make haste, my beloved, and come quickly…"

Download your FREE copy: www.ProphecyCountdown.com

Or from Amazon.com–Available in Paperback and/or Kindle Edition

Perplexed by the book of Revelation? Not sure what all the signs, symbols and metaphors really mean? Jim Harman's latest work unravels Apostle John's remarkable revelation of Jesus Christ and what's in store for the inhabitants of planet Earth. This extraordinary commentary is not another cookie-cutter rehash of the popular teachings fostered by the *Left Behind* phenomena so prevalent in today's church.

One of the central messages in the book of Revelation is that God is calling men to be genuine overcomers. Jesus Christ has been sent out from the throne of God to conquer men's hearts so they can also be overcomers.

The purpose of this book is to encourage people to embrace Him as the King of their heart and allow His life to reign in theirs. He wants you to be able to overcome by His mighty power and strength living inside of you just as He overcame for all of us. Jesus will be looking for a faithful remnant qualified to rule and reign with Him when He returns. This book will help you prepare to be the overcomer for which Jesus is looking.

The reader will come away with a new and enlightened understanding of what the last book in God's Word is all about. Understand the book of Revelation and why it is so important for believers living in the last days of the Church age.

Download your FREE copy: www.ProphecyCountdown.com

Or from Amazon.com–Available in Paperback and/or Kindle Edition

Once a person is saved, the number one priority should be seeking entrance into the Kingdom through the salvation of their soul. It is pictured as a runner in a race seeking a prize represented by a crown that will last forever.

The salvation of the soul and entrance into the coming Kingdom are only achieved through much testing and the trial of one's faith. If you are going through difficulty, then REJOICE:

> *"Blessed is the man who perseveres under trial, because when he has stood the test, he will receive the crown of life that God has promised to those who love Him."* (James 1:12)

The "Traditional" teaching on the "THE KINGDOM" has taken the Church captive into believing all Christians will rule and reign with Christ no matter if they have lived faithful and obedient lives, or if they have been slothful and disobedient with the talents God has given them. Find out the important Truth before Jesus Christ returns.

MUST READING FOR EVERY CHRISTIAN

Jesus Christ is returning for His faithful overcoming followers. Don't miss the opportunity of ruling and reigning with Christ in the coming KINGDOM!

Download your FREE copy: www.ProphecyCountdown.com

Or from Amazon.com – Available in Paperback and or Kindle Edition

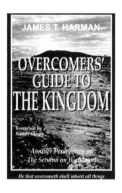

Get ready to climb back up the Mountain to listen to Christ's teachings once again. Though you may have read this great Sermon many times, discover exciting promises that many have missed.

The purpose of this book is to help Christians be the Overcomers Jesus wants them to be and to help them gain their own entrance in the coming Kingdom. Learn what seeking the Kingdom of God is all about and be among the chosen few who will "enter into" the coming Kingdom. *"Whoever hears these sayings of Mine, and does them, I will liken him to a wise man who built his house upon the rock."* (Matthew 7:24)

Also learn about:
- The link between Beatitudes and Fruit of the Spirit
- What the "law of Christ" really is
- The critical importance of the "Lord's prayer"
- How to be an Overcomer
- THE SIGN of Christ's soon Coming
- A new song entitled: LOOKING FOR THE SON which has the message of how vitally important it is to be Watching for the Lord's return and the consequences to those who are not looking.

Download your free copy: www.ProphecyCountdown.com

Or from Amazon.com – Available in Paperback and or Kindle Edition

LOOKING FOR THE SON
Lyrics by Jim Harman
Listen to this Song on the Home Page of Prophecy Countdown

Lyric	Scripture
There's a fire burning in my heart	Luke 24:32
Yearning for the Lord to come,	Rev. 22:17, Mat. 6:33
and His Kingdom come to start	
Soon He'll come.....so enter the narrow gate	Lk. 21:34-36,Mat.7:13
Even though you mock me now...	II Peter 3:4
He'll come to set things straight	
Watch how I'll leave in the twinkling of an eye	I Corinthians 15:52
Don't be surprised when I go up in the sky	Revelation 3:10
There's a fire burning in my heart	Luke 24:32
Yearning for my precious Lord	Revelation 22:17
And His Kingdom come to start	Revelation 20:4-6
Your love of this world, has forsaken His	I John 2:15
It leaves me knowing that you could have had it all	Revelation 21:7
Your love of this world, was oh so reckless	Revelation 3:14-22
I can't help thinking	Philippians 1:3-6
You would have had it all	Revelation 21:7
Looking for the Son	Titus 2:13, Luke 21:36
(Tears are gonna fall, not looking for the Son)	Matthew 25:10-13
You had His holy Word in your hand	II Timothy 3:16
(You're gonna wish you had listened to me)	Jeremiah 25:4-8
And you missed it...for your self	Matthew 22:11-14
(Tears are gonna fall, not looking for the Son)	Matthew 25:10-13
Brother, I have a story to be told	Habakkuk 2:2
It's the only one that's true	John 3:16-17
And it should've made your heart turn	II Peter 3:9
Remember me when I rise up in the air	I Corinthians 15:52
Leaving your home down here	I Corinthians 15:52
For true Treasures beyond compare	Matthew 6:20
Your love of this world, has forsaken His	I John 2:15
It leaves me knowing that you could have had it all	Revelation 21:7
Your love of this world, was oh so reckless	Revelation 3:14-22
I can't help thinking	Philippians 1:3-6
You would have had it all	Revelation 21:7

(Lyrics in parentheses represent background vocals)

(CONTINUED)

Lyric	Scripture
Looking for the Son	Titus 2:13, Lk. 21:36
(Tears are gonna fall, not looking for the Son)	Matthew 25:10-13
You had His holy Word in your hand	II Timothy 3:16
(You're gonna wish you had listened to me)	Jeremiah 25:4-8
And you lost it...for your self	Matthew 22:11-14
(Tears are gonna fall, not looking for the Son)	Matthew 25:10-13
You would have had it all	Revelation 21:7
Looking for the Son	Titus 2:13, Lk. 21:36
You had His holy Word in your hand	II Timothy 3:16
But you missed it... for your self	Matthew 22:11-14

Lov'n the world....not the open door I Jn. 2:15, Rev. 4:1
Down the broad way... blind to what life's really for Matthew 7:13-14
Turn around now...while there still is time I Jn. 1:9, II Pet. 3:9
Learn your lesson now or you'll reap just what you sow Galatians 6:7
(You're gonna wish you had listened to me)
You would have had it all
(Tears are gonna fall, not looking for the Son)
You would have had it all
(You're gonna wish you had listened to me)
It all, it all, it all
(Tears are gonna fall, not looking for the Son)

You would have had it all
(You're gonna wish you had listened to me)
Looking for the Son
(Tears are gonna fall, not looking for the Son)
You had His holy Word in your hand
(You're gonna wish you had listened to me)
And you missed it...for your self
(Tears are gonna fall, not looking for the Son)

You would have had it all
(You're gonna wish you had listened to me)
Looking for the Son
(Tears are gonna fall, not looking for the Son)
You had His holy Word in your hand
(You're gonna wish you had listened to me)
But you missed it
You missed it
You missed it
You missed it. ...for your self

Scripture Summary
Jeremiah 25:4-8
Habakkuk 2:2
Matthew 6:20
Matthew 6:33
Matthew 7:13
Matthew 22:11-14
Matthew 25:10-13
Luke 21:34-36
Luke 24:332
John 3:16-17
I Corinthians 15:52
Galatians 6:7
Philippians 1:3-6
II Timothy 3:16
Titus 2:13
II Peter 3:9
II Peter 3:4
I John 1:9
I John 2:15
Revelation 3:10
Revelation 3:14-22
Revelation 4:1
Revelation 20:4-6
Revelation 21:7
Revelation 22:17

(See www.ProphecyCountdown.com for more information)

The Day of the Lord is Near!

The Coming Spiritual Earthquake

by James T. Harman

"The Message presented in this book is greatly needed to awaken believers to the false ideas many have when it comes to the Rapture. I might have titled it: THE RAPTURE EARTH-QUAKE!"
Ray Brubaker - God's News Behind the News

"If I am wrong, anyone who follows the directions given in this book will be better off spiritually. If I am right, they will be among the few to escape the great-est spiritual calamity of the ages."
Jim Harman - Author

MUST READING FOR EVERY CHRISTIAN!
HURRY! BEFORE IT IS TOO LATE!